"Perhaps no movement in Christian history has suffered more from both its detractors and its admirers than Calvinism. In this book, Kenneth Stewart shatters ten persistent stereotypes about the Calvinist way of being a Christian and helps us to see why the Reformed faith continues to attract so many believers to the God of John Calvin."

Timothy George, Beeson Divinity School of Samford University, Birmingham

"While some may find even the word 'Calvinism' to be unhelpful, it is a standard term used by both its friends and enemies. Thus, Kenneth Stewart has done us all a service by writing a book which highlights and refutes many of the misconceptions about Calvinism propagated by both its adherents and its opponents. This book will provoke healthy and thoughtful discussions both among Reformed people and between the Reformed and Christians who belong to other traditions."

Carl R. Trueman, Westminster Theological Seminary, Philadelphia

"Calvinism—in various strains—has been one of the most powerful forces shaping Protestant Christianity. And despite being repeatedly consigned to the dustbin of history, it just keeps bouncing back. Yet it is frequently misunderstood and misrepresented by friend and foe alike. In this richly detailed study, Ken Stewart harvests a wealth of historical research in order to bust some popular myths and reveal the dynamism and diversity of the Reformed tradition. Given the contemporary resurgence of Calvinism, this book is recommended reading for Christians who call themselves Calvinists, but also for those of us who don't."

John Coffey, University of Leicester, England

"This work is insightful, illuminating, informative and fascinating. The breadth and depth of Stewart's historical research is impressive. The study aims to help Calvinists primarily, but it will be helpful to detractors wishing to be just in their criticisms. Four of the erroneous ideas Stewart identifies as myths are widely held by Calvinists themselves, and six of them are common among non-Calvinists. This well-informed exposition of controversial aspects of the history of Reformed theology and practice should foster profitable discussions among evangelicals of diverse traditions."

Terrance Tiessen, Emeritus Professor, Providence Theological Seminary, Manitoba

Ten Myths About Calvinism

Recovering the Breadth
of the Reformed Tradition

KENNETH J. STEWART

IVP Academic

An imprint of InterVarsity Press
Downers Grove, Illinois

Apollos
Nottingham, England

InterVarsity Press, USA
P.O. Box 1400
Downers Grove, IL 60515-1426, USA
World Wide Web: www.ivpress.com
Email: email@ivpress.com

APOLLOS (an imprint of Inter-Varsity Press, England)
Norton Street
Nottingham NG7 3HR, England
Website: www.ivpbooks.com
Email: ivp@ivpbooks.com

InterVarsity Press®, USA, is the book-publishing division of InterVarsity Christian Fellowship/USA® <www.intervarsity.org> and a member movement of the International Fellowship of Evangelical Students.

Inter-Varsity Press, England, is closely linked with the Universities and Colleges Christian Fellowship, a student movement connecting Christian Unions throughout Great Britain, and a member movement of the International Fellowship of Evangelical Students. Website: www.uccf.org.uk

All Scripture quotations, unless otherwise indicated, are taken from the Holy Bible, New International Version®. NIV®. Copyright © 1973, 1978, 1984 by International Bible Society. Used by permission of Zondervan Publishing House. Distributed in the U.K. by permission of Hodder and Stoughton Ltd. All rights reserved. "NIV" is a registered trademark of International Bible Society. UK trademark number 1448790.

Design: Cindy Kiple
Images: Northwind Picture Archives

USA ISBN 978-0-8308-3898-1
UK ISBN 978-1-84474-513-5

Printed in the United States of America ∞

Library of Congress Cataloging-in-Publication Data

Stewart, Kenneth J.
 Ten myths about Calvinism: recovering the breadth of the reformed
tradition / Kenneth J. Stewart.
   p. cm.
 Includes bibliographical references and index.
 ISBN 978-0-8308-3898-1 (pbk.: alk. paper)
 1. Calvinism. 2. Reformed Church—Doctrines. I. Title.
 BX9422.3.S76 2011
 230'.42—dc22

                                                                        2010040602

British Library Cataloguing in Publication Data
A catalogue record for this book is available from the British Library.

P   20   19   18   17   16   15   14   13   12   11   10   9   8   7   6   5   4   3   2   1

Y   28   27   26   25   24   23   22   21   20   19   18   17   16   15   14   13   12   11

For Jane

Heir with me of the gracious gift of life

(1 Pet 3:7)

Contents

Acknowledgments

A project of this kind cannot go far without supporting friends and backers. The investigation began in Edinburgh in the summer of 2006 with a grant from the then Kaleo Center of Covenant College, directed by Dr. Kevin Eames. More recently Covenant College has assisted with a six-month sabbatical, January-June 2009. I have been assisted at every step of the way by Covenant College librarians John Holberg and Tom Horner, who were unstinting in securing Inter-Library Loan materials. A variety of friends (some gained purely through the advance of this project) assisted me by reading and commenting on various chapters. Among these are Lyle Bierma, David Calhoun, Reid Ferguson, Cameron Fraser, Michael Haykin, Ed Kellogg, Travis Myers, A. J. deVisser, Herb Ward, Jack Whytock and Jason Zuidema.

Two chapters of this work have already appeared elsewhere. Chapter four appeared in an earlier draft as "The Points of Calvinism: Retrospect and Prospect," *Scottish Bulletin of Evangelical Theology* 26, no. 2 (2008): 187-203, while chapter five appeared in an earlier draft as "Calvinism and Missions: The Contested Relationship Revisited," *Themelios* 34, no. 1 (2009): 63-78.

Here I also record my gratitude to my oldest son, Andrew, a rising graphic designer. He closely consulted with me in gathering and editing the images that introduce each of the chapters in this book.

INTRODUCTION

Why Pinpoint Ten Myths?

This book is written with Calvinists in mind, yet I hope it will also prove useful both to those who hold no "opposite" theological position as well as those who have consciously decided that the Calvinist position is not for them.

I have now adhered to what can be called the Calvinist theological position for almost forty years, after being raised and converted to Christ in an evangelical setting in which neither this theological position nor the one generally reckoned as its opposite was pressed.[1] Yet by my early adulthood I had come to see this attempt at "doctrinal balance" (as it was indeed called) as a minus rather than a plus. My pietistic evangelical background had leaned toward what could be called revivalism; in this setting many a zealous evangelist had succeeded in convincing me that I, a struggling adolescent Christian, was no real believer at all and that the only thing to do was to begin with Christ (yet) again. In hindsight this utterly unstable way of living as a Christian seems very much like the children's table game Chutes and Ladders: one wrong move and I find myself starting over at the beginning! The question of God's fixed opinion of me, or whether God had any interest in preserving me in a state of salvation once I was there, was for me a deep question with no certain answer. Certainty was very elusive

---

[1]I hope to rapidly make clear that this language of "Calvinist" and "Calvinism" is less than desirable and ought to be replaced by references to "Reformed theology" and the "Reformed theological position." Here, I use these terms for introductory purposes and do so acknowledging that they have an accustomed use built up over the last two hundred years.

in this pietistic and revivalist stream of evangelicalism.

Some Christians known to me held what were called Calvinist views, and these individuals seemed to possess a kind of swagger and certainty about such questions; I found this to be simultaneously unnerving and attractive. There were many late-night debates and certain recommended authors, but I was not won over easily. Embracing this understanding of God's dealings with humans and the world took some time. Yet, incrementally, I came to embrace what is called Calvinism. This new loyalty also involved my taking what I now recognize to be some wrong turns. For a considerable time I became a true zealot for the new cause.[2] I did not cease to be a pietistic evangelical; I became a pietistic evangelical with a Calvinist backbone. Paramount in my embrace of this new perspective was the consideration that God's own initiative in my salvation had preceded my reception of it. His antecedent intention had undergirded and enabled my response; I had nothing that I had not received (1 Cor 4:7); if I was in Christ it was "because of him" (1 Cor 1:30). God has long-term commitments.

So, why have I, who have embraced Calvinism, written a book like this for those who are already consciously Calvinist? I can think of five reasons:

1. Like some other strands of Christianity, the Calvinist strain has a tendency to generate its share of extremists. Call them high-flyers or ultras if you like, but Calvinism has generated its share. I am not referring here to people who are rude or crude (though there are in fact Calvinists of this type too) but more particularly to those who know no limits; to use an aeronautical metaphor, they fly without an altimeter. Certain aspects of Calvinism are their hobbyhorses; all discussions will eventually return to their pet Calvinist doctrines. It troubles me that the Calvinist movement seems to be reluctant to admit that this tendency to extremes exists; no one seems to blow a whistle on those who are out on the rim of things. I suppose that the expectation is that since

---

[2]As a mark of my zeal for Calvin, our wedding in 1976 included singing Calvin's hymn "I Greet Thee Who My Sure Redeemer Art." At a still earlier stage I took over, uncritically, the perspective of a professor who encouraged us to think that the Dutch were the best Calvinists of all.

Calvinism is good, it is impossible to have too much of a good thing. I myself was positioned on this rim for a period.

The tendency to extremism is not unique to Calvinism; Methodism in its Holiness tendency became known for those who promoted not only the second blessing but a third and fourth.[3] The Baptist movement has had to contend with Landmarkism, which consigned all nonbaptistic forms of Christianity to the margins. Pentecostalism has not only promoted ecstatic speaking in tongues as the evidence of baptism in the Spirit but a portion of its constituency became known as holy rollers; in contemporary times this tendency has extended to those who have uttered animal sounds under a claimed divine influence.[4]

Yet it seems to me that Calvinism has had more trouble restraining its "ultras" than some other forms of Christianity. Perhaps Calvinism's reluctance to do this reflects the prominence given by the movement to the conception of God as omnipotent (a belief which I do not dispute). Calvinists are united in a strong conviction of God's sovereign power; they expect to see this divine sovereignty exercised in the ultimate triumph of the gospel and of certain theological principles; why then think about boundaries or limits? But this obsession with omnipotence is lopsided; it is not sufficiently recognized today that because of it Calvinism is quite capable of assuming degenerate forms.

The biographer of a much-admired Scottish minister John Erskine (1721-1803) insisted that his subject had been "Calvinistical, but not of the vulgar sort,"[5] while two chroniclers from the same era, David Bogue and James Bennett, lamented the tendency of those who gloried in attempting to "stand higher" than Calvin. They believed George Whitefield, the flaming evangelist of the eighteenth century, to have been "a judicious Scriptural Calvinist"; but they described a flock of preachers

---

[3]See Vincent Synan, *The Holiness and Pentecostal Movements* (Grand Rapids: Eerdmans, 1997), pp. 52-57.

[4]See Guy Chevreau, *Catch the Fire: The Toronto Blessing as an Experience of Renewal and Revival* (Grand Rapids: Zondervan, 1995). An interesting part of this narrative was that the Vineyard Churches *did* conclude that certain phenomena at Toronto were "off the charts." So some limits did apply.

[5]Henry Moncrieff Wellwood, *Account of the Life and Writings of John Erskine, D.D.* (Edinburgh: n.p., 1818), p. 380.

influenced by his example as "exceedingly rude and uninformed."[6] A nineteenth-century Scottish-Canadian writer, Thomas McCulloch, observed this also and remarked that Calvinism had sometimes "suffered from the mistaken views of its friends and also from their unguarded expressions."[7] The French have a proverb that goes *plus ça change, plus c'est la même* (the more things change, the more they remain the same). Because tendencies to the extreme recur, I am writing in the hope of encouraging Calvinists to stay in their movement's mainstream and to learn to say no more confidently to upstarts who claim, alone, to have the inside track on the Calvinist tradition.

2. Like some other strains of Christianity, Calvinism nurtures a primeval tendency that cripples well-intentioned attempts to come to terms with cultures and societies very different from the one the movement was birthed in. If there are Methodist believers for whom annual camp meetings are the high watermark of spirituality, or Baptists for whom quoting John Bunyan or Charles Spurgeon is always a good idea, Calvinists have a default tendency to quote John Calvin and to prefer the sixteenth century. An early-nineteenth-century writer, introducing a collection of translated essays from the Swiss Protestant historian of the Reformation, J. H. Merle D'Aubigné, meant to flatter him when he wrote:

> Of all the men of this age, it may safely be said, Dr. Merle D'Aubigné is the most thoroughly imbued with the spirit of the Reformers. In fact, he hardly lives in the present era, though he does move bodily about among the men of our times. Sure I am, his whole spiritual man is at least as much conversant with the events and with the age of the Reformers, as with those of our own day.[8]

This, though intended as a compliment, should raise eyebrows! D'Aubigné, the Swiss historian, was in fact a man quite immersed in the questions of his own day, even while he carried out his vast re-

---

[6]David Bogue and James Bennett, *History of Dissenters from the Revolution to the Year 1838* (1839; reprint, Stoke-on-Trent, U.K.: Tentmaker, 2000), 2:37.

[7]Thomas MacCulloch, *Calvinism: The Doctrine of the Scriptures* (Glasgow: Collins, 1844), p. vii.

[8]Robert Baird, introduction to J. H. Merle D'Aubigné, *Discourses and Essays* (Glasgow: Collins, 1846), p. iv.

searches. Yet, among many contemporary Calvinists who are also inclined to revere this era, an opportune quotation from John Calvin
regularly serves like a trump card in any debate or discussion. An allusion to what was or was not the Genevan policy on something is
considered determinative. This preference among Calvinists for the
"primeval" or "Edenic" has been making the rounds for a long while.

The love for the primeval is not to be confused with mere tradition-
alism; no, to embrace this Calvinist tendency is to incline to the view
that the sixteenth century was the definitive epoch of this expression of
Christianity and to suppose that our great need is to maintain conformity with it and to make it the measure of all subsequent ages. It is not
sufficiently recognized that this tendency of thought is an outworking
of romanticism and that, unless kept in check, it will militate against all
real possibility of genuine development or improvement of thought. On
this view, the century of the Reformation is apparently incapable of
being improved.

3. Calvinism also suffers from seriously underestimating its own potential for diverse development. This difficulty seems to be an outworking of the prior issue, that is, the supposition that the sixteenth
century has provided us with a good script, and that we have only to
adhere to that script and all will go well. But this notion of one size fits
all seriously misjudges the diversity evident even in the century of the
Reformation. Some regions of Europe that embraced the Swiss and
South German Reformed pattern of reformation were more liturgical
and some less; some managed to work in a degree of harmony under a
prince or monarch, while others struggled to survive under royal or
imperial hostility. Some Calvinist churches had presiding bishops while
others repudiated the very idea of any nonparity between pastors. Not
all early Calvinists exclusively sang Psalms, and not all sang unaccom-
panied by instruments. Yet parts of the Calvinist movement of the
present day are unduly obsessed with following in a way that is termed
truly Reformed (a sentiment that is an outgrowth of the primeval
tendency). Let me be frank: this is the notion of hewing to some prim-
itive distinctive or distinctives, when very often there were and are
alternatives.

I mean to make no arguments here in favor of laxity; I affirm the honored place Calvinists grant to the catechisms and confessions of the Reformation era. I only caution against the default tendency to tenaciously resist diversity of thought and practice because it is reckoned to be intrinsically inauthentic—an unwarranted departure from a script carefully furnished to us long ago.

4. Calvinism as a movement also tends to underestimate its own complexity; that is, it is a whole composed of parts—some of which regularly prove very difficult. Advocates of Calvinism do not often enough acknowledge this absence of simplicity. Calvinism's *origins* are composite: we have to account for how and why sixteenth-century European Christians who wished for reform started with Luther but did not stop there. Some proceeded far beyond Luther, and others less far. There was a complexity of *leadership:* we will find (on inspection) that Calvin himself was not the solitary colossus in his time that Calvinist lore has so often made him out to be. Calvinism's *doctrines* may also be reckoned to be complex. Calvinists have not been and are not now equally fixated on the doctrine of predestination; while many have insisted that it be treated as part of God's sovereign governance of the whole universe (in this instance, as it also applies to individual destiny), just as many have held this doctrine in the background from where it can serve to explain how adverse-minded sinners have become and will remain Christian believers. Similarly, very different attitudes to Sunday-keeping grew up simultaneously in different parts of the Calvinist world. It was once common to contrast the Puritan with the Continental view of the sabbath.

Calvinist approaches to the *communication of the gospel* have been complex. Some Calvinists have been fervent evangelists and missionaries, while others have been cool toward both enterprises on the questionable assumption that God will see to the spread of the gospel somehow, in his own way. In between these poles there are some who think that nurture of believers' children is the be all and end all of the growth of the church. Some Calvinists have suffered passively in face of harassment and persecution, while others have justified armed resistance against their oppressors. How can a single movement generate such different tendencies? I hope to help readers grasp that these divergences cannot be explained by making appeals to an original script; not every question over which Calvinists have reached different positions arose in the first decades of the Reformation.

5. Finally, the Calvinist movement has often stood and still stands opposed by persons and parties who perceive that in one or more aspects this expression of the Christian faith is defective and dangerous. The list of such complaints is quite staggering! Has Calvinism been antimissionary? Has it truly been culturally Philistine? Does it encourage passivity in the face of temptation and sin? I write in part because I am not convinced that today's burgeoning Calvinist movement is taking these appeals and complaints with sufficient seriousness, yet it must! Paying greater attention to these recurring complaints (I will name six) from the unconvinced will help to keep today's Calvinist movement from a false triumphalism; it will also help to keep it circumspect. In certain cases it may well be necessary for Calvinists to meet their critics halfway.

Decades ago I came on board this Calvinist ship. I do not propose jumping ship now, even though some heavy weather has been encountered. In writing, I have often stopped to ponder the irony that I—a first-generation Calvinist—should be writing a "guide to the galaxy" aimed at promoting Calvinist discernment. I have concluded that the still-greater irony is that we live in a time when most of the champions of this movement have no better credentials than I: the first-generation crowd seems to rule the roost. My hope and prayer in writing this volume is that this movement will learn to be more adept at self-criticism, more discerning about who does and does not stand firmly in the movement's mainstream, less characterized by a default tendency to resist cultural change and even more concerned with reaching our admittedly changed culture with the gospel.

From European beginnings, the Calvinist family is now global and multiracial. I cannot hope to analyze or describe more than a portion of it. While I am familiar with certain aspects of the Calvinist family as it exists in Francophone Europe and the Netherlands, my focus here is primarily on the Calvinist story as it has unfolded and been advocated in English-speaking lands. This book does not assume any great specialist knowledge in readers. However, a familiarity with Calvin's own career and influence, such as can be had in standard biographies of Calvin, such as those of Williston Walker (1906), Emmanuel Stickelberger (1954), Jean Cadier (1960), T. H. L. Parker (1975), Alister McGrath (1990), Wulfert de Greef (1993, rev. 2008) or Herman Selderhuis (2009), will substantially assist the reader as we investigate the spread of Calvinism's influence and ideas.

PART ONE

Four Myths Calvinists
Should Not Be Circulating
(But Are)

Wall of the Reformers, Geneva (Calvin is second from left)
Image: Wikipedia

MYTH ONE

One Man (Calvin) and
One City (Geneva) Are Determinative

IN 1909, THE CITY OF GENEVA authorized the preparation of a public monument that still functions as a major attraction for Christians who visit the city. The one hundred meter Wall of the Reformers depicts John Calvin flanked by Guillaume Farel, Theodore Beza and John Knox; each figure is five meters tall. The first of these, Farel (1489-1565), had come to Geneva from nearby Bern in 1535, one year prior to Calvin's arrival, to implement a course of religious reformation agreed to by the city fathers; he was the actual pioneer of Geneva's Reformation. The second, Beza (1519-1605), was invited to Geneva at Calvin's urging in 1558 as a minister and Greek scholar; at Calvin's passing in 1564, Beza became the most prominent Genevan minister. The last, the fiery Scot, Knox (c. 1514-1572), was associated with Geneva and with Calvin during years 1555-1559, when he was a fugitive from religious persecution in England and Scotland.

Flanking these five-meter figures, on the right and on the left, are figures of six other individuals; each is three meters high.[1] Each of

---

[1]These are Prince William of Orange (1533-1584), the French Protestant leader Gaspard de Coligny (1519-1572), Prince Frederick William of Brandenburg (1620-1688), the New England colonist Roger Williams (1603-1683), the English soldier-politician Oliver Cromwell

these is reckoned to have been the continuator of Geneva's Reformation principles in another place. As well, there are inscribed on separate cubes of stone the names (but not the likenesses) of Martin Luther (1483-1546), the reformer of Saxony, and Ulrich Zwingli (1484-1531), the pioneer of Zurich's Reformation.[2]

Though it was not the intention of Geneva to suggest by this monument that Calvin had no wider circle of relationships among his contemporaries than the three pictured standing at his side, or that the city had no indebtednesses to other centers of the Reformation, the principle of selection employed in the sculpture can seem to suggest this narrower focus to many who view it. In actuality the usual supposition of Christians standing in the Reformed or Presbyterian branch of the Christian family is that the Reformation as it has come down to us is the legacy of this man, John Calvin, and this city, Geneva. And the sober fact is that such a judgment is far older than the Wall of the Reformers, commissioned in 1909. The notion of Calvin's and of Geneva's dominance was a common nineteenth-century belief, which had roots extending almost back to the age of the Reformation itself. Yet this belief has always stood on a suspect foundation. From where had such an idea come?

THE REFORMATION ERA WAS LITTLE UNDERSTOOD PRIOR TO THE NINETEENTH CENTURY

Prior to the early nineteenth century there were few persons in the English-speaking world who had undertaken deep researches into the Reformation era and its leading characters. Earlier, historians who interpreted the Reformation era tended to do so in very broad brush strokes.[3] The nineteenth century, by contrast, was an era when well-

---

(1599-1658) and the leader of the Hungarian Reformation, Stephen Bocskay (1557-1606).

[2]In 2002, four additional names were chiseled into the stone wall: Marie Dentière (c.1491-1561), a French woman of high theological acumen; Peter Valdes (c. 1140-c. 1217), founder of the Waldensian movement; John Wycliffe (c. 1330-1384), English proto-reformer; and John Hus (c. 1369-1415) the Bohemian reformer who was executed at the Council of Constance.

[3]This is illustrated clearly in the essays of J. H. S. Burleigh, "The Scottish Reformation as Seen in 1660 and 1670," *Records of the Scottish Church History Society* 13 (1959): 241-56; and Ian Henderson, "Reassessment of the Reformers," in *Reformation and Revolution*, ed Duncan Shaw (Edinburgh: St. Andrews Press, 1967), pp. 34-41. As illustrative of the approach taken by

researched treatments of the Reformation and its leaders began to be available.

The first modern biography of Calvin had been composed by a Francophone minister at Berlin, Paul Henry in 1835, but it was not available in English until 1849.[4] After the 1838 publication of his *A History of the Reformation in the Sixteenth Century*, the Swiss historian J. H. Merle D'Aubigné was complimented by the Scottish professor of divinity Thomas Chalmers, who reported to him that until the release of this work, "the Swiss Reformation was very much unknown to the people of this country."[5] Longstanding assumptions in the English-speaking world about the dominant role in Reformation history played by Calvin and Geneva, while very much in evidence, seemed to lack a solid foundation. How had popular impressions been established prior to that time? We must look into the more distant past.

Durable impressions from the Tudor era. Even before the heightened curiosity in the Reformation exhibited in the Victorian age, the English-speaking world had received impressions of a central significance of Calvin and Geneva. John Knox, who is depicted next to Calvin in the Genevan Reformers Wall, had spent the greater part of the years 1555-1559 there, during the time when English Queen Mary Tudor had tried in vain to reinstate Catholicism in England. Knox had been so enamored with Calvin and Geneva that he pronounced it to be "the most perfect school of Christ that ever was in the earth since the days of the Apostles," and on another occasion, "the most godly reformed church and city of the world."[6] Both claims were made for the benefit of readers in his homeland.

Other refugees from England in Geneva spent those years of exile

---

English-speaking church historians in the late eighteenth century, consider the multivolume work of Joseph Milner, *History of the Church of Christ* (London: n.p., 1794).

[4]The two-volume work was *Leben Johann Calvins des grossen Reformators* (1835), translated as *The Life and Times of John Calvin, the Great Reformer* (London and New York: n.p., 1849).

[5]"Thomas Chalmers to J. H. Merle D'Aubigne," February 14, 1846, in *Selections from the Correspondence of the Late Thomas Chalmers, D.D., L.L.D*, ed. W. Hannah (Edinburgh, 1853), p. 447.

[6]John Knox, *Works*, ed. David Laing (Edinburgh: Wodrow Society, 1864), 4:240; *History of the Reformation in Scotland*, ed. W. C. Dickinson (New York: Philosophical Library, 1950), 1:283.

profitably by carrying out the translation of the Geneva Bible. This English translation of 1560 would reign supreme until the middle of the seventeenth century, even though its successor, the Authorized Version, had been published in 1611.[7] The widespread influence of this Bible can only have served, like Knox's dicta, to fix Geneva and Calvin in the Protestant mind as of unrivaled influence. Still later in the sixteenth century, Geneva again became a haven for English-speaking Christian leaders who could not endorse the kind of gradual Reformation endorsed by Queen Elizabeth I and her post-Marian government. Individuals such as Walter Travers (1548-1635) and Thomas Cartwright (c. 1535-1603) found Cambridge University no longer congenial once they criticized the continuation of bishops in the Elizabethan church; Geneva in the era of Theodore Beza now became their place of refuge (Calvin having passed away in 1564). In the same years the emerging Scottish Protestant leader, so prominent among the generation that followed John Knox, Andrew Melville (1545-1622) returned to his homeland (and militant action) following his own interval with Beza at Geneva. For Cartwright, Travers and Melville, Geneva—with or without Calvin still on the scene—epitomized what the "best Reformed churches" stood for; their lament was that the advance of Reformation in their homelands seemed to lag so far behind.[8] Geneva enjoyed this reputation as a bastion of Reformation orthodoxy and zeal throughout the sixteenth century. In that century also theological stu-

---

[7]The origin of the Geneva Bible is described in F. F. Bruce, *The English Bible* (London: Lutterworth, 1961), pp. 86-95. The decades between the publication of the Authorized Version of 1611 and its displacement of the Geneva Bible in popular usage is a testimony to the affection in which it was held.

[8]On these proto-Presbyterians of Elizabethan England, see S. J. Knox and Walter Travers, *Paragon of Elizabethan Puritanism* (London: Methuen, 1962); and A. F. Scott Pearson, *Thomas Cartwright and Elizabethan Puritanism* (Cambridge: Cambridge University Press, 1925). For Melville, see Thomas McCrie, *Life of Andrew Melville* (Edinburgh: n.p., 1824), and Michael Lynch, "Calvinism and Scotland: 1559-1638," in *International Calvinism*, ed. Menna Prestwich, (New York: Oxford University Press, 1985), pp. 225-56. It is the view of Francis Higman, in the essay "Calvin's Works in Translation," in Andrew Pettegree et al., *Calvinism in Europe: 1540-1620* (Cambridge: Cambridge University Press, 1996), pp. 97-99, that the too-close identification of Geneva with these "square-peg" late-Tudor refugees, who could not accept the state of the Reformation at home, served to discredit the Calvin tradition associated with the city. Calvin's English literary influence peaked in the 1570s.

dents from across Europe flocked there in great numbers.[9]

After the seventeenth century. It was generally acknowledged that the Geneva of Calvin had lost its exemplary reputation for rigorous Christianity during the eighteenth century. Such were the concessions to the age of Enlightenment that fundamental doctrines of the faith, such as the deity of Christ, came to be openly questioned. The perception from afar was that Geneva had fallen from her former greatness as a "city set on a hill." By 1800 an Anglican evangelical writer, Thomas Haweis (1732-1820), said, "I doubt if there remains a single professor or pastor at Geneva who adheres to Calvin, either in principle or practice, but the lowest form of moral essay, and Socinian Christianity prevails."[10]

This sense that Geneva was in disarray showed itself well into the nineteenth century; in 1835 the Church of Scotland declined an invitation from Geneva to send representatives the next year to share in festivities marking the tercentennial of the coming of the Reformation to that city. The church at Geneva was deemed by the Scots to have become "deplorably corrupt in doctrine."[11]

Despite this decline in confidence, the trickled-down Tudor ideas of Calvin's and Geneva's original greatness seemed remarkably hardy. A Scottish preacher and philanthropist, Robert Haldane (1764-1842), who visited Geneva in 1816-1817, scolded the canton's council of pastors over their doctrinal waffling. Their countercharge that he was a "rigid Calvinist" prompted him to respond (in print): "Are you afraid of Calvinism? Has the ghost of Calvin, whom you thought dead and buried, and forgotten, appeared among you? Is he again raising his voice

---

[9]So, for example, Jacob Arminius was one of seventy-nine Dutch students who entered the Geneva Academy between 1581 and 1585 (Carl Bangs, *Arminius: A Study in the Dutch Reformation* [Nashville: Abingdon, 1971], p. 66). Yet it is the contention of Gillian Lewis in the essay "The Geneva Academy," in *Calvinism in Europe 1540-1620*, ed. Andrew Pettegree et al. (Cambridge: Cambridge University Press, 1996), p. 62, that the best days of the Academy were already past by 1572; thereafter the theological faculty of the University of Heidelberg surpassed it in renown and drew students away.

[10]Thomas Haweis, *An Impartial History of the Church of Christ* (London: 1800), 3:290.

[11]"Acts of the General Assembly, Church of Scotland," Friday, May 22, 1835, as quoted in Kenneth J. Stewart, *Restoring the Reformation: British Evangelicalism and the Francophone Réveil 1816-1849* (Milton Keynes, U.K.: Paternoster, 2006), p. 196.

from the chair which he once occupied?"[12]

A contemporary, the London minister and future Anglican missionary-bishop of Calcutta Daniel Wilson (1778-1858), visited the city in 1823 and demonstrated that he was equally in the grip of these legendary ideas about Calvin and the Reformation: "I approach Geneva with feelings of peculiar veneration. The name of Calvin stands highest among the Reformers, Divines and Scholars of the sixteenth century. There is no man to whom I owe so much as a commentator."[13]

These nineteenth-century sentiments are inexplicable without our making reference to the persistence of ideas passed down from Tudor times. But acknowledging the persistence of this legendary lore about Geneva and Calvin tells only one part of the story. There remains another.

The selectivity of those early impressions. This lore, implying the centrality of Calvin and Geneva passed down from the sixteenth to the nineteenth century, was flawed inasmuch as it was based on a kind of selective reporting about places and persons. John Knox, who had been so eager to extol Geneva's virtues, had also been present briefly (in 1554) as a refugee in the south German city of Frankfurt-am-Main. Knox was less liturgically oriented than some of the other English-speaking refugees who had made this their safe haven in Queen Mary's times of persecution, and had resisted the proposal to follow the Anglican Book of Common Prayer in what he considered to be a slavish manner.[14] He would later extol the perfections of Geneva, rather than Frankfurt, in large part because the refugee congregation in the former had agreed to no such constraints on their way of worshiping God. Geneva seemed to him more congenial, but it was not, after all, such a solitary haven for refugees like him.

In point of fact, for every John Knox who would later recall happy

---

[12]Robert Haldane, *Letter to Chenevière* (Edinburgh: n.p., 1824), p. 21.

[13]Daniel Wilson, *Letters of an Absent Brother*, 3rd ed. (London: n.p., 1825), 2:289.

[14]Knox, it should be pointed out, had been serving the Church of England while a Scottish Protestant refugee during young King Edward's reign. His reservation about the use of the Book of Common Prayer was therefore the reservation of one who had gained familiarity with it by prior use.

associations in Calvin's Geneva,[15] there were other refugees, such as the future Archbishop of Canterbury, Edmund Grindal (c. 1519-1583), and the future Archbishop of York Edwin Sandys (c. 1516-1588), who had the same happy recollections of Strasbourg. The future Anglican bishop of Salisbury John Jewell (1522-1571) recorded his happy recollections of Zurich, to which he had proceeded after spending the first part of his exile in Strasbourg.[16] John Knox's own eventual co-reformer of Scotland, John Willock (1515-1585), who, like Knox had served the Church of England temporarily in the reign of King Edward, spent his exile in Mary's reign at Emden, a North Sea port city in what is now the Netherlands; at Emden the links were not with Geneva and Calvin but with Zurich and Heinrich Bullinger.[17] Miles Coverdale (1488-1568), the continuator of William Tyndale's Bible translation work, spent his years of exile in the Rhine valley city of Wesel as well as Geneva. The chronicler of Christian martyrs from Roman antiquity to bloody Queen Mary's reign, John Foxe (1516-1587), sojourned at both Frankfurt and Basel. Still-additional European cities of the Reformation such as Cologne and Aarau proved every bit as hospitable. Beyond these Protestant cities, refugees even landed in Padua and Venice.[18] The question naturally arises, therefore, as to why Geneva's

---

[15]With Knox in Geneva there had also been refugees such as William Whittingham (c. 1524-1579) eventual primary translator of the Geneva Bible.

[16]"Oh Zurich, Zurich how much oftener do I now think of thee than I thought of England when I was in Zurich!" was how Jewell expressed his sense of loss in 1560 of the company of that city and his former mentor Peter Martyr Vermigli, whom he had followed to Zurich during the Marian exile (see Hastings Robinson, ed. *The Zurich Letters: Comprising the Correspondence of Several Bishops of the English Church and others with the Helvetian Reformers* [Cambridge: Cambridge University Press, 1842], 1:23).

[17]Duncan Shaw, "John Willock," in *Reformation and Revolution*, ed. Duncan Shaw (Edinburgh: St. Andrew Press, 1969), pp. 42-69.

[18]This wider pattern of English-speaking involvement with other European cities of the Reformation began to reemerge from obscurity in the nineteenth century with the publication of such volumes as *Original Letters Relative to the English Reformation* (Cambridge: Cambridge University Press, 1846); *The Zurich Letters* (Cambridge: Cambridge University Press, 1842); and Edward Arber, ed., *A Brief Discourse of the Troubles at Frankfort* (London: Elliot Stock, 1908). In the twentieth century the body of refugees, numbering some eight hundred, have been researched by Christina Garrett, *The Marian Exiles* (Cambridge: Cambridge University Press, 1938); Martin Simpson, "On the Troubles at Frankfort," in *Reformation and Revolution*, ed. Duncan Shaw (Edinburgh: St. Andrew Press, 1967); and most recently Dan G. Danner, *Pilgrimage to Puritanism: History and Theology of the Marian Exiles at Geneva 1555-1560* (New York: Peter Lang, 1999).

story was remembered and not that of the others.

But this is to concentrate our quest only back to the tumultuous years of Queen Mary Tudor's reign (1553-1558) and to the persons who gained impressions of the Reformation on the Continent when they were refugees. On closer examination, however, these multiple links with European Protestantism had roots extending back to the reign of Henry VIII. It is clear that Calvin's influence was being exerted in England by the closing years of that reign. He willingly entered into correspondence with those who presided over England's government in the minority of Henry's son and heir, Edward.[19] Yet, on the other hand, staunch John Hooper, bishop of Gloucester from 1551, had found refuge with Heinrich Bullinger in Zurich in the closing years of aged King Henry VIII's reign. And from Strasbourg in 1547 there had come to England the distinguished theologians Martin Bucer (1491-1551), who took a post at Cambridge, and Peter Martyr Vermigli (1499-1562), who took a post at Oxford. The city of Emden furnished to London in those same years of young King Edward's reign the distinguished reformer of Polish extraction John à Lasco (1499-1560).

And as to literary influence, Zwingli's successor at Zurich, Heinrich Bullinger (1504-1575), had an influence in Tudor England equal to or surpassing that of Calvin of Geneva; his theological expositions (popularly known as *The Decades*) were available in English from as early as 1549;[20] they were on recommended-reading lists for ministers in the Elizabethan period. It thus emerges that there is an important story here which has not received equal telling.

An actual diminution of John Calvin's role in intervening centuries. Though it may sound very odd, given the persistence of these legends

---

[19]So, for example A. G. Dickens, *The English Reformation* (London: Batsford, 1964), chap. 9.

[20]Bullinger's earliest known work translated into English is *The Christian State of Matrimony* (London, 1541). His *Decades* (originally titled in English, *Fiftie godlie and learned sermons divided into five decades*) were reissued by the Parker Society, London, in four volumes 1849-1852. Peter Opitz, "Heinrich Bullinger's *Decades:* Instruction in Faith and Conduct," in *Architect of Reformation: An Introduction to Heinrich Bullinger, 1504-1575*, ed. Bruce Gordon and Emidio Campi (Grand Rapids: Baker, 2004), pp. 101-2 demonstrates that this influence in late Tudor England was replicated across Europe in both German and Dutch editions. Bullinger's Tudor influence has recently been explored afresh by J. Torrance Kirby, *The Zurich Connection and Tudor Political Theology* (Leiden, Netherlands: E. J. Brill, 2007).

of Calvin and of Geneva's perpetual eminence in wider Protestant Christianity, the fact is that Calvin's literary and theological influence had actually gone into eclipse by the late sixteenth century. This was no particular indication of antipathy toward Calvin, for we can recall that even Jacobus Arminius (1560-1609), that dissenter from Calvinist orthodoxy, had praised his biblical commentaries.[21] The decline of influence only meant that Calvin and the generation of his contemporaries had left very capable theological and literary successors who were rightly famous in their own times.[22] The time had come for a move "beyond Calvin," and beyond his contemporaries also.[23] This meant that in the seventeenth century the prominent names in Reformed theology were "Beza, Junius, Danaeus, Ursinus, and above all Zanchius," but not Calvin.[24]

The transmission of Swiss Reformed theology into English-speaking lands in this period also contributed to the emergence of a kind of hybridized Reformed theology that various writers have called "Anglo-Calvinism";[25] certain elements of the earlier Lutheran phase of the Reformation in England were also incorporated. Theologians such as William Perkins (1558-1602), William Ames (1576-1633), John Cameron

---

[21]Arminius relates that "in the interpretation of Scripture, Calvin's *Commentaries* are more valuable than anything that is handed down to us in the writings of the Fathers," in Jacobus Arminius, "Letter to Sebastian Egbertsz, May 3, 1607," in Nathan Bangs, *Arminius: A Study in the Dutch Reformation* (Nashville: Abingdon, 1971), pp. 287-88.

[22]Thus, B. B. Warfield, describing the history of the various editions of Calvin's *Institutes* notes the marked decline in the number of printed editions after 1609—a trend not reversed until the early nineteenth century. Cf. "The Literary History of Calvin's *Institutes*," in *Works of B. B. Warfield* (Grand Rapids: Baker, 1981), 5:373-428.

[23]Graeme Murdoch, *Beyond Calvin* (Basingstoke and New York: Palgrave Macmillan, 2004). Murdoch's book deals with developments in the international Reformed movement into the seventeenth century.

[24]Patrick Collinson, "England and International Calvinism: 1558-1640," in *International Calvinism 1541-1715*, ed. Menna Prestwich (Oxford: Oxford University Press, 1986), pp. 214-15. John H. Primus has illustrated this relative "eclipse" of Calvin by 1600 in his demonstration of the change of sabbatarian views of the Puritan, Nicholas Bound. Bound's two books on the sabbath (1595, 1606) demonstrate a shift in deference *from* Calvin *to* Jerome Zanchius. See John H. Primus, "Calvin and the Puritan Sabbath," in *Exploring the Heritage of John Calvin*, ed. David E. Holwerda (Grand Rapids: Eerdmans, 1976), p. 58

[25]The attempt to define the indigenization of the Reformed theology within English-speaking countries through a hybridization with preexistent lingering Lollard and earlier Lutheran influences has been attempted by writers such as Gordon Rupp, *Religion in England: 1688-1791* (Oxford: Clarendon, 1986), pp. 325, 483; and Richard L. Greaves, *John Bunyan* (Grand Rapids: Eerdmans, 1969), pp. 24, 29, 33.

(1579-1625), David Dickson (1583-1663), James Ussher (1581-1656) and John Owen (1616-1683) gained renown in their lifetimes, and this extended well beyond their own England, Ireland and Scotland. By the eighteenth century the "names" in Reformed theology were still less likely to be led by that of Calvin; rather, students of theology were reading English-speaking writers William Ames (1576-1633) and Richard Baxter (1615-1691) as well as Johannes Wollebius (1586-1629) of Basel, the Genevan François Turretin (1623-1687) and his son, John Alphonse Turretin (1671-1737). They read Benedict Pictet (1655-1724) of the same city and John Marck (1655-1731) of Leyden. Those wishing to read theology that was more pliable in the face of the Enlightenment could consult Geneva's Jacob Vernet (1698-1789).[26] All this is to say that by the early seventeenth century Calvin had been eclipsed.

A NINETEENTH-CENTURY CALVIN RENAISSANCE: FOUR FACTORS

Romanticism in theology. For complex reasons that can only be touched on here, the eclipse of Calvin's influence began to be reversed at just about the point in European history when Napoleon met his Waterloo and peace returned to Europe (1815). The primary factor working to stimulate interest in Calvin (and the Reformation era, generally) was the rising romantic spirit of the times. Just as popular writers such as Sir Walter Scott were churning out bestsellers such as *Ivanhoe* (1819), which re-created misty medieval times, replete with castles, jousts and chivalry, so also were there authors and a readership for historical and biographical works exploring the events and heroes of the sixteenth century. The year 1817, three centuries after Martin Luther nailed his "Ninety-Five Theses" to the church door at Wittenberg, seems to have

---

[26]H. McLachlan, *English Education Under the Test Acts* (Manchester, U.K.: Manchester University Press, 1931), pp. 22, 300-303; David Bogue and James Bennett, *History of Dissenters* (London: n.p., 1808), 3:333, 361. David Sorkin, "Geneva's 'Enlightened Orthodoxy': The Middle Way of Jacob Vernet (1689-1789)," *Church History* 74, no. 2 (2005): 286-305. The influence of post-sixteenth-century European Reformed theology in Scotland is helpfully explored by G. D. Henderson, "Dutch Influences on Scottish Theology," *Evangelical Quarterly* 5, no. 1 (1933): 33-45. The significance of this move "beyond Calvin" has been lost on many twentieth-century commentators who, conscious that seventeenth-century Protestant theology contained scholastic tendencies, *blame* Protestantism for moving forward with writers such as Marck, Pictet and Turretin. This attitude itself seems to bespeak the primeval tendency I have already indicated that has been so unrealistic and romantic.

triggered a great wave of historical curiosity in many people. A wealthy British visitor to Geneva in this postwar period, Henry Drummond (1786-1860), a man who was decidedly affected by this romantic out-look, found no edition of Calvin's *Institutes* for sale at his visit there in 1817. Before he departed, he had personally financed the republication of the *Institutes* in the French language.[27]

Resurgent Catholicism after the 1815 Council of Vienna. European and English-speaking Protestants had reason to be apprehensive about stirrings in international Roman Catholicism, as well, stirrings which had repercussions in their cities and towns.[28] After having to reach an accommodation with Emperor Napoleon to weather the era of revolution,[29] the papacy after the Council of Vienna (which attempted to restore a pre-revolutionary state of affairs in Europe after Napoleon's demise) sought to assert its authority where it had not been felt for some time. In England in 1850 the papacy reestablished a range of Catholic bishops to oversee its clergy, its members and adherents.[30] This devel-opment was termed "the papal aggression" by the English, whose pre-Reformation episcopal bishoprics had been absorbed into the protes-tantized Church of England. It is quite plain that the Church of Rome was perceived at this time to be contesting a state of affairs vis-à-vis Protestant Europe that had lain fallow for a very long time.[31] The emergence of the Tractarian movement beginning in 1833 was per-ceived as similarly threatening. This was a campaign of agitation and publication of pamphlets advocating the appropriation of certain ele-ments of Catholic belief and devotion within the national Church of England. Such uncertainties as these helped create a climate of uncer-tainty in which a fresh appeal to the various Reformers of the sixteenth

---

[27]The early nineteenth century witnessed the first rigorously investigative biography of John Knox , the Scots Reformer, in a two-volume work by Thomas McCrie (1811, 1813) (Kenneth J. Stewart, *Restoring the Reformation: British Evangelicalism and the Francophone Réveil 1816-1849* [Carlisle, U.K.: Paternoster, 2006], p. 206).

[28]See B. G. Worral, *The Making of the Modern Church: Christianity in England Since 1800* (Lon-don: SPCK, 2004), chap. 9.

[29]A concordat was signed between the pope and Napoleon in 1803.

[30]In place of bishops, Roman Catholicism had relied on persons termed "vicars apostolic," who responsible directly to the pope, had a roaming commission throughout a country.

[31]Worral, *Making of the Modern Church*, p. 171.

century seemed very timely. Calvin, some remembered, had shown himself an able anti-Roman controversialist.

An evangelical resurgence at Geneva. If, in 1800, the view of Protestants across Europe and the new world was that Geneva had deplorably declined from its past position as a bastion of the Reformation, this opinion began to be reversed in the era after Napoleon's defeat in 1815. In those years a movement of spiritual awakening began to unfold at Geneva and extended into other French-speaking regions of western Europe. The awakening drew on a variety of strands: the work of traveling Moravian evangelists, elements of surviving Reformed orthodoxy in and around Geneva, and the foreign influences of visitors from Britain and America such as Robert Haldane (1764-1842) and John Mitchell Mason (1770-1829). The state church of Canton Geneva was only marginally affected by this awakening, and took obstructive efforts to hamper its influence in the churches and among theological students in the Geneva Academy. But by 1831 a new school of theology was erected and its graduates went in all directions from Geneva to preach the gospel in the French language. Prominent Genevans such as historian J. H. Merle D'Aubigne (1794-1872), soon to gain great renown as author of the multivolume *History of the Reformation in the Sixteenth Century*, and a pastor-theologian Louis Gaussen (1790-1863), author of the famous book on inspiration, *Theopneustia*, were associated with the new school. These teachers became the exemplars of a new phase of evangelical vitality at Geneva; they were lionized as leading Christian thinkers across the Protestant world. D'Aubigne in particular traveled widely in the English-speaking world.[32]

A flurry of Calvin republication. Symptomatic of a changed climate was the creation of the Calvin Translation Society at Edinburgh in 1843. Within the space of two decades this society commissioned and published a fresh edition of John Calvin's *Institutes of the Christian Religion* (1845), a three-volume edition of his *Tracts and Treatises*, and each of his commentaries on books of the Old and New Testaments.[33] The net effect

---

[32]The repercussions of this awakening or "réveil" at Geneva are discussed in two recent books: Timothy F. S. Stunt, *From Awakening to Secession* (Edinburgh: T & T Clark, 2000); and Stewart, *Restoring the Reformation*.

[33]This second nineteenth-century English translation of the *Institutes* came to be known as the Beveridge translation, after Henry Beveridge, the translator who was an Anglican clergyman.

of this re-release of so much of Calvin's published material was a virtual Calvin renaissance. Calvin, the early Reformed theologian and commentator, was in consequence more of a force to be reckoned with in 1864 (the tercentennial of his death at Geneva) than in 1764 or 1664. His reputation now went from being the "great Reformer" on the basis of lore about him transmitted from Tudor times to being the "still-greater Reformer" whose posthumous literary influence now grew by leaps and bounds. It is in such a context that we observe Victorian Christianity exalting John Calvin to a degree not customary a century earlier.

Accordingly, William Cunningham, the theologian of New College, Edinburgh, extolled the Genevan Reformer in 1864 by stating:

> The *Institutes* of Calvin is the most important work in the history of theological science, that which is more than any other creditable to its author, and has exerted directly or indirectly the greatest and most beneficial influence upon the opinions of intelligent men on theological subjects.[34]

This judgment reflected to a very high degree the proliferation of editions of Calvin's writings that had come about in the two decades preceding. It was not a verdict one would have heard pronounced fifty or a hundred years before. That long before the Calvin "renaissance" Protestant theological study was still in its beyond-Calvin mode. It was this determination to pursue a Reformed theology that had advanced beyond the sixteenth century which explains the use of the writers Turretin, Pictet, Doddridge and others through the eighteenth into the nineteenth centuries.

Charles Spurgeon's counsel to the students in his London Pastor's College in 1876 also reflected this Calvin renaissance. Addressing the subject of classic Bible commentaries suitable for the pastor's library, he urged:

The *Tracts and Treatises* (Edinburgh: Calvin Translation Society, 1844) included Calvin's anti-Roman *Reply to Cardinal Sadoleto* and *An Antidote to the Council of Trent*. The commentaries were kept in print over the whole of the nineteenth century and were eventually reprinted, without change, in the 1950s by Eerdmans of Grand Rapids. This nineteenth-century edition of the commentaries has been reprinted yet again by Baker of Grand Rapids.

[34]William Cunningham, *The Reformers and the Theology of the Reformation* (Edinburgh: T & T Clark, 1866), p. 295.

It would not be possible for me too earnestly to press upon you the importance of reading the expositions of that prince among men, John Calvin! I am afraid that scant purses may debar you from their purchase, but if it be possible, procure them. . . . You will find forty-two or more goodly volumes worth their weight in gold.[35]

The memory of Calvin had been revived on a scale that was out of sync with earlier centuries. The ground was inadvertently being prepared by this Calvin renaissance for what I have termed the *primeval* appeals to the authority and writings of the Genevan Reformer that would characterize much of Protestant life in the past century and a half. Let us consider some of the changes this proliferation of Calvin's writings in English would bring with it.

In the seventeenth and eighteenth centuries, when Christians called themselves Calvinists, they scarcely ever meant by this that they had a library well-stocked with books penned by the Genevan; these books were still largely unobtainable because long out of print. People who used the term *Calvinist* acquired their theological systems by other means and from other authors. The great evangelist George Whitefield (1714-1770), for example, seems to have developed his theological views by reading authors such as the late Puritan commentator Matthew Henry (1662-1714), the Scotts Episcopal writer Henry Scougal (1650-1678), and his evangelical Scots contemporaries Ebenezer Erskine (1680-1754) and Ralph Erskine (1685-1752). On one occasion this self-consciously Calvinist preacher insisted that he had never read a word of Calvin.[36] Examples of the contrary kind were uncommon. Yet by 1850 this had changed dramatically. There was a general resurgence of interest in the Reformation of the sixteenth century for the reasons described earlier.

To be sure, from the 1840s onward, there were also republication projects of the works of some other Reformers. The reprinting of the writings of English Reformers Cranmer, Ridley, Hooper and Jewell was undertaken by the Parker Society (established 1840). In Scotland the works of Knox were collected and published by 1848. Yet plainly

---

[35]C. H. Spurgeon, *Commenting and Commentaries* (New York: Sheldon, 1876), p. 15.
[36]Arnold Dallimore, *George Whitefield*, 2 vols. (London: Banner, 1970, 1980), 1:82, 574.

the republication programs of these decades did more to boost the influence of Calvin and Geneva than of any other Reformer or of any other city of the Reformation. I am not saying that Calvin's influence has been at a constant high pitch during the past 150 years. In fact there seem to have been identifiable waves of fresh interest in Calvin since that time, with the most recent emerging in about 1994. I am only affirming that it rose to a much higher pitch then, and subsequently, than in the centuries preceding.

CALVIN AND GENEVA RECONSIDERED

Given that the legend of the central importance of Calvin and Geneva was originally overplayed in the aftermath of the Reformation era by those who returned from refuge there, that it declined in seventeenth and eighteenth centuries, only to undergo massive rediscovery in the nineteenth, where do we stand now in our attempts to understand how this powerful movement has come down to us?

It seems that we cannot escape a kind of reformulation of these things, things which so many have previously treated as instinctive and straightforward. Despite what conservative Calvinist literature continues to reiterate by profuse references to Calvin and the city he labored in, it is not justifiable to continue to think in terms of a preeminent Reformer and city being the prime mediators of this theological movement down to our own time. On the basis of the experience of the English-speaking refugees to Europe in Mary's time alone, we are required to consider that Geneva was but one of more than a half dozen Reformation cities that, in welcoming the English refugees during their exile, also ensured that their literature, liturgy and piety were taken up and made the basis of comparisons with things at home. Recent Reformation research points very clearly in this direction.

Two recent writers, Philip Benedict and Graeme Murdoch, have written masterful treatments that consolidate many recent studies of the century of Reformation, studies centering in the various Swiss cantons.[37] Both help us to discover more accurately how, across Western

---

[37]Philip Benedict, *Christ's Churches Purely Reformed: A Social History of Calvinism* (New Haven, Conn.: Yale University Press, 2002); and Murdoch, *Beyond Calvin*.

Europe, there were available what an older historian, the late Gordon Rupp, called various "patterns of Reformation."[38] These patterns emerged in settings such as these cantons, and were eventually transmitted across land and sea to new homes, where they were grafted onto earlier, local strivings after reform. Benedict and Murdoch help us to understand how, like the ever-widening ripples emanating from a pebble dropped into water, the Reformation movements, not at Geneva alone, but also at Zurich, Basel, Strasbourg, Emden and Bern, each had their own spheres or circles of influence east and west across Europe. While our focus is on English-speaking lands, we find our questions answered as part of this larger canvas. The implications of attempting to see what English-speakers have called Calvinism in this wider framework are not far to seek. Here are several.

Calvin's relationships with other Reformers. A cursory investigation of Calvin's own life rapidly brings to light his own indebtedness to and relationships with Reformers both senior to and contemporary with him. As a student in France in the 1520s, he along with others had been accused of Lutheran heresy and fled the fires of persecution that claimed even his own brother.[39] It has been seriously maintained that Luther's Small Catechism was a significant influence on Calvin in the composition of the first edition of his *Institutes*.[40] We know that Calvin admired Luther, and that the senior Reformer thought well of some of Calvin's early writings.[41] Thus we are obliged to speak of some measure of debt owed by Calvin to this senior Reformer.

Just prior to his arrival at Geneva in 1536, that canton had embraced the Reformation cause at the instigation of neighboring canton Bern.[42] The Bernese influence, while indispensable initially, proved to be a

---

[38]Gordon Rupp, *Patterns of Reformation* (Philadelphia: Fortress Press, 1969).

[39]So, for example T. H. L. Parker, *John Calvin: A Life* (Philadelphia: Westminster Press, 1975), chap. 2; Wulfert de Greef, *The Writings of John Calvin* (Grand Rapids: Baker, 1989), pp. 20-21.

[40]De Greef, *Writings of Calvin*, pp. 27-28.

[41]Jules Bonnet, *Letters of John Calvin*, 4 vols. (Philadelphia: Presbyterian Board of Publication, 1858), 1:167. In the November 20, 1539, letter of Calvin (at Strasbourg) to Farel, Calvin repeats praise relayed from Luther through his new colleague, Martin Bucer.

[42]Bern, having embraced the Reformation on a model very much like that of Zurich, placed inordinate ecclesiastical power in the hands of the city government. This tendency, which infringed on the domain of the church, was always resisted by Calvin.

mixed blessing in later years, as it was following a pattern of Reformation drawn very extensively from Zurich in Zwingli's day. After his very brief initial ministry at Geneva (1536-1538), Calvin's sudden exile to Strasbourg through 1541 enabled him to expand his understanding of various issues, with senior Reformer Martin Bucer (1491-1551) as his mentor. The importance of discipline in the maintenance of the purity of the congregation and the supervisory ministry of congregational elders were but two issues about which his understanding advanced in this mentoring relationship.[43] Heinrich Bullinger and the Zurich ministers were consulted (along with other such sister churches) in the controversy stirred up over predestination by Jerome Bolsec in 1551, and in the awkward Servetus affair of 1553. It was important for the Genevan authorities, and for Calvin, that their city be seen to act in solidarity with others of like faith. And when there began to appear doctrinal fissures between the Swiss Reformed cantons that had embraced the Reformation, these two leaders (with others) collaborated in the composition of the *Mutual Consent in Regard to the Sacraments Between the Ministers of the Church in Zurich and John Calvin, Minister of the Church in Geneva* (1549).[44] When Calvin had departed this life in 1564, his Zurich contemporary, Bullinger, pressed ahead in completing the Second Helvetic Confession (1566) as a means of consolidating the witness of the Reformed Swiss; Geneva under the guidance of Calvin's successor, Theodore Beza, took up the creed.[45] The composite picture emerging is not one that supports a view of the solitary greatness of one single Reformer and a single city.

Calvin's influence in the English-speaking world simultaneous with but not eclipsing that of contemporaries. From the mere fact that Calvin vied with Martin Bucer, Peter Martyr Vermigli and Heinrich Bullinger

---

[43]On the Bucer-Calvin relationship in these Strasbourg years, see Wilhelm Pauck, *The Heritage of the Reformation* (New York: Oxford University Press, 1961), chap. 6; Willem van't Spijker, "Bucer's Influence on Calvin: Church and Community," in *Martin Bucer: Reforming Church and Community*, ed. David F. Wright (Cambridge: Cambridge University Press, 1994), chap. 3.

[44]This *Mutual Consent* was made public in 1554, having been composed in 1549. It is usually referred to as the *Consensus Tigurensis*. The document is printed in Calvin's *Tracts and Treatises* (Edinburgh: Calvin Translation Society, 1849), vol. 2.

[45]This document is most readily available in the Arthur C. Cochrane, ed. *Reformed Confessions of the Sixteenth Century* (Philadelphia: Westminster Press, 1966), pp. 220-301.

for the attention of English-speaking readers in the Tudor period, we have little basis for supposing, as have many, that Calvin stood like a solitary colossus above the scene.[46] Bucer and Martyr, while resident in England, were called on to assist in the revisions of the first Protestant prayer book, which had been produced in 1549. Calvin's influence in official circles in England declined because of his suspected concurrence with the writings of John Knox, some of which called into question the right of women to rule.[47] In 1563, when thirty-seven advanced Protestant Anglican preachers were suspended from their offices for their refusal to wear the prescribed clerical garments, Bullinger and the Zurich ministers were called on to advise as to what prudent steps ought to be next taken.[48] By 1570, when Elizabeth's government needed assistance in dealing with a papacy ready to excommunicate her for her failure to follow in the Catholicizing steps of her half-sister, the English government turned to the same Heinrich Bullinger for literary assistance. Calvin, who had passed from the scene in 1564, never had the same leverage with Tudor governments after the Knox episode. In Scotland, Knox was the solitary representative among the six men (all named John) who led the reform in the crucial period of 1559-1560 who had known links with Geneva and the theology of Calvin. The ongoing influence of Luther's thought, as well as the principles of Zwingli and Bullinger, were just as current among the six Johns as was Calvin's theology.[49]

The witness of the exiles not determinative of which city was preeminent. From the mere fact that English-speaking refugees in Queen Mary's time went as willingly to Zurich as to Basel, to Emden as to Strasbourg, to Wesel as to Geneva to await providential developments

---

[46]C. D. Cremeans, who if anything was accustomed to detect Calvin's influence beyond what was verifiable, nevertheless concluded that by the time of young King Edward's reign (1548-1553) "Calvin wielded nothing like a dominant influence at this time" (*The Reception of Calvinistic Thought in England* [Urbana: University of Illinois Press, 1949], p. 30).

[47]One particular writing of Knox, *First Blast of the Trumpet Against the Monstrous Regiment of Women*, had been composed in 1558 while the persecuting Mary Tudor was still on the throne. By the time of its publication (and Calvin warned against its release), Mary was deceased and her Protestant half-sister, Elizabeth, installed on the throne.

[48]Cf. Patrick Collinson, *The Elizabethan Puritan Movement* (London and New York: Methuen, 1967), pp. 71-83.

[49]Lynch, "Calvinism and Scotland," p. 229.

that would make it safe for them to return home, and went knowing full well that these Reformation cities had characteristic liturgical and theological features, we ought to grant that notions of Genevan preeminence or dominance in the age of Reformation are exaggerated. If alumni of the Marian exile looked back fondly on their sojourn in Geneva, so also did their compatriots remember Zurich, Strasbourg, Frankfurt and Emden.

We need therefore to accept that our readiness to suppose Calvin's dominance in that age is as much a product of old literary iconography, now centuries old, combined with the well-intentioned republication programs of the Victorian period. We cannot know, at present, why those Victorian editors who made it their business to reprint Calvin's works on such a massive scale did not show the same zeal for the writings of Zwingli, Bullinger and Peter Martyr. It might very well be that these well-intentioned editors were themselves influenced too much by the surviving stories from the Tudor age. It seems entirely possible that they did not launch those other republishing programs because they accepted Calvin's preeminence as self-evident.[50] We must be ready to consider the possibility that our still-current fixation on Calvin above other Reformers is as much a reflection of the wide availability of his translated works in the past century and a half as it is a reflection of his early greatness. The next time we hear someone try to win a theological discussion with an apt quotation from the Genevan Reformer, we should remind ourselves that while the mere availability of texts may seem to enhance their authority, this availability by itself cannot prove their original preeminence.

WHAT DIFFERENCE DOES THIS MAKE?

One implication of all this is that we must, in consequence, learn to

---

[50]Zwingli's works were not made available in English translation until 1912, when Samuel Macaulay Jackson edited the *Shorter Works of Zwingli* for G. P. Putnam of New York. Bullinger was left untranslated, apart from the Victorian edition of his *Decades*. Mere excerpts of this were published in *Zwingli and Bullinger*, edited by G. W. Bromiley for Westminster Press of Philadelphia in 1953. Translation of Peter Martyr was utterly neglected since the Tudor age, when his *Common Places* rivaled Calvin's *Institutes* as a standard text in theology. However, a *Peter Martyr Library* of translated texts (commenced in 1994) had reached nine volumes at the time of this writing. The publisher is Thomas Jefferson University, Kirksville, Missouri.

express ourselves differently. The terms *Calvinism* and *Calvinist* have been in the English language since the 1570s, but their enduring and widespread usage has reflected the embrace of a series of assumptions about Calvin and Geneva that are, on examination, overplayed.[51] *Calvinist* and *Calvinism* are not ideal terms to describe an approach to Christian faith and theology descending from multiple centers that knew few boundaries and had a high degree of fraternal cooperation within Swiss-South German Protestantism.[52] And if such terms as *Calvinist* are to be discontinued, what then? It seems that we have no choice but to adopt the broader and slightly more generic terminology *Reformed*. This is the historical terminology actually used by the pan-European movement of Christians and churches of the sixteenth century that understood themselves to be in solidarity with the Swiss.

It is understandable that there will be some for whom this proposal is problematic. For these the term *Calvinist* does not necessarily connote support for covenant theology or for the baptism of infants, whereas (they suppose) the term *Reformed* implies both. I can appreciate the anxiety but not the logic. The distinction of terms appears to only to have this implication in the English-speaking world, whereas in Europe the terms seem to be used more interchangeably. Besides, surely those who prefer the time-honored terminology of *Calvinist* for reasons such as these know that they do not have the Genevan Reformer's backing in their doctrinal reservations. And what is more, all the good historical reasons for abandoning the terminology of *Calvinist* and *Calvinism* as misrepresentative of a multicitied, multileader and international movement still apply.

Beyond this concern about labels, what other difference can we expect the preceding review to make? The difference can be seen by taking a known issue emerging in Calvin's career and asking what we are to make of it. Simply because it is a question being discussed by many Christians today, we can ask, Did John Calvin have an opinion about

---

[51]The compact edition of the *Oxford English Dictionary* of 1971 records an earliest usage of 1566 for the archaic form *Calvynian*, of 1570 for *Calvynisme* and of 1579 for *Calvynyste;* by contrast, the form *Calvinistic* does not appear until Sir Walter Scott employed it in 1820.

[52]The late David F. Wright wrote in 1972 that it was "surely far nearer the mark historically to describe Calvin as a 'Buceran' than Bucer as a Calvinist" (David F. Wright, trans. and ed., *The Common Places of Martin Bucer* [Appleford, U.K.: Sutton Courtenay, 1972], p. 17).

the frequency of the administration of the Lord's Supper?[53]

It is not difficult to uncover evidence that the young Calvin favored weekly observance. When he had only been in Geneva a matter of months in 1537, he presented "Articles Concerning the Church and Worship" to the city fathers; he went on record as favoring "at least weekly" celebration of the holy meal.[54] Agreement was not given by the council of Geneva to Calvin's stated preference; if they had implemented his request, it would have marked a very great revision from what had been pre-Reformation practice. By 1541, the time of his return to Geneva after the three-year exile to Strasbourg, he proposed a monthly administration of the Supper in one of the linked congregations in the city with the understanding that each congregation would have the sacrament administered at least four times per year.[55] In the final edition of the *Institutes of the Christian Religion* (1559), Calvin once more endorsed his 1537 opinion.[56]

That Calvin had such fluctuating opinions about the administration of the Lord's Supper is a matter of historical record; there can be no dispute about that. But the difficulty arises when we ask the more difficult questions, How significant is Calvin's opinion on this subject? and, Are we under any necessity of agreeing with his final opinion about this? The point of view I mean to caution against here is the one that, once armed with the reliable information that such an opinion was Calvin's, is ready to brandish Calvin's opinion in a way that places a burden of proof on believers within the Reformed tradition who see the matter differently. This "Calvin trumps all" argument is untenable.

Any obligation to adopt Calvin's view on this or any other question must first be carefully established on scriptural grounds, then in light of the wider circle of Reformers who were Calvin's contemporaries and successors, and then in light of the subsequent transmission of Re-

---

[53]The third chapter of this book examines Calvin's view of predestination within this same framework.

[54]John Calvin, "Articles Concerning the Organization of the Church" (1537), in *Calvin's Theological Treatises*, ed. J. K. S. Reid (London: SCM Press, 1954), p. 49.

[55]John Calvin, "Draft Ecclesiastical Ordinances" (1541), in *Calvin's Theological Treatises*, ed. J. K. S. Reid (London: SCM Press, 1954), p. 60.

[56]John Calvin, *Institutes of the Christian Religion*, ed. John T. McNeill (Philadelphia: Westminster Press, 1960), 4.17.43

formed theology across intervening centuries in confessions and articles of faith adopted by churches. On this, as on so many other questions, there has been no necessary "falling into step" with Calvin because these named criteria do not require it.[57] Geneva and Calvin represent one of the beginning points of the Reformed tradition, but not the only beginning and not the endpoint either! This is the kind of problem that has vexed the Reformed tradition, especially since the massive revival of interest in Calvin following the large-scale republication of his works since 1843. We need to move beyond it now.

DISCUSSION QUESTIONS

1. In what open or subtle ways have you encountered the suggestion that Geneva and Calvin were dominant among non-Lutheran Protestants in the age of the Reform?

2. If you are familiar with the outline of Calvin's life, are you as familiar with the life of any of his friends or contemporary Reformers? If not, why?

3. If you are accustomed to quoting John Calvin or to hearing him quoted, how do you guard against giving his opinions a prominence that slights his important contemporaries and successors?

4. If you are ready to describe yourself as a Calvinist, is there some reason why you would hesitate to alternately describe yourself as Reformed or standing in the Reformed tradition? What is the advantage of one form of terminology over the other?

5. John Calvin's original influence faded for good and natural reasons. How can we guard now against vesting his writings and opinions with an authority that sidesteps the question of why that original influence faded?

---

[57]The New Testament does not directly address the question of the frequency of the Lord's Supper; far too much weight is placed by those who affirm the contrary on Acts 20:7, where it is supposed that the reference to "breaking of bread" on the first day of the week is an unambiguous reference to this sacrament, observed weekly. The repetition of the same phrase in Acts 20:11 (with reference to the recuperating Eusebius) strongly suggests that this idiom means only the sharing of food. For lack of clear scriptural guidance, the Reformed churches did not require the weekly celebration of the Lord's Supper.

6. Famous musical composers' works are sometimes neglected after their passing, and only subsequently rediscovered and appreciated. J. S. Bach is a good example of this. What are the advantages and the limitations of thinking about the renewed fascination with Calvin in this way? Calvin and Bach were both rediscovered in the nineteenth century.

FURTHER READING

Calvin

Seven good biographies of John Calvin are listed at the end of the introductory chapter.

Calvin's Contemporaries

Gerrish, Brian. *Reformers in Profile*. 1967. Reprint, Philadelphia: Fortress, 2004.

Raitt, Jill, ed. *Shapers of Religious Traditions in Germany, Switzerland, and Poland, 1560-1600*. New Haven, Conn.: Yale University Press, 1981.

Steinmetz, David C. *Reformers in the Wings*. 1971. Reprint, Philadelphia: Fortress, 2001.

Stjerna, Kirsi. *Women and the Reformation*. Oxford: Blackwell, 2009.

Van den Berg, Machiel A. *Friends of Calvin*. Grand Rapids: Eerdmans, 2009.

The Wider Reformed Movement

Benedict, Philip. *Christ's Churches Purely Reformed: A Social History of Calvinism*. New Haven, Conn.: Yale University Press, 2002.

Murdoch, Graeme. *Beyond Calvin: The Intellectual, Political and Cultural World of Europe's Reformed Churches c. 1540-1620*. New York: Palgrave Macmillan, 2004.

Geneva in Calvin's Time

Monter, William. *Calvin's Geneva*. New York: John Wiley, 1967.

Naphy, William G. *Calvin and the Consolidation of the Genevan Reformation*. Louisville: Westminster/John Knox, 2003.

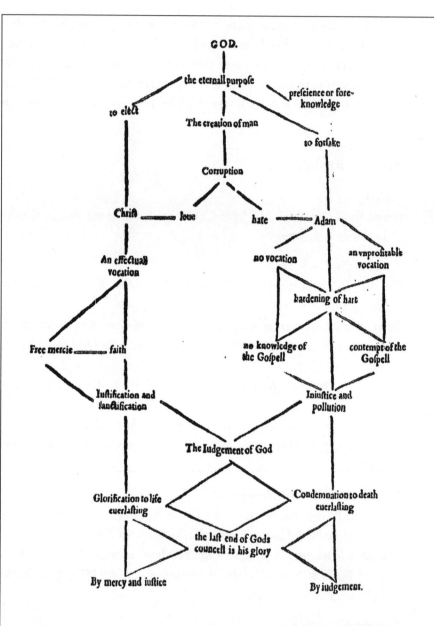

GOD.

the eternall purpose

prescience or fore-
knowledge

to elect

The creation of man

to forsake

Corruption

Christ ——— loue

hate ——— Adam

An effectuall
vocation

no vocation

an vnprofitable
vocation

hardening of hart

Free mercie ——— faith

no knowledge of
the Gospell

contempt of the
Gospell

Iustification and
sanctification

Iniustice and
pollution

The Iudgement of God

Glorification to life
euerlasting

Condemnation to death
euerlasting

the last end of Gods
councell is his glory

By mercy and iustice

By iudgement.

A Table of Predestination from Theodore Beza's A Brief Declaration of the Chief Poyntes of the Christian Religion, (E.T. 1613)
Image: S.T.C. 2002, accessed from Early English Books Online

MYTH 2

Calvin's View of Predestination
Must Be Ours

IN CHAPTER ONE A CAUTION was given against the tendency to utilize John Calvin's opinions as a kind of trump intended to instantly outrank the opinions of persons living in his time or our own. As an illustration, I cited the current penchant for stressing Calvin's preference for a weekly administration of the Lord's Supper. It would have been just as easy to cite the ongoing habit of appealing to John Calvin's understanding of predestination as the standard view, which needs to be embraced by those loyal to the Reformed theological tradition.

This line of argument was already in evidence in the nineteenth century when there was such enthusiasm for translating and publishing a vast proportion of Calvin's writings in English; at the same time, by contrast, almost none of his reforming contemporaries' works were being made available in the same way. In 1855 the English Calvinist-writer Henry Cole prefaced his translation of Calvin's 1552 treatise *Concerning the Eternal Predestination of God* with the protest that there were, currently "almost as many different shades, phases, kinds and degrees of Calvinism as there are Calvinists."[1] He was determined, by the republication of Calvin's treatise, to enforce that Reformer's view as the *only* tenable one. The tendency continued well into the twentieth century. The noted author Loraine Boettner (1901-1990), in writing the oft-quoted *Reformed Doctrine of Predestination* (1932) treated the views of two Reformers (Calvin and Jerome Zanchius) on predestination as representative of the *entire* Swiss Reformed position.[2] We will see that this was not a very fair representation of things. Exalting Calvin's understanding of predestination raises a host of questions. Was predestination a doctrine Calvin introduced to the church? Was his exposition of this doctrine such that there was nothing left to be said about it? As some readers will sense, we are opening a Pandora's box!

A HISTORY OF DISAGREEMENT

Twentieth-century theologian Paul King Jewett spoke the truth when, in 1985, he said:

> There are two things about the doctrine of election that cannot be gainsaid: it is important and it is controversial. . . . Here is an argument that has endured so long and engendered so much feeling that the very terms *predestination, foreordination*, and *election* have become symbols of divisiveness.[3]

In our discussion we will understand two of these terms in the following way: *predestination* is an aspect of that all-comprehending purpose according to which God directs and guides whatever comes to pass (Eph 1:11). If this suggests to you what Christians customarily call providence, you are quite right. But because predestination is what could be called an application of this general providence to the matter

---

[1]Cole, intro to *Calvin's Calvinism*, 7. Cole published *Concerning the Eternal Predestination of God* under the title *Calvin's Calvinism* (London: 1855), lamenting that a decision had been made to exclude the treatise "Concerning the Eternal Predestination" from the three-volume *Tracts and Treatises of Calvin*, published in 1850. His volume was reprinted by Eerdmans in 1950.

[2]Loraine Boettner, *The Reformed Doctrine of Predestination* (Grand Rapids: Eerdmans, 1932). This volume, which began its life as a Th.M. dissertation at Princeton Seminary under the late Caspar Wistar Hodge, has been kept in print constantly by P & R Publishing. For this writer, Boettner's readiness to present as representative the views of two of the higher predestinarians within Swiss Protestantism tells us that something was lacking in the rigor of his investigations.

[3]Paul K. Jewett, *Election and Predestination* (Grand Rapids: Eerdmans, 1985), p. 1.

of human destiny, it is properly accompanied by the added phrase "to life," because predestination is *saving providence*. It is noteworthy that the term *predestination* is *not* used in Scripture to describe the situation of those who will eventually be condemned at the last judgment. The terminology therefore indicates that as surely as God governs and sustains all things—generally considered—so also does he guide and ensure that a multitude of persons, who are in and of themselves sinful and unworthy, will be brought to enjoy salvation in Jesus Christ.

The term *election*, though highly similar, has a distinguishable shade of meaning. It refers to the manner in which such persons, sinful in and of themselves, come to be encompassed in God's plan of predestination to life: they are chosen for this by God and in Christ. Election is chosen-ness; and it is chosen-ness without respect to merit (of which sinners have none).

A mistake to suppose that Calvin was the originator of these doctrines. We begin on the wrong foot if we suppose that a sixteenth-century writer such as John Calvin was the originator of these conceptions, and for two reasons. First, it is evident that Luther (1483-1546) and Zwingli (1484-1531)—sixteenth-century Reformers in the generation before Calvin—themselves emphasized this same general doctrine of predestination (i.e., understood as selection for life).

Particularly in his treatise *On the Bondage of the Will* (1525) Martin Luther endorsed a strong predestinarian position. Writing against Erasmus's treatise *On the Freedom of the Will* (1524) Luther defended a position which could be called "necessitarian," that is, that all things (including the faith we are saved by) happen by divine necessity. The Saxon Reformer found antecedents for such necessitarian views in ancient classical writers such as Virgil, and he claimed that in the ancient world "the knowledge of God's predestination and foreknowledge remained with the common people no less than the awareness of his existence itself."[4] He found such views taught in familiar Scriptures as

---

[4]Martin Luther, "The Bondage of the Will," in *Luther's Works*, ed. Philip S. Watson (Philadelphia: Fortress Press, 1972), 33:40-41. Luther's utilization of ancient pagan ideas of fate as anticipating the Christian idea of predestination would seem to have opened him to the charge that the second was as impersonal as the first.

2 Timothy 2:19, Romans 9:18 and Matthew 22:14. Lutheran historical theologian Paul Althaus sympathetically described Luther's position as entailing "an unconditional, eternal predestination both to salvation and to damnation."[5]

Ulrich Zwingli of Zurich called providence "the mother of predestination," yet generally he preferred to utilize the term *election* rather than *predestination* when speaking of such things.[6] Only gradually did such elementary ideas of predestination (understood as election) come to have a more prominent role in his theology. By 1526 he indicated that it was only by election that the universal effects of original sin were overcome. He believed that divine election, properly understood, undermined the then-prevalent Roman Catholic belief that salvation was overtly tied to the administration of baptism and the Eucharist.[7] Controversy with the Swiss Anabaptists in 1526-1527 brought the matter still more to the fore. The latter, examining election, argued that as surely as Esau (in Rom 9), a descendant of Abraham, was not among the elect, so there could be no advance assurance of the salvation of any particular infant born to Christian parents—and, by extension, no proper basis for the baptism of such a child. Only upon their believing can anyone identify the elect, urged the Anabaptists. But Zwingli, while acknowledging that the identity of the elect is somewhat shrouded, also insisted that election was nevertheless a reality *in advance* of any particular individual believing the gospel.[8] This definite, but non-elaborate, understanding of election is found in Zwingli's other writings through to his last, *An Exposition of the Faith* (1529).[9]

Second, Luther and Zwingli had themselves taken over this conception of predestination from theologians of the medieval period: Isidore

[5]Paul Althaus, *The Theology of Martin Luther* (Philadelphia: Fortress Press, 1966), p. 275. It is worth noting that Lutheran theology recognizes that this strong predestinarian emphasis was not fully transmitted to Luther's successors. See the discussion of this in David P. Scaer, "The Doctrine of Election: A Lutheran Note," in *Perspectives on Evangelical Theology*, ed. Kenneth Kantzer and Stanley Gundry (Grand Rapids: Baker, 1979), pp. 105-16.
[6]Huldrych Zwingli, *Latin Works*, trans. C. N. Heller (Philadelphia, 1929), 3:270-71, quoted in W. P. Stephens, *The Theology of Huldrych Zwingli* (Oxford: Clarendon Press, 1986), p. 97.
[7]Stephens, *Theology of Zwingli*, p. 99.
[8]Ibid.
[9]Huldrych Zwingli, *An Exposition of the Faith*, in, *Zwingli and Bullinger*, trans. Geoffrey Bromiley (Philadelphia: Westminster Press, 1953), pp. 268-69.

of Seville, Gottschalk of Orbais and Thomas Aquinas, as well as later medieval theologians Thomas Bradwardine, John Wyclif and Gregory of Rimini. And all these were indebted ultimately to the ideas about predestination set out by Augustine of Hippo.[10] We find little in predestinarian thought in the Reformation era that is truly new.

THE GROWTH OF CALVIN'S OWN CONCEPTION

To speak now of Calvin, who was a generation younger than Luther and Zwingli, his earliest utterances on this subject in his first edition of the *Institutes* (1536), published at Basel, comprised only two brief, mild paragraphs. There he introduced the theme of predestination in connection with his teaching about the endurance of the church. There will always be a church, Calvin said, and that church will prevail because "those whom the Lord has chosen, have been turned over to the care and keeping of Christ his Son so that 'he may lose none of them but may revive all on the last day' [Jn 6:39]." It is evident that in 1536 Calvin's view is simply that predestination concerns the rescue of the fallen: "from this, as it were polluted mass, he sanctifies some vessels unto honor [Rom 9:21] so that there is no age that does not experience his mercy [2 Tim 2:20]."[11] No one will call this high-flying.

Consistent with this reticence of 1536, Calvin, in November of the same year—and by now resident at Geneva—composed a brief "Confession," adherence to which was required of all residents of the city wishing to be included in the newly reformed church, which had only months before been under the jurisdiction of Rome. Neither predestination nor election finds any mention in this elementary summary of

---

[10]See the helpful discussion in Jewett, *Election and Predestination*, pp. 5-10. The medieval period is sketched in greater detail in the helpful work of John V. Fesko, *Diversity Within the Reformed Tradition: Supra and Infralapsarianism in Calvin, Dort, and Westminster* (Greenville, S.C.: Reformed Academic Press, 2001), pp. 21-55; and Jaroslav Pelikan, *The Christian Tradition*, vol. 3, *The Growth of Medieval Theology* (Chicago: University of Chicago Press, 1978), pp. 80-95, and *Reformation of Church and Dogma*, vol. 4 (Chicago: University of Chicago Press, 1984), pp. 28-35. The discussion of the question in the late medieval period was taken up by Heiko Oberman, *Forerunners of the Reformation* (London: Lutterworth, 1967), chap. 3, and the same author's *Harvest of Medieval Theology* (1963; reprint, Grand Rapids: Baker, 2000).

[11]John Calvin, *Institutes of the Christian Religion* (1536 ed.), trans. and ed. Ford Lewis Battles (Grand Rapids: Eerdmans, 1975), 2.4.59.

Geneva's Reformation belief.[12] Evidently, in 1536 a citizen of Geneva might hold no opinion whatsoever regarding predestination and still be welcomed into the fellowship of the Reformed Church.

Before he was abruptly exiled from the city of Geneva in 1538, Calvin composed a catechism that gave the doctrine of predestination only slightly more attention than the *Institutes* of two years previously. In this catechism Calvin's earlier reticence on this doctrine begins to fade. Now, predestination is linked not only with the existence and endurance of the church but with the question of believing. This new emphasis in Calvin perhaps reflected the experience he had acquired in pastoral ministry; as a preacher he now had reason to ponder the question of why many more hear the gospel than ever respond to it. On this subject, Calvin is frank in saying,

> The seed of God's Word takes root and bears fruit only in those whom the Lord has predestined as his children and heirs of the kingdom of heaven; for all the rest, who were condemned by this same plan of God before the foundation of the world, the utterly clear preaching of truth can be nothing but the stench of death unto death. Now why should the Lord deem the former worthy of his mercy, but exercise his severe judgment on the latter? Let us leave the cause in his hand.[13]

Here, I think we may safely say that Calvin has moved beyond the assertion of the "consolatory" value of election (considered as the foundation of the church and the anchor of the Christian life) to something rather more analytical. Especially in his focus on the persistence of unbelief, he was now readier to explain its existence by referring to its place in the eternal plan of God than he was ready to focus on the obvious disobedience and spiritual rebellion of wayward hearers. Of course, he did not and would not deny the significance of the latter.

The next window we have into the development of Calvin's thinking about predestination and election is his Romans commentary, which he completed at Strasbourg in October 1539. He had arrived at

---

[12]See the text of this in "The Geneva Confession," in *Calvin's Theological Treatises*, ed. J. K. S. Reid (London: SCM Press, 1954), pp. 26-33.

[13]John Calvin, *Catechism* (1538), in *Calvin's First Catechism: A Commentary*, ed. John L. Hesselink (Louisville, Ky.: Westminster John Knox Press, 1997), p. 17.

that city as an exile from Geneva only twelve months before and was dividing his time between pastoral work in the city's Francophone exile congregation and lecturing in New Testament in an advanced school presided over by the French Protestant refugee John Sturm. The Romans commentary (his first), especially chapters 8-9, provided further opportunity for him to comment on this doctrinal question. Commenting on the well-known passage of Romans 8:28-29, Calvin took the opportunity to distinguish between what he considered to be the proper understanding of election and predestination, and another view. On the phrase "those who are called according to his purpose," he wrote:

> There is no doubt, however, that Paul expressly stated here that our salvation is based on the selection of God, in order that he might pass from this to the subject which he immediately added, viz. that the afflictions which conform us to Christ have been determined for us by the same heavenly decree.

And on the following phrase, "for whom he foreknew, he also predestined," he added:

> The foreknowledge of God here mentioned by Paul is not mere prescience, as some inexperienced people foolishly imagine, but adoption, by which he has always distinguished His children from the reprobate. . . . Those therefore to whom I have referred, foolishly conclude that God has elected none but those whom He foresaw would be worthy of his grace. . . . (But) this knowledge depends on God's good pleasure, because in adopting those whom He would, God had no foreknowledge of anything outside Himself, but simply marked out those whom He purposed to elect.[14]

He elaborated these opinions still more emphatically in commenting on the ninth chapter.

There, in conjunction with the discussion of the varying fortunes of Jacob and Esau (whom he took simply to represent brothers, rather than peoples or nations descended from them), Calvin acknowledges

---

[14]John Calvin, *Commentary on Paul's Epistle to the Romans*, trans. R. Mackenzie (1539; reprint, Grand Rapids: Eerdmans, 1973), pp. 181-82.

that Esau's foreseen evil deeds did provide a kind of ground for his being rejected by God, yet continued: "Nevertheless, Paul withdraws us from this view, so that we may learn to rest in the bare and simple good pleasure of God, until he has established the doctrine that God has a sufficiently just cause for election and reprobation in His own will."[15]

If we may speak of Calvin as having an overriding concern, that concern would be to establish the absolute freedom of God in the matter of the salvation of humans. God is compelled by no obligation outside himself in the matter of salvation. Calvin's views expressed at Strasbourg in 1539 are essentially what we observed them to be prior to his departure from Geneva. We are not wise to think at this stage of some relentless trajectory wafting Calvin ever higher in his writings on this theme.

Having said this, it is also necessary to acknowledge that in those Strasbourg years, Calvin will only have been further encouraged in this predestinarian orientation through extended contact with the senior Reformer Martin Bucer. Bucer had just recently published (1536) his own distinct approach to this doctrine, emphasizing on the one hand what might be called the positive aspect:

> Predetermination (proorismos) then, which we commonly call "predestination," is that act of designation on the part of God whereby in his secret counsel he designates and actually selects and separates from the rest of mankind those whom he will draw to his Son, Jesus our Lord, and engrafts them into him (having brought them into this life at his own good time).

However, Bucer also allowed the existence of what could be called a general predestination by which "God accomplishes all things by his predeterminate counsel, assigning each and every thing to its own use." Bucer went on to explain that

> In this sense there is even a predestination of the wicked, for just as God forms them out of nothing, so he forms them for a definite end. God does everything in wisdom, not excepting the predetermined and good

---

[15]Ibid, pp. 200-201.

use of the wicked, for even the godless are the tools and instruments of God.[16]

Having acknowledged this, we can still note that at his return to Geneva in 1541, Calvin began to work at producing a second catechism for the canton (eventually put forward in 1545), in which all reference to predestination and election is confined to a single question. The thrust of that piece of instruction is that the existence and perseverance on earth of the church of God is ensured by the operation of God's secret election; here we see once more the nonspeculative approach taken in the first edition of the *Institutes*.[17] It is fair to say that regarding this doctrine Calvin carefully gauged his audience as to the level of detail appropriate to them. For church members, no more was requested than a simple acknowledgment that there was an election of grace. From pastors and theological students he expected much more.

THE EXPANSION OF CALVIN'S VIEWPOINT

Yet, having rubbed shoulders with Martin Bucer at Strasbourg in the years 1538-1541, having revised and expanded his 1536 *Institutes* in 1539, and elaborated on these doctrines in response to sometimes-violent criticism of his published views, his treatment of predestination and election did grow more extended.[18] There were conflicts in 1543 with Albert Pighius, in 1551 with Jerome Bolsec and in 1552 with Jean Trolliet over this doctrine.[19] In the latter year Calvin published a full

---

[16]Martin Bucer, *An Inquiry Concerning Predestination* (1536), in *Martin Bucer's Common Places*, trans. and ed. David F. Wright (Appleford, U.K.: Sutton Courtenay Press, 1972), pp. 96-97. It was the opinion of translator Wright that Bucer's doctrine of predestination "remained for the most part in the background, rather than featuring prominently as a visible mark of his theology," (ibid., p. 95).

[17]"The Catechism of the Church at Geneva" (1545), in *Calvin: Theological Treatises*, ed. J. K. S. Reid (London: SCM Press, 1954), p. 103.

[18]As to the question of Bucer's influence on Calvin in the 1538-1541 period at Strasbourg, consult Wilhelm Pauck, *The Heritage of the Reformation* (New York: Oxford University Press, 1968), p. 90; and Willem van't Spijker, "Bucer's Influence on Calvin: Church and Community," in *Martin Bucer: Reforming Church and Community*, ed. David F. Wright (Cambridge: Cambridge University Press, 1994), pp. 32-44. Wulfert de Greef endorses the opinion of van't Spijker that Calvin's doctrine of predestination was strengthened in contact with Bucer (see Wulfert de Greef, *The Writings of John Calvin: An Introductory Guide* [Grand Rapids: Baker, 1993], p. 200).

[19]De Greef, *Writings of John Calvin*, pp. 158-59, 205.

treatise on the subject titled *Concerning the Eternal Predestination of God*. Here was an elaboration of the doctrine that clearly went beyond what had been presented to date.

While occasioned most immediately by the 1551 confrontation with Bolsec, Calvin's treatise also drew extensively on material he had written after conflict in the preceding decade.[20] These opponents of the emerging Reformation doctrine of predestination shared a common conviction that differing human responses to the gospel arise "not from God's free election or His secret counsel, but from the will of each individual. . . . No one may perish except the man who deletes his name from the book of life by his obstinacy."[21] The position staked out by Calvin, however, is:

> If we are not ashamed of the gospel, we must confess what is plainly there declared.
>
> God, by His eternal goodwill, which has no cause outside itself, destined those whom He pleased to salvation, rejecting the rest; those whom He dignified by gratuitous adoption He illumined by His Spirit, so that they receive the life offered in Christ, while others voluntarily disbelieve, so that they remain in darkness destitute of the life of faith.[22]

This is the position Calvin elaborates and defends by explicit appeal to the scriptural writings of Paul, the Gospel of John and the prophet Isaiah; such sentiments were not new from Calvin. The difference in Calvin now lies instead in a more aggressive advocacy than earlier of the conviction that God's predestination is wrapped up with the elaboration of what we might call a doctrine of "meticulous providence."[23]

---

[20]J. Wayne Baker, "Jerome Bolsec," in *Oxford Encyclopedia of the Reformation*, ed. Hans Hillerbrand (Oxford: Oxford University Press, 1996), 1:188-89. Bolsec, a former French Carmelite monk, had embraced the Reformation about 1545 and migrated to the Geneva region after a sojourn at the court of Renée, duchess of Ferrara. Only in the matter of predestination did Bolsec have strong disagreement with Calvin and this he made no attempt to conceal. Calvin's response to the challenge posed by Pighius is now published as John Calvin, *The Bondage and Liberation of the Will: A Defence of the Orthodox Doctrine of Human Choice Against Pighius*; ed. A. N. S. Lane, trans. G. I. Davies (Carlisle, U.K.: Paternoster; Grand Rapids: Baker, 1996).

[21]John Calvin, *Concerning the Eternal Predestination of God*, ed. and trans. J. K. S. Reid (London: James Clark, 1961), p. 55.

[22]Calvin, *Concerning the Eternal Predestination of God*, p. 58.

[23]I have previously noted that Calvin had earlier associated predestination and election with the

On Calvin's understanding, "it is certain that not one drop of rain falls without God's sure command." The absence of rain, the spread of blight in grain fields or the onslaught of hail or storms was, in Calvin's understanding, nothing less than the outworking of a comprehensive, direct willing by God.[24]

In the treatise of 1552 Calvin expounds the idea of meticulous providence thus:

> First, it must be observed that the will of God is the cause of all things that happen in the world; and yet God is not the author of evil. . . . Whatever things are done wrongly and unjustly by man, these very things are the right and just works of God. . . . This may seem paradoxical at first sight to some; but at least they should not be so offended that they will not suffer me to search the word of God for a little to find out what should be thought here. . . . That God directs by His counsel the things that seem most fortuitous, is clearly attested by Scripture when it says: The lot is thrown in the lap, but the judgment of things is from the Lord (Prov. 16.33). . . . What I hold is, in my judgment simple, and needs no force to accommodate it usefully to life. What necessarily happens is what God decrees, and is therefore not exactly or of itself necessary by nature.[25]

This belief in meticulous providence did not involve a disbelief in the operation of secondary causes (Calvin called them "inferior causes"); Calvin affirmed as clearly as any opponent of his that human behavior and choices are significant and unforced. Yet he believed also that human choices, even when poor and hurtful, serve ends known to God.

---

foundation of the church and the stability of the Christian believer. Though even in the final edition of the *Institutes* in 1559, these doctrines will be considered as a means of understanding how a particular sinner finds him- or herself in a state of grace and forgiveness; it is undeniable that Calvin's defense of predestination and election come more and more to be wrapped up with his doctrine of God.

[24]Calvin, *Institutes*, 1.16.5. When we read these sections of the *Institutes*, we find that while Calvin embraces the notion that aspects of the natural world possess what might be called "properties," these properties are not exercised *apart from* the direct willing of the Creator. See the discussion of this problem in Calvin in Gary B. Deason, "Reformation Theology and the Mechanistic Conception of Nature," in *God and Nature: Historical Essays on the Encounter Between Christianity and Science*, ed. David C. Lindberg and Ronald L. Numbers (Berkeley: University of California Press, 1986), pp. 177-78.

[25]Calvin, *Concerning the Eternal Predestination*, p. 168.

"Nothing happens but by His assent; . . . men can deliberately do nothing unless He inspires it. . . .There can be no doubt that the will of God is the chief and principal cause of all things."[26] The added difficulty, however, is that under this conception of meticulous providence, the primary cause of eternal human condemnation is traceable back to the determination of God in eternity and only secondarily to human sin. Now it was this expanded elaboration of the doctrines of predestination and election that found its capstone in the 1559 edition of Calvin's *Institutes:*

> We call predestination God's eternal decree, by which he compacted with himself what he willed to become of each man. For all are not created in equal condition; rather eternal life is foreordained for some, eternal damnation for others. Therefore, as any man has been created to one or the other of these ends, we speak of him as predestined to life or to death.[27]

For perfectly good reason, this conception of predestination has come to be called "double."

Locating Calvin's Understanding on a Continuum

Others of the second generation. Among the second generation of Reformers (to which Calvin himself belonged), not all matched this intensity of commitment to predestinarian teaching.[28] Such a statement requires explanation lest it be misconstrued. The front rank of Reformers who were in informal alliance with Calvin shared his com-

---

[26]Ibid., pp. 172, 177.

[27]Calvin, *Institutes*, 3.21.5. It is significant that in this 1559 edition of the *Institutes*, Calvin separated the subject of eternal predestination from his consideration of providence. In all previous editions of this work in the 1536-1554 period, these themes had been treated together. Cf. editors' note 1 in the *Institutes* (1559), 1.16.1, p. 197. Calvin's position as articulated in *Concerning Eternal Predestination* and the final edition (1559) of the *Institutes* have understandably been understood to embrace the notion that God's determination to make distinctions among humans preceded the consideration that they would, in Adam, fall into sin.

[28]Richard A. Muller sanely indicates that the Reformed perspective on this doctrine, after Calvin, "represents a spectrum of opinion rather than a monolithic doctrinal perspective: it moves between the concept of a single predestination to life and the concept of a single predestination to salvation and damnation conceived in the mind of God prior to his permissive willing of the Fall" ("Predestination," in *Oxford Encyclopedia of the Reformation*, ed. Hans Hillerbrand [Oxford: Oxford University Press, 1996], 3:332-38).

mitment to a divine predestination which, linked to providence, secured as certain the eventual salvation of a multitude of sinners. But they did not necessarily stand where Calvin stood on the difficult question of the possible dual predestination of both saved and lost. Some examples will be helpful in illustrating this.

Heinrich Bullinger. Calvin's direct contemporary Heinrich Bullinger of Zurich (1504-1575), for example, while evidently also a predestinarian, was at the same time somewhat more restrained. This successor to Zwingli at Zurich was especially eager to avoid the implication that the ultimate condemnation of any sinner was purposed and planned by God in a manner comparable to the predestinating of one to life and blessedness.[29] Bullinger's position did not involve any denial that the eternal plan and purpose of God envisioned both salvation and destruction, yet his manner of stating the doctrine was circumspect enough to prevent any insinuation that this envisioning of such ends made God the author of sin and evil. He would allow that predestination contemplates and provides for two ends: "The predestination of God is the eternal decree of God, whereby he has ordained either to save or destroy men; a most certain end of life and death being appointed unto them. Whereupon also it is elsewhere called a foreappointment."[30]

Yet he showed no interest in elaborating on this theme more fully, and this almost on the eve of Calvin's extended publication on the subject in 1552. The practical tendency of Bullinger's teaching was to identify predestination and election as one and the same, and to say next to nothing about any connection it might have to the destiny of the lost.[31] Bullinger wished to leave the impression that the eventual damnation of the wicked is entirely due to their failure to believe and heed the gospel message.[32]

---

[29]In this section I make extensive use of Cornelis P. Venema, *Heinrich Bullinger and the Doctrine of Predestination* (Grand Rapids: Baker, 2002), pp. 39-56. Venema typifies Bullinger's approach to this doctrine as "temperate" and "moderate."

[30]Henry Bullinger, *The Decades*, ed. Thomas Harding (1549-1551; reprint, Grand Rapids: Reformation Heritage, 2004), 3:185.

[31]The identification of predestination and election has the net effect of stressing only predestination to life.

[32]Venema, *Heinrich Bullinger*, p. 54.

When the vociferous critic Jerome Bolsec disparaged John Calvin's teaching on predestination in a public meeting at Geneva, the senate of that city temporarily imprisoned him. When required to defend his insolent action, Bolsec argued that the position he was maintaining was only that of Bullinger and the Lutheran Reformers Johannes Brenz (1499-1570) and Philip Melanchthon (1497-1560). In consequence, Bullinger's advice (and that of the church council of his city) was sought by Geneva. In responding, Bullinger referred Calvin and the church council of Geneva to the statements of the Zurich church already committed to writing in the "Consensus Tigurensis" of 1549.[33] Then, as earlier, Bullinger wished it to be understood that the ground of condemnation of the ungodly was "because of their own sin and guilt, because they had not received the savior."[34] The relations of Calvin and Bullinger show a substantial concurrence in the matter of predestination, and yet distinguishable emphases.

Jerome Zanchius. On the other hand, in that second generation we can note the Italian-born Jerome Zanchius (1512-1590), who after flight from his native land as a Protestant refugee taught Old Testament and theology with distinction in Strasbourg and Heidelberg. If we may, without exaggeration term Bullinger a moderate and circumspect predestinarian, it would be appropriate to describe Zanchius as rigorous and thoroughgoing. Though this Reformer was careful to insist that the divine predestination to salvation was from among Adam's "degenerate offspring,"[35] he was not (unlike Bullinger) averse to applying the term *predestination* equally to the situation of those persons on

---

[33]This "Consensus" was the joint work of the Genevan and Zurich churches, and was composed in 1549 (published in 1551) to display their extensive agreement on teaching about baptism and the Lord's Supper in the face of Lutheran criticisms. The doctrine of election was important to such a topic inasmuch as the two churches were in agreement that ultimately only elect persons benefited from the two sacraments. See headings 16 and 17 of the "Consensus Tigurensis," in John Calvin, *Tracts and Treatises* (Edinburgh: Calvin Translation Society, 1849), 2:217. The degree of collaboration necessary between Calvin and Bullinger in this project (with the initiative lying with the former) is helpfully described by Timothy George in his essay "John Calvin and the Agreement of Zurich," in *John Calvin and the Church*, ed. Timothy George (Louisville, Ky.: Westminster John Knox Press, 1990), pp. 42-58.

[34]Heinrich Bullinger, in John Calvin, *Calvini Opera*, ed. Wilhelm Baum, Eduard Cunitz and Eduard Reuss (Brunswick and Berlin, 1863), 14:210, quoted in Venema, *Heinrich Bullinger*, p. 60.

[35]An important indicator that Zanchius took what is called post- or sublapsarian view.

whom God had not determined to show mercy.[36] For Zanchius any hesitation in affirming this "twofold predestination" was implicitly a denial of "God Himself, since His will, decree and foreknowledge are no other than God Himself willing and decreeing and foreknowing."[37] In a way reminiscent of Calvin's formulation, Zanchius was willing to trace both the choice of the elect and the passing by of the nonelect to nothing other than the sovereign good pleasure of God.[38]

Peter Martyr Vermigli. One further example will help us to grasp the fluidity and variety of the understanding of predestination, even among the contemporary allies of John Calvin in the second half of the sixteenth century. Peter Martyr Vermigli was an Italian Protestant refugee who taught successively at Strasbourg, Oxford, Strasbourg (again) and Zurich. On the basis of his service in England for nearly six years, he had an ongoing influence in the English-speaking world through his numerous treatises (many of which were translated). As oriented to the teaching of Aristotle as any Reformation leader of his age, Vermigli wrote with great felicity and clarity. On the matter of predestination we can note two emphases. First, his definition:

> Predestination is the most wise purpose of God whereby he hath from the beginning constantly decreed to call those, whom he hath loved in Christ, to the adoption of his children, to justification by faith, and at length to glory through good works, that they may be made like unto the image of the Son of God.

It is what is *not* included in Vermigli's definition as well as what is there that should stir our interest. Unlike Calvin and Zanchius (and rather more like Bullinger), Vermigli is reluctant to speak of a predestination that enfolds those who will ultimately be lost.

> I separate the reprobate from the predestinate because the Scriptures nowhere (that I know of) call men that shall be damned, predestinate. . . . Reprobation is the most wise purpose of God, whereby he hath before all eternitie, constantly decreed without any injustice, not to have

[36]Jerome Zanchius, *The Doctrine of Absolute Predestination*, trans. and ed. Augustus Toplady (1769; reprint, Grand Rapids: Sovereign Grace, 1971), pp. 49-52.
[37]Ibid., p. 53.
[38]Ibid., p. 75.

mercie on those whome he hath not loved, but hath overhipped [i.e., passed over] them.[39]

If the conception of Calvin and of Zanchius could fairly be called double predestination, that of Bullinger and Vermigli could be called single predestination.

Predestination in the conception of the third generation. It is important, before terminating this rapid survey of sixteenth-century Reformed Protestant thought about predestination, to note that there were additional developments before the century was out. What might be called the third generation of Reformed theologians provided formulations of this doctrine that went somewhat beyond what they had received. We will consider two thinkers in particular, Theodore Beza (1519-1605) and William Perkins (1558-1602).

Beza, an accomplished Greek scholar was, like John Calvin, of French origin.[40] He had taught in a theological academy at Lausanne until 1558, at which time he had been invited to Geneva to assist in the setting up of another academy there. At the death of Calvin in 1564, he had come to be recognized as doyen or chief minister among the Geneva clergy and taught both Greek and theology until his death. Already loyal to Calvin's double understanding of predestination prior to joining the senior Reformer at Geneva, Beza went on to articulate that doctrine in a fashion informed to a heightened degree by a reliance on categories of thought taken from the Greek philosopher Aristotle.[41] While debate is still raging as to whether Beza fundamentally changed Calvin's presentation of this doctrine, there is no disputing that this

---

[39]Peter Martyr Vermigli, *The Common Places* (London: Henry Denham and Henry Middleton, 1583), bk. 3, chap. 1, pp. 8-11. See the helpful commentary on Vermigli's theological emphases in Frank James, "Peter Martyr Vermigli (1499-1562)," in *The Reformation Theologians: An Introduction to Theology in the Early Modern Period*, ed. Carter Lindberg (Oxford: Blackwell, 2002), pp. 198-212, esp. p. 205.

[40]His prowess in Greek is testified to by the fact that one of the earlier codices of the New Testament, dated to the fifth century A.D., having been recovered by him and then donated to Cambridge University in 1581, now bears his name.

[41]Note the discussion of Beza's role as an exemplar of the use of the scholastic method in late Reformed theology in John S. Bray, *Theodore Beza's Doctrine of Predestination* (Niewkoop, Netherlands: DeGraaf, 1975); and Richard A. Muller, "Calvin and the Calvinists: Assessing Continuities and Discontinuities Between the Reformation and Orthodoxy, Part I," *Calvin Theological Journal* 30 (1995): 350, 356.

successor to the older Reformer was even more forthright in his espousal of it. Writing in Lausanne in 1555 (in the immediate aftermath
of Calvin's controversy with Jerome Bolsec), Beza left no doubt whatsoever about which side he supported in this quarrel. In his *Summa totius
Christianismi, sive description et distribution causarum salutis electorum et
exitii reproborum*[42] Beza affirmed, even more forthrightly than Calvin,
that predestination was "double"; this conception carried with it the
principle that certain humans had been created for no other purpose
than destruction:

> God . . . according to the determinate and unchangeable purpose of his
> will . . . hath determined from before all beginning with himself to cre-
> ate all things in their time for his glory and namely men: whom he hath
> made after two sorts, clean contrary one to the other. Whereof he ma-
> keth the one sort (which it pleased him to choose by his secret will and
> purpose) partakers of his glory through his mercy, and these we call ac-
> cording to the word of God, the vessels of honor, the elect, the children
> of promise and predestinate to salvation: and the others, whom likewise
> it pleased him to ordain to damnation (that he might show forth his
> wrath and power to be glorified also in them) we do call the vessels of
> dishonor and wrath, the reprobate cast off from all good works.[43]

The influence of this kind of theological literature was not confined
to the Swiss cantons in which it was produced. At Cambridge, England, the rising young Puritan theologian William Perkins digested it
and incorporated certain of its emphases into his own writings on the
subject. A fellow of that university's Christ College and lecturer in that
city's Great St. Andrews church, Perkins—like Beza—advocated a

---

[42]I have consulted this treatise in its English translation of 1575, *A Briefe Declaration of the Chiefe
Poyntes of Christian Religion Set Foorth in a Table Made by Theodore Beza* (London: 1575). This
work, which was prefaced by a sketched "table" indicating the relationship in which predestination and reprobation stand to the will of God, is unpaginated. Though in 1555 Beza still
resided and taught in Lausanne, the work was published at Geneva. John S. Bray, *Theodore
Beza's Doctrine of Predestination*, pp. 74-75, provides helpful cautions against supposing that
the 1555 treatise provides a kind of key to Beza's entire theological position. I accept Bray's
judgment that however pronounced Beza's views were on this subject, it is nevertheless inac-
curate to suggest that predestination was the central doctrine or the organizing principle of his
theology.

[43]In this quotation from *A Briefe Declaration*, chap. 2, n.p., I have taken the liberty of substitut-
ing modern spelling for the Elizabethan.

high doctrine of predestination; like Beza, he also circulated with his writings on this subject a chart or table sketching out the mutual relations of predestination and reprobation to the will of God. In his *Armilla Aurea* of 1590, one could read by now familiar themes. Like Calvin and Zanchius, he took the high view that nothing occurs in this world which has not been decreed by God:

> The Lord, according to his good pleasure, hath most certainly decreed every thing and action, whether past, present, or to come, together with their circumstances of place, time, means, and end. Yea, he hath most justly decreed the wicked works of the wicked. For if he had nilled them, they should never have been at all. And albeit they of their own nature are and remain wicked, yet in respect of God's decree they are some ways good, for there is not anything absolutely evil. The thing which in its own nature is evil, in God's eternal counsel is respectively good, in that it is some occasion and way to manifest the glory of God in his justice and his mercy. . . . God is not only a bare permissive agent in an evil work, but a powerfule effecter of the same; yet so as he neither in-stilleth an aberration in the action, nor yet supporteth or intendeth the same, but that he most freely suffereth evil and best disposeth of it to his own glory.[44]

Consistent with such views, on the narrower matter of predestination, Perkins wrote, "Predestination . . . is the decree of God by which he hath ordained all men to a certain and everlasting estate, that is either to salvation or condemnation, for his own glory. The means of accomplishing God's predestination are twofold: the creation and the fall."[45]

We have surveyed a three-quarters of a century period in Reformation Europe in which there was widespread support for belief in predestination as discriminating divine mercy. All the figures of the period whose views have been surveyed could have been considered allies in support of this cause. And yet having said this, we can note also both that there has appeared a variation of emphases ranging from the un-

---

[44]William Perkins, *The Golden Chain or the Description of Theology*, trans. and ed. Ian Breward (Appleford, U.K.: Sutton Courtenay Press, 1970), pp. 183, 185.
[45]Ibid., pp. 185-86.

derstated (Bullinger, Vermigli) to the pronounced and explicit (Calvin, Zanchius, Beza, Perkins) and a readiness on the part of the third generation (Beza, Perkins) to amplify and elaborate things declared by those theologians (especially Calvin) with whom they stood in greatest continuity. Now, we take up the question of the wider meaning of what has been displayed.

WHAT CALVIN'S PREDESTINARIAN VIEWS DRAW ATTENTION TO

Calvin's modern followers have long been prone to look on those who diverged from his doctrine of predestination as defectors, that is, as persons who *might* have endorsed his high position but who instead chose to betray it. Such folk are considered to have substituted for it an understanding of predestination that is weak, half-hearted or cowardly.[46]

Friends of Reformed theology too easily suspect that something like this principle of "defection" was at work in the Christian leader of the following century, Jacobus Arminius, of whom I will say more. Yet, this view that such persons were defectors would be much more compelling if Protestant dissent against high views of predestination (like Calvin's) had not arisen until the seventeenth century. But in fact we find these dissenting opinions among persons wishing to be identified with the Reformation cause in the earliest decades of this period. When this pre-Arminian dissent against predestination as Calvin articulated it is acknowledged, it prevents us from so easily treating dissenters with impatience or exasperation. In fact, on closer examination we find that these persons struggled to maintain the variant views of predestination they had already adhered to when they allied themselves with the Reformation cause. Note the variety displayed in the following examples.

Predestination cautiously embraced. While Martin Luther had been stridently predestinarian at the time he wrote his controversial work *On the Bondage of the Will* (against Erasmus), Lutheranism did not follow him in this stridency. The doctrine of predestination eventually preserved in the Formula of Concord (1577) was what could be called consolatory. It explicitly distanced itself from any suggestion that the

---

[46]See for example the opening remarks in the opening paragraphs of this chapter in which Henry Cole and Loraine Boettner are pinpointed as the practitioners of this point of view.

decree of God arbitrarily ensured the damnation of any.[47] This was also the approach taken by the Heidelberg Catechism (1563), which was composed to teach the theological position of the Swiss Reformed in territories formerly Lutheran. In a manner reminiscent of Calvin's initial edition of the *Institutes* (1536), the doctrine of election is introduced by the Heidelberg Catechism purely in support of the permanence and durability of the true church.[48] The Articles of the Church of England, first drafted in 1547 and eventually given royal approval in 1563,[49] similarly concentrated purely on the application of predestination to the redeemed.[50]

Even in territories that embraced Swiss-style Reformed theology with less trepidation, the doctrine of predestination was capable of being stated more circumspectly than Calvin had done. The Belgic Confession of 1559, having affirmed positively that, "God delivers and preserves from . . . perdition all whom he, in his eternal and unchangeable council, of mere goodness hath elected in Christ Jesus our Lord" affirmed also that God was just "in leaving others in the fall and perdition wherein they have involved themselves."[51] This was an emphasis more in keeping with the teaching of Bullinger than of Calvin. Even milder in its statement was the Scots Confession of 1560, which did not advance beyond the generic assertion that God "chose us in His Son Christ Jesus before the foundation of the world was laid."[52] The Second Helvetic Confession of 1566, "the most widely received among the Re-

[47]The Formula of Concord 11, in *The Book of Concord: The Confessions of the Evangelical Lutheran Church*, ed. Theodore Tappert (Philadelphia: Fortress Press, 1959), pp. 616-32.

[48]See question 54 of the Heidelberg Catechism, in *Reformed Confessions of the Sixteenth Century*, ed. Arthur C. Cochrane (Philadelphia: Westminster Press, 1966), p. 314.

[49]In the 1553-1558 period, England saw the pendulum swing back to Catholicism under Queen Mary Tudor, and thus the Articles, which had originated in the reign of her half-brother, Edward VI, could only be ratified belatedly in the reign of Elizabeth I, following Mary's death.

[50]"Thirty-Nine Articles of the Church of England," in *The Creeds of Christendom*, ed. Philip Schaff (New York: Harper, 1877), 3:497.

[51]Belgic Confession, art. 16, in *Reformed Confessions of the Sixteenth Century*, ed. Arthur C. Cochrane (Philadelphia: Westminster Press, 1966), p. 200. I find it to be of interest that the modern biographer of Arminius, Carl Bangs, concurs that this is the tone of the Belgic Confession when touching predestination. See Carl Bangs, *Arminius: A Study in the Dutch Reformation* (Nashville: Abingdon, 1971), p. 102.

[52]Scots Confession, chap. 8, in *Reformed Confessions of the Sixteenth Century*, ed. Arthur C. Cochrane (Philadelphia: Westminster Press, 1966), p. 169.

formed Confessions," was largely the work of Bullinger.[53] Here, the
emphasis is that election is God's gracious purpose toward the undeserving, that it involves being chosen not directly but in Christ, and
that the Christian is elected with a view to service. There is no application of the idea of predestination to the eventual destiny of the unbelieving.[54] Calvin had already passed from the scene when this work was
composed.

Sixteenth-century dissenters against the doctrine. We need also to acknowledge that from across Reformation Europe anecdotal evidence
soon emerged that there were persons allied with the young Protestant
movement who did not endorse any scheme of predestination capable of
being understood as exclusionary. Among those imprisoned in England
during the attempted reintroduction of Catholicism in the reign of Queen
Mary (1553-1558) were Protestants outspoken in their defense of unrestricted free will. These entered into lively debates with prominent Protestant leaders (also imprisoned) who were in the theological orbit of Zurich and Geneva. One of the latter, the Anglican leader John Bradford,
went so far as to write a pacific treatise (while imprisoned) seeking to
persuade these fellow prisoners of the error of their position.[55]

At Zurich a Protestant professor of Hebrew, Theodore Bibliander
(c. 1504-1564) held his post while holding to conditional predestinarian views from 1531 until 1560, at which time his opinions were finally deemed unacceptable. Only after a controversy with fellow professor Peter Martyr Vermigli (who, from the commencement of his
teaching at Zurich in 1556, pressed the "unconditional" view) did
Bibliander leave his post for early retirement (with pension). Bibliander had earlier apparently stifled his differences with the modest predestinarian emphasis of his colleague Bullinger.[56]

---

[53]Second Helvetic Confession, introduction to the Second Helvetic Confession, *Reformed Confessions of the Sixteenth Century*, ed. Arthur C. Cochrane (Philadelphia: Westminster Press,
1966), p. 220.

[54]Ibid., pp. 240-41.

[55]The intraprisoner conflict is helpfully described by Dewey D. Wallace, *Puritans and Predestination 1525-1695* (1982; reprint, Eugene, Ore.: Wipf & Stock, 2004), pp. 21-28.

[56]Note the helpful discussion of this episode in Venema, *Heinrich Bullinger*, pp. 75-79; Frank A.
James, "Peter Martyr Vermigli," in *The Reformation Theologians: An Introduction to Theology in
the Early Modern Period*, ed. Carter Lindberg (Oxford: Blackwell, 2002), pp. 200-201; and

The canton of Bern embraced the Reformation cause in increments after 1523. Without Bern's military assistance, neighboring Geneva would not so easily have declared its political independence from the Duke of Savoy and embraced the Reformation cause in 1536. But such alliances did not imply that Bern would be stridently predestinarian. For a long time after Bern's embrace of the Reformation, any advocacy of predestination in pulpits and lecture rooms was forbidden. The strife over predestination illustrated by the Calvin-Bolsec controversy of 1551-1552 threatened to polarize canton Bern also; the canton took preemptive action in 1554 to ban all public disputes on the doctrine. Only in 1588 was a doctrine of predestination akin to that advocated in Geneva endorsed in this canton.[57]

Later than canton Bern made its peace with this doctrine, Cambridge University witnessed a revolt against the predestinarian theology, which had for two decades been entrenched in its instruction. Peter Baro, the Lady Margaret Professor of Divinity at Cambridge, was of French extraction and had been ordained at Geneva by Calvin. He was at least undogmatic in his adherence to the doctrines under review here. Concerned that the earlier Calvinist consensus was waning in the university, and provoked by a 1595 sermon of William Barrett (who had been Baro's student) the university heads, in conjunction with Archbishop of Canterbury John Whitgift introduced the Lambeth Articles. These were intended to clarify the sense in which the Church of England's Articles of Religion were to be understood in Cambridge as touching predestination. Against these amplificatory measures Baro railed to such an extent that his professorship was not renewed.[58]

Reaction in the seventeenth century. We can observe the continuation of this resistance into the opening decades of the seventeenth century. There is no more obvious example of this than Jacobus Arminius.

J. Wayne Baker, "Bibliander, Theodor," in *The Oxford Encyclopedia of the Reformation*, ed. Hans J. Hillerbrand (New York: Oxford University Press, 1996), 1:171-72.

[57]Heinrich Richard Schmidt, "Bern," in *Oxford Encyclopedia of the Reformation*, ed. Hans Hillerbrand (New York: Oxford University Press, 1996), pp. 143-45.

[58]Wallace, *Puritans and Predestination*, pp. 67-68. The text of the Lambeth Articles is provided in Schaff, *Creeds of Christendom*, 3:523-25.

Though after graduation from Leiden University he had pursued advanced theological study in Basel and Geneva in the 1581-1586 period and produced a commendatory letter from Theodore Beza at the time of his own subsequent ministerial examination at Amsterdam, it was never clear that Arminius endorsed the strident predestinarian teaching he found taught at Geneva. While the Belgic Confession had been introduced into the Reformed Churches of the Netherlands as a standard of common teaching in the 1571 Synod of Emden, Arminius's modern biographer has found no evidence to suggest that at his Amsterdam ordination in 1588 he was required to endorse it.[59] He was plainly familiar with the Reformed writers of his age, and took special note of the theological writings of the Cambridge theologian, William Perkins (noted above); in writings only published after his own death in 1609, the young Arminius made plain how objectionable he found Perkins' predestinarian views.[60]

Whatever Arminius may have thought on these themes in his years as an Amsterdam pastor (1588-1603), he published nothing. He was only drawn into open controversy about predestination after his selection as professor of theology in his alma mater, the University of Leiden. Once there, within a year he found himself in conflict with the senior professor of theology, Franciscus Gomarus. With Gomarus, he shared the experience of having studied in the premier institutions of Reformed theological learning in Germany and Switzerland. They diverged, however, in their adherence to the strident elaborations of the doctrine of predestination associated with contemporary scholars Beza and Perkins. Arminius, motivated by ethical concerns, leaned to the view that divine predestination both presumed the existence of sinful humanity (rather than being contemplated in the divine mind prior to the idea of the creation of unfallen humans) and was based on divine prescience of how particular sinners would respond to the gospel.[61]

---

[59]Bangs, *Arminius*, pp. 101, 116.
[60]Ibid., pp. 208-9.
[61]In this first concern, Arminius's outlook would have overlapped with that of many cautious predestinarians. This is what is called the sublapsarian or infralapsarian position.

Arminius's premature death, attributable to tuberculosis, in 1609 ended the academic struggle between the two Leiden theologians. But the publication and circulation of Arminius's academic treatises (some composed prior to his arrival at Leiden) after his death helped to galvanize into formal existence a hitherto loose coalition of ministers and church leaders Arminius's views largely overlapped with. This group put forward in 1610 the list of concerns that would eventually comprise the subject matter deliberated over by the famous Synod of Dordt in 1618-1619. It is not our purpose here to review the proceedings of that synod; it is our purpose to note that in common with other dissenters against predestination named already, Arminius and the party loosely affiliated with him would not endorse a doctrine they judged to involve divine partiality. Among their list of formulations was this alternative understanding of predestination:

> God has immutably decreed, from eternity, to save those men who, by the grace of the Holy Spirit, believe in Jesus Christ, and by the same grace persevere in the obedience of faith to the end; and on the other hand to condemn the unbelievers and unconverted (John III.36).[62]

On this understanding (and the understanding of most other dissenters named earlier) divine predestination involved the divine ratification of a foreseen positive response to the gospel, as presented.

RESPONSES TO THIS DISSENT

Those concerned Protestants who raised their voices or took up their pens to object to the Reformed understanding of predestination received a variety of responses. In some cases—as in Cambridge of the 1590s, the response given to dissent was a more forceful and detailed defense of the previously articulated doctrine in the form of the Lambeth Articles. In Reformation Zurich the eminent Hebrew professor Bibliander found himself in an involuntary early retirement. After the eventual Synod of Dordt, called in Holland to answer the protests of the coalition that shared Arminius's sense of uneasiness of predestina-

---

[62]"The Remonstrance," art. 1, in *The Creeds of Christendom*, ed. Philip Schaff (New York: Harper, 1877), 1:517.

tion as usually taught, there were eventually two hundred ministers who forfeited their pastoral positions because they would not conform.[63] But it would be a mistake to stop here.

Predestination ameliorated. If we compare the formulations of the doctrine of predestination among the Reformed in the decades following these expressions of dissent, we can detect amelioration or improvement in two particular respects.[64] As regards the vexatious question of the possible relationship between an omnipotent God's providential control of all things and the existence of sin and evil in a world originally declared "good," Reformed theology gradually moved—across the space of a century—from denying that there was such a thing as mere divine "permission" of evil but instead only a "willing" (this had been Calvin's own view) to a ready embracing of the language of "permission" in an attempt to make plain that there was no divine approbation or endorsement of sin and evil in his creation.[65] The use of *permission* language is already endorsed by Zanchius, Calvin's near contemporary.[66] The language is taken up and utilized in the treatment of providence in the Westminster Confession of Faith (1646).[67]

Acknowledging this modification is to acknowledge that the earlier Reformation statements on this subject had contained moral and ethical ambiguities that could not be left unattended any longer. Dissenters suffered dislocation and disadvantage in the meantime, but the force of their protest made its mark.

More particularly, in the matter of predestination itself, there was a comparable amelioration in the handling of the question of the relation in which elect and nonelect persons stand to the all-comprehensive

---

[63]Schaff, *Creeds of Christendom,* 3:514.

[64]I am indebted to Alan P. F. Sell's work *The Great Debate: Calvinism, Arminianism, and Salvation* (Worthing, U.K.: Henry E. Walter, 1982), p. 23, for this terminology.

[65]Note Calvin's emphatic denial of this conception of mere divine permission in the *Institutes,* 3.23.8

[66]Zanchius, *Absolute Predestination,* p. 12. The significance of this development is commented on by Richard A. Muller in "Calvin and the Calvinists, Part 2," in *Calvin Theological Journal* 31 (1996): 155. Muller speaks of the "modification" of Calvin's emphasis. The alteration is also noted by Carl Trueman in his essay "Calvin and Calvinism," in *The Cambridge Companion to John Calvin,* ed. Donald K. McKim (Cambridge: Cambridge University Press, 2004), p. 237.

[67]Westminster Confession of Faith, 5.4.

will of God. While a whole succession of sixteenth-century Reformed theologians (including Beza and Perkins) had essentially reiterated the view of Bucer and the later Calvin that all men are predestined to one of two ends, a movement had begun before that century expired to limit the language of predestination to persons made the object of God's saving mercy. This was the conception of predestination *to life*. Bullinger, Vermigli—and in time—the Canons of Dordt and the Westminster Confession themselves took the view that the ultimate end of the unsaved did *not* proceed from the eternal will of God in the same manner as the end of the saved. The cause of ultimate condemnation, according to this second understanding was none other than the unbelief and sin of the condemned.[68]

This chapter has pointed out that Calvin was by no means the originator of the doctrine of predestination, even though it is overassociated with him in the public mind. It has been shown that Calvin's own views expanded over time and through bitter controversy. It has been indicated that some of Calvin's close allies did not necessarily state the matter as he did and avoided some extremities perceived to be attached to his opinions. Within even a half-century of Calvin's death, the doctrine of predestination—because it had justifiably engendered protest— was being stated with greater care and circumspection than in Calvin's time. Is there some obligation that we simply take over his view as it continues to be available to us in his widely republished works? Far from it! As one wise writer has recently said,

> It is too often assumed that Calvin's theology has, or had at some point in the past, some kind of normative status within the Reformed tradition. This is historically and ecclesiastically not so. . . . The historic identity of Reformed theology has always been expressed through public confessional documents such as the First and Second Helvetic Confessions, the *Consensus Tigurensis*, the Heidelberg Catechism, the Belgic Confession and the Westminster Standards.[69]

---

[68]The relevant portion of the Canons of Dordt is head 1, article 15, the concluding segment of which begins "the non-elect are simply left to the just condemnation of their own sins." The Westminster Confession is very circumspect also in handling this matter; see 3.3 and 3.7. Nonelect persons are "passed by for their sins."

[69]Carl Trueman, "Calvin and Calvinism," in *The Cambridge Companion to John Calvin*, ed. Don-

When it is so evident that thoughtful Reformed theology has moved *beyond* Calvin on this doctrine, it is—to say the least—very unhelpful to be urged or encouraged to hold this doctrine *just as Calvin did*. Today's Calvinists ought, at very least, to have observed that predestination as addressed in the major confessions of the Reformation era is shorn of some excesses attached to Calvin's own views. According to these, God's relation to evil is one of permission, *not* causation; predestination is "to life" and not "to death"; those not embraced in God's electing mercy are passed by "for their sins." These are the sentiments of co-Reformers and successors of Calvin who were more circumspect and measured, on this theme, than he.

DISCUSSION QUESTIONS

1. Can you pinpoint what is the major issue that separates the Reformed tradition's understanding of predestination from the understanding of rival positions?

2. Given a general agreement about predestination among the Swiss Reformers, at what point(s) did Calvin's view stake out distinctive ground?

3. What factor or factors moved Calvin's successors to ameliorate or modify his teaching on this matter?

4. If a person today insists that he or she holds Calvin's own view of predestination, what is a thoughtful way of interacting with this assertion?

FURTHER READING

Jewett, Paul K. *Election and Predestination*. Grand Rapids: Eerdmans, 1985.

Olson, Roger. *Arminian Theology: Myths and Realities*. Downers Grove, Ill.: InterVarsity Press, 2006.

Klooster, Fred. *Calvin's Doctrine of Predestination*. Grand Rapids: Baker, 1977.

---

ald K. McKim (Cambridge: Cambridge University Press, 2004), pp. 225-26.

Venema, Cornelis P. *Heinrich Bullinger and the Doctrine of Predestina-tion.* Grand Rapids: Baker, 2002.

Wallace, Dewey D., Jr. *Puritans and Predestination: Grace in English Protestant Theology.* 1982. Reprint, Eugene, Ore.: Wipf & Stock, 2004.

The International Synod of Dordt, 1618-1619 by Bernard Picart, 1729
Image: Wikipedia

MYTH THREE

TULIP Is the Yardstick
of the Truly Reformed

IF WE WERE TO DECIDE THE matter on the basis of anecdotal evidence, we might conclude that the venerable "Five Points of Calvinism," customarily summarized by the acronym of T-U-L-I-P, have an unclouded future.[1] To name just three pieces of evidence, I could point to the publication by Zondervan in 2004 of Richard Mouw's intriguing title *Calvinism in the Las Vegas Airport*, the September 2006 *Christianity Today* feature story by Collin Hansen, "Young, Restless and Reformed," and the recognition by *Time* magazine's David Van Biema of this "New Calvinism" as "One of Ten Ideas Changing the World Right Now."[2] Surely, any movement with enough momentum to generate a sympa-

---

[1]This chapter will challenge the fitness of TULIP to represent Reformed theology and show that the usage of this acronym has varied widely and subjectively. But lest there be any doubt about what is at stake, the majority of those who rely on this formula reckon that the T = Total Depravity, U = Unconditional Election, L = Limited Atonement, I = Irresistible Grace and P = Perseverance. An earlier version of this chapter appeared in the *Scottish Bulletin of Evangelical Theology* 26, no. 2 (2008), under the title "The Points of Calvinism: Retrospect and Prospect."

[2]Richard Mouw, *Calvinism in the Las Vegas Airport* (Grand Rapids: Zondervan, 2004); Collin Hansen, "Young, Restless and Reformed," *Christianity Today*, September 2006, pp. 32-38. Hansen has expanded his magazine article into a book of the same name, *Young, Restless and Reformed* (Wheaton, Ill.: Crossway, 2008). David Van Biema, "The New Calvinism," *Time*, March 12, 2009.

thetic volume from the pen of a major seminary president, a story in America's widest-read Christian periodical reflecting a massive twenty-something movement newly enamored with these same ideas, and enough momentum to draw *Time*'s attention is not about to expire. In particular, who would have ever anticipated that the evangelicalism of middle America reflected in *Christianity Today* would be displaying Calvinism's contested points in a story sidebar? And yet, there they were for all to see in the September 2006 issue.

Yet, it is my contention that all such recent appearances of a Calvinist resurgence notwithstanding, the modern Calvinist movement is conflicted over the manner in which appeals to these very points (those summarized by the acronym TULIP) are to be made.

A DISTINCTION IN HOW APPEALS ARE BEING MADE TO TULIP

There exists what I will term a "sovereign grace" school and an "apologetic" school of Calvinism. Before elaborating on this distinction I must first maintain that both tendencies accept that the points summarized by TULIP are a faithful kind of theological shorthand for a much more comprehensive statement of Calvinist theology delivered at the international Reformed Synod hosted at Dordrecht, the Netherlands, in 1618-1619.[3] Both tendencies acknowledge that this was a synod summoned to deal with the challenge to Calvinist orthodoxy associated with the pastoral and academic career of Jacobus Arminius.

The first tendency, which I designate "sovereign grace," is concerned first and foremost to champion God's purposing an omnipotent electing grace toward undeserving persons who belonged to the common mass of fallen humanity.[4] For the sovereign grace Calvinist, the TULIP acronym is sacrosanct; it is a historic formula understood to have been passed down to us by our forebears. Dislike and scorn of

---

[3]The best two accounts in English of the international synod at Dordrecht are Alan P. F. Sell, *The Great Debate* (Grand Rapids: Baker, 1983); and P. Y. De Jong, ed., *Crisis in the Reformed Churches* (Grand Rapids: Reformed Fellowship, 1968).

[4]Examples of this "sovereign grace" approach are such authors as David Steele and Curtis C. Thomas, *The Five Points of Calvinism Defined, Defended, Documented* (Philadelphia: Presbyterian & Reformed, 1963); Jack Seaton, *The Five Points of Calvinism* (Edinburgh: Banner of Truth, 1970); and Arthur C. Custance, *The Sovereignty of Grace* (Phillipsburg, N.J.: Presbyterian & Reformed, 1979).

TULIP is reckoned as being akin to negative attitudes toward the Bible and gospel; unbelievers misjudge them all. The second tendency I designate "apologetic," not because those displaying this tendency are any less zealous in their advocacy of an omnipotent electing grace but because they show a heightened awareness that the doctrines summarized under the rubric of TULIP are capable of being grossly misunderstood. (Total depravity, limited atonement and irresistible grace are the items most often admitted to be problematic.) The Calvinist writers I term *apologetic* are ready both to restate the doctrines summarized in TULIP and to alter that acronym, as necessary, to more effectively communicate what they consider to be the actual meaning of the points.[5]

BOTH TENDENCIES LABOR UNDER A COMMON MISUNDERSTANDING

Though my personal sympathies are entirely with the apologetic tendency, united in its determination to prevent gross misunderstandings of what TULIP represents, it appears that both tendencies are unwittingly working from a mistaken premise. And that mistaken premise is the common assumption that the acronym TULIP is itself historic. Both sovereign-grace and apologetic Calvinists equally suppose that the points are a time-honored and authentic representation from the dim Calvinist past that gives us a proper distillation of what was achieved at Dordt in the face of the early Arminian challenge. This chapter aims to establish that this is an unwarranted belief; in consequence we should be able to locate both more historically accurate methods of summarizing the message of Dordt *and* to consider some faithful contemporary ways of

---

[5]Examples of the apologetic school include such writers as Edwin H. Palmer, *The Five Points of Calvinism: A Study Guide* (Grand Rapids: Baker, 1972); John R. DeWitt, *What Is the Reformed Faith?* (Edinburgh: Banner of Truth, 1981); R. C. Sproul, *Grace Unknown* (Grand Rapids: Baker, 1997); Roger Nicole, *Our Sovereign Savior* (Fearn, U.K.: Christian Focus, 2002); James Boice and Philip Ryken, *The Doctrines of Grace* (Wheaton, Ill.: Crossway, 2002); and more recently both Richard Mouw, *Calvinism in the Las Vegas Airport* (Grand Rapids: Zondervan, 2004); and Robert Peterson and Michael Williams, *Why I Am Not an Arminian* (Downers Grove, Ill.: InterVarsity Press, 2004). In a class by itself is the winsome popular work of Timothy F. George, *Amazing Grace: God's Initiative—Our Response* (Nashville: LifeWay, 2002). Designed for Southern Baptist readers unfamiliar with or suspicious of TULIP, the author substitutes the alternate acrostic ROSES.

rearticulating this message. Let us proceed by moving from our own times to earlier days.

USE OF THE FIVE POINTS IN RETROSPECT

TULIP may be of twentieth-century origin. Many can remember initially encountering the points of Calvinism through the large booklet of the writers David N. Steele and Curtis C. Thomas. In 1963, when Steele and Thomas released their *The Five Points of Calvinism: Defined, Defended, Documented* and in the process helped to popularize the T-U-L-I-P acronym, a reader might easily have supposed that they were relaying a formula of considerable vintage.[6] Steele and Thomas apparently believed so, and it appears that they were in good company. The renowned Reformation historian, the late Lewis W. Spitz of Stanford University, though he disapproved of the acronym, spoke of it in 1971 as by then a "familiar caricature of Calvin's theology."[7] Wheaton College's Earle E. Cairns had just as confidently used the acronym to describe the Calvinist position in his 1953 *Christianity Through the Centuries* (he called it a mnemonic device).[8]

The intriguing thing we find on reading Steele and Thomas's booklet closely is that of the older works on Calvinist history and theology that they relied on in their preparation to write on this subject, only *one* utilized the TULIP acronym. Ben A. Warburton, whose 1955 work *Calvinism: Its History and Basic Principles* was one of their chief authorities, did not.[9] B. B. Warfield (1851-1921), the late professor of theology at Princeton, had neither in his short work *The Plan of Salvation* (1915) nor in the shorter pieces published in the posthumous collection of

---

[6]Roger Nicole, then of Gordon Divinity School, the predecessor of today's Gordon-Conwell Theological Seminary, supplied a preface. The 2004 expanded reprint edition of the 1963 volume makes plain that the authors, Steele (now deceased) and Thomas wrote from within a "Bible Church" stance.

[7]Lewis W. Spitz, *The Renaissance and Reformation Movements* (St. Louis: Concordia, 1971), 2:417.

[8]Earle E. Cairns, *Christianity Through the Centuries* (Grand Rapids: Zondervan, 1953), pp. 336-77.

[9]Ben A. Warburton, *Calvinism: Its History and Basic Principles* (Grand Rapids: Eerdmans, 1955). In a reading of Warburton I discern that he writes from a context outside North America.

writings, *Calvin and Calvinism* (1929).[10] J. I. Packer, who contributed an introductory essay to the 1959 reprint of John Owen's particularistic *The Death of Death in the Death of Christ* (1647), was clearly a resource for these authors; yet Packer did not use the acronym.[11] The one clear source drawn on by Steele and Thomas which *did* employ the TULIP acronym is Loraine Boettner's *The Reformed Doctrine of Predestination* (1932).[12] Therefore, Steele and Thomas were not the originators of TULIP but only among its most successful popularizers; the acronym has a shadowy history extending back to Boettner's utilization of it.[13] Can we go back earlier? Yes, we can.

The earliest twentieth-century usage of the acronym to have come to light is one found in an article in a New York periodical called *The Outlook* in 1913. There, the writer, William H. Vail of Newark, New Jersey, both recalled details of hearing an address on the subject eight years earlier by a Dr. McAfee of Brooklyn and described his own current attempts to ascertain what some of his contemporary Presbyterian ministers held the points of Calvinism to be.[14] It is enough to say that there was no standardized way of answering, though the persons whose opinions he sought were quite able to paraphrase the concerns of the points of doctrine enunciated by the Synod of Dordt.

---

[10]Warfield's essay, "Calvinism," which had originally appeared in the second volume of the *New Schaff-Herzog Encyclopedia of Religious Knowledge*, is reprinted in the *Works of Benjamin B. Warfield* (Grand Rapids: Baker, 1981), 5:353-72. At p. 363, Warfield describes the points of Calvinism but does not employ the acronym.

[11]I have consulted the introductory essay in a free-standing undated reprint, produced c. 1969. Note especially Packer's description of the five points at p. 4.

[12]Loraine Boettner, *The Reformed Doctrine of Predestination* (Grand Rapids: Eerdmans, 1932), pp. 59-60.

[13]Boettner's discussion and use of TULIP is cautious and restrained.

[14]I am indebted to two Internet acquaintances, Ched Spellman of Dallas/Ft. Worth, Texas, and Bart Byl of Vancouver, British Columbia, for simultaneously locating this source in a search through Google Books: William H. Vail, "The Five Points of Calvinism Historically Considered," *The Outlook*, June 21, 1913. Vail must have taken down notes from McAfee's presentation, c. 1905. He records that McAfee's use of the TULIP acronym diverged from what is popularly held, at present, only in the "U," to which he assigned the meaning "Universal Sovereignty." On the other hand, Vail's attempt to learn whether his contemporaries concurred with McAfee's earlier construction brought a clearly negative result. His contemporaries, much like the nineteenth-century Christian leaders we next deal with, could give indications of the *content* of the points of Dordt—all the while showing no concern to prop up any acronym. This important document of 1913 is reprinted as an appendix to this book as appendix A: "The Earliest Known Use of TULIP?"

TULIP is even more elusive in the nineteenth century. The nineteenth century had many advocates for Calvinism and for the theology of Dordt, but not one emerges as an advocate of this acronym. Robert L. Dabney (1820-1898) of Union Seminary, Virginia, and subsequently Austin Seminary, Texas, composed a small volume on the subject in 1895. The Presbyterian from the American South was hardly an eager beaver for the points, for he introduced his volume with the words "this title *(The Five Points of Calvinism)* is of little accuracy or worth; I use it to denote certain points of doctrine, because custom has made it familiar."[15] Like many writers of that century, he wrote on behalf of the points of Dordt and yet took liberty to describe them in his own way.

He discussed total depravity, but as part of a wider discussion of original sin and the inability of the will; he would *not* expound irresistible grace but rather effectual calling or regeneration.[16] Election he expounded primarily in terms taken from his own denomination's Westminster Confession of Faith; particular redemption, *not* limited atonement, was the way he expressed his conviction that the death of Christ served a design.[17] He *did* espouse the perseverance of the saints in language familiar to those who know TULIP.

William Parks was the mid-Victorian Anglican vicar of Openshaw, near Manchester. A high Calvinist in the tradition of Augustus Toplady (1740-1778), he utilized the season of Lent in 1856 to preach a series of sermons on Calvinism, published as *Sermons on the Five Points of Calvinism*.[18] The high Calvinist organization Sovereign Grace Union kept these sermons in print into the twentieth century.[19] But for all their associations with rigor, Parks's sermon themes were hardly abra-

---

[15]Robert L. Dabney, *The Five Points of Calvinism* (Richmond: n.p., 1895), p. 3.

[16]Ibid., pp. 8, 25.

[17]Ibid., pp. 38, 60. This same doctrinal posture is discernible in the ministerial career of Dabney's contemporary, B. M. Palmer (1818-1902). His biographer, Thomas Carey Johnson, reports of Palmer, of New Orleans, "He even preached boldly and frequently on those points of Calvinism which have been so bitterly attacked in every generation, viz: total depravity, unconditional election, particular redemption, efficacious grace, and perseverance therein unto the end" (Thomas Cary Johnson, *Life of B. M. Palmer* [1906; reprint, Edinburgh: Banner of Truth, 1987], p. 660). I am indebted to my colleague Dr. Daphne Haddad for this reference.

[18]Note the brief reference to Parks in Ian J. Shaw, *High Calvinists in Action: Calvinism and the City, Manchester and London, 1810-1860* (New York: Oxford University Press, 2002), p. 17 n. 33.

[19]I have used the edition produced by Farncombe (London: n.p., 1915).

sive; "The Fall of Man," "Election," "Particular Redemption," "Effectual Calling" and "Final Perseverance" were his way of articulating what he took to be the doctrinal legacy of Dordt. Horatius Bonar (1808-1889), a Scottish minister and hymn writer, had written in defense of Calvinistic doctrines in 1846 in a small volume of published letters titled *Truth and Error.*[20] In this volume Bonar took up the doctrines emphasized at Dordt and felt at liberty to rephrase them in what he believed to be a timely way. What under TULIP would be called total depravity, Bonar tackled as "God's Will and Man's Will"; rather than unconditional election, he spoke of "Predestination and Foreknowledge." He spoke of neither limited nor particular atonement by name but simply of "The Work of Christ."[21]

In the same era the Scottish-Canadian theologian Thomas McCulloch (1776-1843) addressed these questions in a volume titled *Calvinism, the Doctrine of the Scriptures.*[22] The work has a distinct eighteenth-century feel and is largely taken up with the refutation of anti-Calvinist writers of the earlier period. What is significant for our purposes, however, is the fact that in defending the theological system to which he is loyal against such attacks, he avoids the use of terminology we have come to consider customary. As with Dabney there is a preference for terminology of his own or his confession of faith's choosing, rather than any cant formulas. Original sin comes under examination, not total depravity; in considering the atonement of Christ, the sacrifice as constituting a form of satisfaction to God draws his defense, while the question of the efficacy of the atonement receives only a minor discussion. Election is defended in a conventional discus-

---

[20]Horatius Bonar, *Truth and Error*, 3rd ed. (New York: Carter, 1850). The volume seems to reflect the Scottish upheaval over Calvinism in the 1840s stirred up by James Morrison, who left the Scottish Secession Church to found the Evangelical Union. The theological controversies of the period are surveyed in Ian Hamilton, *The Erosion of Calvinist Orthodoxy: Seceders and Subscription in Scottish Presbyterianism* (Edinburgh: Rutherford House, 1990).

[21]Bonar, *Truth and Error*, letters 2, 4, 5.

[22]The work was published posthumously, Thomas McCulloch, *Calvinism, the Doctrine of the Scriptures* (Glasgow: William Collins, 1846). McCulloch, an Antiburgher Presbyterian, became, on his arrival in Nova Scotia, the principal of Pictou Academy from 1818 and the principal of Dalhousie College (later University) from 1838 (N. R. Needham, "McCulloch, Thomas," in the *Dictionary of Scottish Church History and Theology*, ed. Nigel M. de S. Cameron [Downers Grove, Ill.: InterVarsity Press, 1993], p. 507).

sion; McCulloch allows but does not belabor the fact that this election is not based on mere prescience of the condition of the fallen individual.

Charles H. Spurgeon (1834-1892) devoted a chapter of his autobiography to describing his own Calvinist stance. He gladly identified himself as believing and preaching the five Calvinist points, and yet he refrained from identifying them in the manner we have grown accustomed to. Typical of his viewpoint are the lines:

> I do not believe we can preach the gospel if we do not preach justification by faith, without works; nor unless we preach the sovereignty of God in His dispensation of grace; nor unless we exalt the electing, unchangeable, eternal, immutable, conquering love of Jehovah; nor do I think we can preach the gospel, unless we base it upon the special and particular redemption of His elect and chosen people which Christ wrought out upon the cross; nor can I comprehend a gospel which lets saints fall away after they are called.[23]

Here, admittedly, is but a sample of nineteenth-century Calvinism, yet neither in the United States, England or Scotland were those ready to stand up for Calvinism concerned to state the doctrines in any particularly aggressive or uniform way. Their concern was to restate the doctrines carefully and modestly in an era when theological change was in the wind.

TULIP is similarly elusive in the eighteenth century. You may not be surprised to learn that the acronym cannot be located in the eighteenth century, which followed immediately after the epoch of the Synod of Dordt and the Westminster Assembly. As the eighteenth century closed, there were Anglican evangelicals like Thomas Scott (of *Commentary* fame) and his contemporary Thomas Haweis (a founding sponsor of the London Missionary Society in 1795) doing battle with their bishop of Lincoln, George Tomline. The latter, both in his *Elements of Christian Theology* (1801) and *Refutation of Modern Calvinism* (1811) laid at the feet of these Georgian evangelicals charges that they believed the fall of Adam had meant that his descendants had "lost all

---

[23]Charles H. Spurgeon, *C. H. Spurgeon: The Early Years, 1834-1859* (London: Banner of Truth, 1967), p. 168.

distinctions of right and wrong" and that they preached their "favourite tenets of instantaneous conversion and indefectible grace"; he was certain that their "preaching of free justification" had led to the neglect of good works and denied that in the atonement of Christ there was any design to redeem particular persons.[24]

Haweis and Scott each replied to Tomline in defense of what they took to be the basic Calvinism of their Elizabethan Anglican Articles of Religion. Each knew that their English church had been represented by delegates at the seventeenth-century Synod of Dordt; each also believed that it was the recovery of the gospel of free justification in the awakening of the eighteenth century that was the real target of their bishop's criticisms. Scott believed that if left unanswered, his bishop would "sweep away at once the labors of his whole life."[25] Yet their response to this provocation was measured; they were determined not to contend for the Calvinist system so much as what they termed "our common Christianity," that is, things held in common by all scriptural Christians. Within this framework Haweis and Scott were prepared to contend for Calvinist doctrine of the broad-brush variety. They write in defense of "Original Sin and Incorrigible Depravity," "On Free Will" and on "Regeneration and Conversion." As to the extent of redemption, Scott, like the Anglican delegates to Dordt, preferred "general redemption," and yet allowed that there were others holding a narrower view. He maintained "perseverance," while allowing that "not all who contend for perseverance will enjoy it."[26] In a further attempt to resist the

---

[24]George Tomline, *A Refutation of Modern Calvinism* (London: n.p., 1811), pp. 3, 91, 94, 166, 185.

[25]Thomas Scott, *A Reply to Tomline's "Refutation of Calvinism"* (London: n.p., 1811), p. xiv. Beyond Scott and Haweis, there were at least two other evangelical Protestant responses to the provocation issued by Tomline. The Congregationalist divine of Rotherham Academy, Edward Williams (1750-1813) published his *A Defense of Modern Calvinism: A Reply to the Bishop of Lincoln* (London, 1812), while another individual, a nonconformist school teacher of Truro, Cornwall, John Allen (1771-1839), rose to the occasion by providing the first nineteenth-century English translation of Calvin's *Institutes*. On Williams, see "Williams, Edward," in *Biographical Dictionary of Evangelicals*, ed. Timothy Larsen (Downers Grove, Ill.: InterVarsity Press, 2003); Allen's translation of Calvin is discussed in "The Literary History of Calvin's *Institutes*," in *The Works of B. B. Warfield* (Grand Rapids: Baker, 1981), 5:421

[26]Scott, *Reply to Tomline's "Refutation of Calvinism,"* pp. 2-9, 51, 227, 473, 634. The role and stance of the delegates to Dordt appointed by the current monarch, James I, has been explored in two articles by Michael Dewar, "The British Delegation at the Synod of Dort," *Evangelical Quarterly* 46, no. 2 (1974): 103-16, and "The British Delegation at the Synod of Dort: Assem-

disparaging of these central evangelical doctrines, Thomas Scott provided his readers with the first nineteenth-century translation, in English, of the actual Canons of Dordt, from the Latin text made available at Oxford in 1804 as *Sylloge Confessionum*.[27]

The hymnwriter and theological controversialist Augustus Toplady (1740-1778), so fierce in his attempts to counter John Wesley's Arminian teaching, similarly conforms to the pattern I have described. In two treatises, *The Church of England Vindicated from the Charge of Arminianism* (1769) and *Historic Proof of the Doctrinal Calvinism of the Church of England* (1774), we come no closer to a rehearsing of the five points (TULIP) than references to "predestination unto life and regeneration by the Spirit of God" and "gratuitous and irreversible election . . . from whence a limited redemption necessarily follows."[28] Only *this* from him who was the best source of information about Dordt, in English, in the eighteenth century![29] The point is *not* that Toplady is a reticent Calvinist but only that his attempts to uphold the integrity of the system he holds dear do not involve him in the use of the Procrustean formula many have come to accept uncritically as a hallmark of Calvinist orthodoxy.[30]

In certain broad features this approach to the points of Calvinism had been anticipated in the early decades of the century by three writers: a Baptist, a Congregationalist and an Anglican. All three took up their pens in a context dominated by the writings of the liberal Anglican writer Daniel Whitby (1638-1726); the latter had thrown down the gauntlet to Calvinists by his work *A Discourse on the True Import of the*

---

bling and Assembled; Returning and Returned," *Churchman* 106, no. 2 (1992): 131-46. See also John Platt, "Eirenical Anglicans at the Synod of Dort," in *Reform and Reformation*, ed. Derek Baker (Oxford: Blackwell, 1979), pp. 221-43.

[27]Scott, *Reply to Tomline's "Refutation of Calvinism,"* p. 725. Scott provided an enlarged edition of the Canons of Dordt in 1818, with historical commentary. An American edition, with an endorsement by Samuel Miller of Princeton, was published in 1840.

[28]Augustus M. Toplady, *Works*, vols. 1, 2, 5 (London: n.p., 1828), 5:5, 46.

[29]In his *Historic Proof of the Doctrinal Calvinism*, vols. 1-2, Toplady provides an epoch by epoch account of the embrace of and influence of Reformed theology in the Church of England from Henry VIII forward. He shows that he has digested all the standard seventeenth-century correspondence and eyewitness accounts of the English delegates to Dordt (see ibid., 2:226-68).

[30]I introduce "Procrustean formula" advisedly, using it in the sense of "aiming to produce a conformity by arbitrary means."

Words Election and Reprobation (London, 1710). In this, Whitby had assailed the theological legacy of Dordt by writing dismissively of the imputation of Adam's sin, of election and particular atonement.[31] Taking the respondents beginning with the more recent, we can note that John Gill issued a three-part work, *The Cause of God and Truth*, commencing in 1735. It is significant that the headings under which Gill defends the Calvinist scheme are, once more, not the heads that have become familiar to us in recent times. Gill writes in defense of reprobation, election, redemption, efficacious grace and perseverance.[32]

Thomas Ridgley (1667-1734) was a Congregationalist divine and tutor. His *A Body of Divinity* (1731) was a thoughtful statement of Reformed theology using the framework of the Westminster Larger Catechism.[33] As in Gill, the theology of Dordt was safeguarded and protected, but without any fixed method of referring to it. Written as a vindication of orthodoxy against current misrepresentation, the *Body of Divinity* is also straightforward theological exposition.[34] Ridgley steers deftly through the contested questions of the decrees of God, election and predestination, original sin, effectual calling, the extent of the atonement, and perseverance—all with an eye to judicious and moderate statement. There is no doubt that Ridgley is a Dordtian Calvinist, and yet he is a writer who feels compelled to be generous and expansive, and above all scriptural.[35]

The Anglican John Edwards (1637-1716) wrote two works in de-

---

[31]Whitby had circulated these attacks in his *Paraphrase and Commentary on the New Testament* (1700-1703) and his *A Discourse on the True Import of the Words Election and Reprobation* (London: n.p., 1710). This latter title was popularly known as *Whitby on the Five Points*. I have argued in an earlier, still-unpublished paper, "The Strange Reemergence of the Points of Calvinism, 1700-1820," that the polemical writing of Whitby after 1700 provided an occasion for Calvinist theologians to rally around Dordt, when this might not otherwise have been their priority. This period has now helpfully been investigated by Stephen Hampton, *Anti-Arminians: The Anglican Reformed Tradition from Charles II to George I* (Oxford: Oxford University Press, 2008).

[32]Gill's separate treatment of the doctrine of reprobation (discussed in conjunction with election in the Canons of Dordt) tells us something of importance about the theological tendency of this high Calvinist.

[33]The best modern source of information about Ridgley is the recent work of Alan P. F. Sell, *Hinterland Theology: A Stimulus to Theological Construction* (Milton Keynes, U.K.: Paternoster, 2008), chap. 2.

[34]Ridgley, preface to *Body of Divinity* (London: n.p., 1731).

[35]Ridgley, *Body of Divinity*, 1:204-48.

fense of the points of Calvinism: *Veritas Redux* (1707) and a smaller
book-pamphlet *The Scripture Doctrine of the Five Points* (1715).[36] Though
the volumes differed in bulk, they were the same in tone. Edwards—a
kind of J. I. Packer in his day—used his vivacious writing skills to help
his readers to see that Whitby's attack on Calvinism was an attack on
the vitals of evangelical religion.

> The Divine decrees, the impotency of man's free will, original sin, grace
> and conversion, the extent of Christ's redemption, and perseverance are
> interwoven with the greatest and most substantial articles of the Chris-
> tian faith. . . . There is a necessity of preaching these in order to under-
> stand the main principles of our Christian belief.[37]

As for the five points themselves, Edwards provided a paraphrase
based on his own direct knowledge of the Canons of Dordt. He was
ready to sketch out "The Eternal Decrees," "Free Will," "Grace and
Conversion," "The Extent of Christ's Redemption and Universal
Grace," and "The Perseverance of the Saints."[38] His way of doing so
created the impression that there was no rigid form of the points need-
ing to be adhered to at all costs.

I believe that a sufficient sampling has been surveyed so that we may
now move beyond it to something more demanding still—an attempt
to learn lessons for the present and future use of the Calvinist points.

OBSERVATIONS AND INFERENCES

Loyalty to TULIP is based on misunderstanding. Late twentieth- and
early twenty-first-century advocates of five-point Calvinism—whether
of the sovereign-grace or apologetic school—have been wedded to the
TULIP formula since at least 1932 in a fashion uncharacteristic of Calvinists of any earlier era.[39] Even those who have felt that the acronym

---

[36]Edwards intimated in his *Veritas Redux* that he envisioned this volume being but the first part
of a more extensive *Body of Divinity*. There is no clear evidence that this larger project was ever
realized. It is commendable that Steele and Thomas, in their *Five Points of Calvinism* (1963),
are conversant with Edwards and list him in their bibliography.

[37]John Edwards, *Veritas Redux* (London: n.p., 1707), pp. vii, x.

[38]John Edwards, *The Scripture Doctrine of the Five Points* (London: n.p., 1715).

[39]It is not my belief that Loraine Boettner himself devised this acronym at the time of the writing of his *Reformed Doctrine of Predestination* in 1932. This seems also to be the conclusion

could be improved have done their fine-tuning of it wearing kid gloves as it were; they were that anxious to avoid the appearance of tampering with what they took to be a time-honored and venerable formula. As the acronym is apparently no older than the early twentieth century, we must ask ourselves what the pervasive use of this acronym says about those who have utilized and still utilize it. At very least this use suggests that users of the acronym have not understood the Calvinist past very well. There has been too great a willingness to reiterate, as though venerable, something with a relatively short and checkered history. Could it also mean that they have willingly consented to take a very loose rendering of the theology of Dordt in place of the actual burden of Dordt?

Fixation on TULIP enshrines emphases that are "off." The obverse of the first principle is that Calvinists of the nineteenth century and earlier could be positively breezy in their handling of and naming the points of Calvinism, all the while defending their actual substance. Would any early twenty-first-century conservative Calvinist worth his or her salt speak so casually as Dabney, who—as has been indicated—said that "this title (*Five Points of Calvinism*) is of little accuracy or worth. . . . I use it because custom has made it familiar"? This open-minded eclecticism has given way to a more slavish, unquestioning loyalty and use. Today, in many conservative theological circles, TULIP functions as a ready-made index for gauging the orthodoxy of a theological student, a minister or a professor.

We have not often enough heeded the cautions of those twentieth-century writers who, while embracing or alluding to the TULIP framework, have themselves cautioned us *not* to equate the acronym—or even the doctrines summarized by the acronym—with the Reformed theol-

---

drawn by Roger Nicole. In his preface to the fortieth-anniversary edition of Steele and Thomas's *Five Points of Calvinism*, he simply states, "Ever since the appearance of Loraine Boettner's magisterial *The Reformed Doctrine of Predestination* it has been customary to refer to the five points according to the acrostic TULIP" (ibid., p. xiv). For a possible allusion to the idea of limitation in the atonement prior to 1932, see n. 48 of this chapter, where there is some indication that Spurgeon was familiar with this conception and dismissive of it. At this point the best judgment would seem to be that Boettner, writing in 1932, popularized a conception that had been in circulation in print in the United States since at least 1913. See footnote 14 of this chapter.

ogy itself. Boettner himself judiciously warned, early in the twentieth century, against "a too close identification of the Five Points and the Calvinist system."[40] Palmer, in 1972, made essentially the same point when he began by writing, "Calvinism does not have five points and neither is Calvin the author of the five points."[41] Packer, while not endorsing the acronym, gave out similar cautions in 1959: "It would not be correct simply to equate Calvinism with the five points," and "the five points present Calvinistic soteriology in a negative and polemical form."[42]

Our failure to heed such cautions and our still-current tendency to revel in this acronym (however fine-tuned) may indicate that the Calvinism of our age has a vehement, belligerent streak to it. Earlier ages than our own were capable of distinguishing between a Calvinism that was sound and one that was bellicose, between a Calvinism that was soberminded and one that was extravagant.[43] Spurgeon, for example, insisted that with regard to the hyper-Calvinists of his day, he "differed from them in what they do *not* believe." He maintained that distinctions between Calvinist emphases were necessary. Just as a navigational compass, in addition to having North, South, East and West, also has "a Northeast and a Northwest," so there are expressions of Calvinism which have subtly shifted from the "true."[44] If such a readiness to draw distinctions between the comparative emphases of various preachers and writers has been lost, the modern Calvinist movement is the poorer for it.

Our use of TULIP fragments when we should aim at inclusion. Earlier defenders of Calvinism's points were frequently accommodating, ready to go some distance toward meeting the concerns expressed in the views of objectors. This is nowhere so obvious as when older writers took up the always-controversial question of the extent of the atonement. The vast majority of older writers surveyed here preferred the

[40]Boettner, *Reformed Doctrine of Predestination*, p. 59.
[41]Palmer, *Five Points*, p. i.
[42]Packer, introductory essay to Owen's *Death of Death* (1647), p. 5.
[43]Such distinctions about the Calvinism at the end of the eighteenth century were drawn by David Bogue and James Bennet, *History of Dissenters from the Revolution Under King William to the Year 1838* (London: n.p., 1839), 2:37; and Henry Moncrieff Wellwood, *Account of the Life and Writings of John Erskine, D.D.* (Edinburgh: n.p., 1818), p. 380.
[44]Spurgeon, *C. H. Spurgeon*, p. 173.

language of "definite atonement" or "particular redemption" to the acronym's suggestion (L) of an atonement that is "limited."[45] But more than this, it is evident that in keeping with Dordt's original insistence that, as to the sheer value of Christ's dying, his death was "abundantly sufficient to expiate the sins of the whole world,"[46] older writers often took pains to spell out the senses in which there were *universal* benefits in that particular redemption won by Christ. John Edwards listed two such benefits and Thomas Ridgley three.[47] In the following century Charles Hodge of Princeton established the same point in his *Systematic Theology*, while Robert L. Dabney acknowledged it in his *Lectures in Theology*.[48] Spurgeon, for his own part, was adamant in resisting "some who think it necessary to their system of theology to limit the merit of the blood of Jesus; if my theological system needed such a limitation, I would cast it to the winds."[49]

There is no pretending here that "limited atonement" was just another name for "particular redemption." The latter view, but not the former, carried with it suggestions of adequacy and capaciousness, ideas which are both noble and capable of addressing the question of "room at the cross." Where Calvinist writers today show no such generous interest in defining and articulating their Calvinism, it may be an indication that they have accepted that they are now theologizing for an identifiable Calvinist narrow way, a Calvinism on the margins, rather than for the evangelical Protestant tradition as a whole. Such a tendency, if it in fact exists, represents a dramatic reversal, a self-imposed ghettoization compared even to the nineteenth century. It is time to ask

---

[45]I find it intriguing that Steele and Thomas, writing in 1963, ostensibly to uphold the *L* of limited atonement, *still* evince the strongest preference for the older language of particular redemption. This is a clear example of the way that the venerated acronym had become a Procrustean formula by the 1960s. See their *Five Points*, pp. 39-47. With the exception of Augustus Toplady (cf. p. 84) the literature produced by Calvinists in the eighteenth and nineteenth centuries consistently spoke of the atonement as "particular" rather than "limited."

[46]This is the actual language of the Canons of Dordt, 2.3.

[47]Edwards, *Veritas Redux*, pp. 383-84; Ridgley, *Body of Divinity*, 1:434.

[48]Charles Hodge, *Systematic Theology*, 2:558; Dabney, *Lectures in Theology*, p. 527. This emphasis is not present, however, in John Murray's *Redemption Accomplished and Applied* (Grand Rapids: Eerdmans, 1955). In his fourth chapter Murray stoutly defends the acceptability of the term *limited* with respect to the atonement, while maintaining his firm belief in a free gospel offer.

[49]Spurgeon, *C. H. Spurgeon*, p. 173.

hard questions as to who led the way in this retreat. Is this ghettoization an unacknowledged remnant of the fundamentalist era of the early
twentieth century?

This leads to the related observation that earlier Calvinist theologians
believed that in upholding the points of Calvinism (described in broad-
brush fashion) they were performing a service to the *whole* of evangelical
Christianity rather than pursuing mere party interest. Thomas Haweis
and Thomas Scott saw this presciently; their diocesan bishop either could
not tell the difference or did not care to distinguish between his clergy of
Wesleyan and Calvinist sympathy. He blamed them all for holding
gloomy views of human nature, of discouraging human moral effort, of
bordering on enthusiasm by holding to belief in a sensible calling to salvation in this life (as opposed to a baptismal regeneration) and teaching
that believers might enjoy strong impressions of assurance of salvation.
They answered him, as writers consciously standing in the stream of
Dordt-style Calvinism in defense of what they perceived to belong to
"our common Christianity," that is, scriptural religion. One can certainly
find the same stance in the nineteenth-century Princeton theologian
Charles Hodge, who claimed (however accurately) that he wrote in support of the views of evangelical Christianity as a whole and was only
enunciating "the church doctrine."[50] When TULIP is used in an exclusionary way, meant to draw the circle tight rather than as a means of
rallying evangelical Christians to central pillar principles, a great reversal
has taken place among Calvinists who call themselves evangelical.

Is TULIP related to the actual doctrinal articles of our churches? One
portion of today's Calvinist movement is found in the churches that
have an explicit loyalty to the Canons approved by the Synod of Dordt.[51]
Yet this is atypical. By contrast, the Presbyterian world owes *no* explicit
loyalty to the Canons of Dordt, except in so far as those elaborations of
Calvinist theology are reflected in the Westminster Confession of Faith

---

[50]This feature of Hodge's writing, so evident in his *Systematic Theology*, was highlighted by
David Wells in "The Stout and Persistent Theology of Charles Hodge," *Christianity Today*,
August 30, 1974, pp. 10-12.

[51]The Reformed Church of America and the Christian Reformed Church are examples of such
churches. The Canons of Dordt are one of the "Three Forms of Unity" (the others being the
Heidelberg Catechism and the Belgic Confession).

and Catechisms. But we are not done yet. Whole portions of today's burgeoning Calvinist movement—whether Anglican, Baptist, charismatic, Free Church or Bible church are connected to churches whose doctrinal articles make little or no acknowledgment of the importance of Dordt's points; the doctrinal articles of many such churches are deliberately designed to provide for the free continuance of viewpoints the Synod of Dordt opposed. The point I raise here is not that the Canons of Dordt are off-limits to all but those whose churches have explicitly endorsed them. But it is the question of how the points of Dordt can function with integrity in any setting in which they have not been formally embraced. Let me break this down three ways.

First, believers affiliated with churches that explicitly align themselves with the Canons of Dordt have the Canons set out in their official doctrinal standards and also have guides and materials available to help them study these themes as they stand in relation to Scripture and the rest of Reformed theology. These materials can be of help to others too.[52] A fine scholar from this branch of the Reformed family pointed out, for example, in 1989, that the *I* in TULIP was actually a caricature of the position championed in the Synod of Dordt. Those who derided the Reformed idea of effectual calling or prevailing grace branded it "irresistible."[53] This is the kind of inside information that needs circulating. It should change popular Calvinism's use of TULIP.

Second, believers affiliated with other Presbyterian and Reformed churches that have no specific allegiance to the Canons of Dordt should pursue how and to what extent Dordt's Calvinist points are echoed or reflected in the standards their churches uphold. A Presbyterian will find, for example, that the Westminster Confession and Catechisms, being composed *after* the Synod of Dordt had deliberated, to a large

---

[52]Examples are the works of Cornelius Plantinga, *A Place to Stand: A Reformed Study of Creeds and Confessions* (Grand Rapids: Christian Reformed Church, 1979); and Henry Petersen, *The Canons of Dordt: A Study Guide* (Grand Rapids: Baker, 1968).

[53]The "I" of the acronym T-U-L-I-P, far from encapsulating Dordt's intended emphasis, actually relays the protest of the Dutch Remonstrants *against* early seventeenth-century Calvinism in a way dependent on Jesuit writers of that time. How is it possible that *irresistible*, a term intended to besmirch and caricature the concept of a grace that eventually prevails over all opposition, has been taken up and championed by those it was meant to portray unfavorably? See Anthony Hoekema, *Saved by Grace* (Grand Rapids: Eerdmans, 1989), pp. 104-5.

extent concur with things emphasized there. Yet, they should not expect to find a one-to-one correspondence! So, for example, "total depravity" is not in the Westminster Confession of Faith (WCF), but a
chapter, "The Fall of Man" (embracing the intensiveness and exten-
siveness of sin), is. Limited atonement is not in the WCF, but a chapter, "Of Christ the Mediator" (embracing in paragraph 8 the application of redemption "to all those for whom Christ purchased" it) is.
Irresistible grace is not present, while "Effectual Calling" forms a
chapter that indicates that awakened sinners are enabled to "come
most freely, being made willing by his grace." TULIP, at least as popularly understood, is not to be found here in any one-to-one fashion.
Rather than judging the actual Presbyterian standards by the points
of Dordt as popularly understood, thoughtful Presbyterians should
want to do the reverse.[54]

But a good proportion of today's Calvinists have not yet been addressed. If you are Anglican, Baptist, charismatic, Free Church and also
Calvinist in sympathy, your doctrinal loyalties may well run *beyond* what
your church actually endorses. For some, this will be only in degree. The
Anglican Articles of Religion (1563), for example, are certainly Reformed
in orientation, but they come from the century before the Calvinist-
Arminian controversy. And Baptist, charismatic or Free Church Calvinists? Their church's doctrinal articles may offer little or no support at all.
What then? My advice is that they borrow from the resources available in
the Presbyterian and Reformed Churches that offer help in understanding the relationship between Dordt and the Reformed Confessions.

All this needs to be stressed because there is strong evidence that
twentieth-century writing on behalf of TULIP has not properly engaged with the actual Canons of Dordt, of which the acronym purports
to be a paraphrase or summary.[55] This meant, and means, that writers

---

[54]Standard explanatory guides to the Westminster Confession of Faith and Catechisms are
those of A. A. Hodge (1869), John MacPherson (1882) and George Hendry (1960). Those in
the Baptist stream of Christianity should become familiar with the interpretation of Reformed
Christianity found in the London Baptist Confession of 1677 (adapted at Philadelphia in
1688) and the New Hampshire Baptist Confession of 1833. The texts of each are supplied in
Schaff, *Creeds of Christendom*, 3 vols. (New York: Harper, 1877), 3:738-48

[55]Welcome exceptions to this rule are found in John R. DeWitt, *What Is the Reformed Faith?*
Edwin H. Palmer, *The Five Points of Calvinism*, and Richard Mouw, *Calvinism in the Las Vegas*

have been implying the fidelity of the acronym as a rendering of Dordt's meaning without ever being pressed to demonstrate that this fidelity exists in fact. Calling the paraphrasing of Dordt by TULIP a broad-brush approach is arguably too kind. TULIP cannot be allowed to function as a creed.

SUMMARY AND CONCLUSION

This chapter began by remarking on the current evidences of the resurgence of Calvinism and its oft-contested points. It was noted that evangelical Calvinists today tend to belong to one of two types ("sovereign grace" or "apologetic"). It was maintained that whatever their differences, they were both more wedded to the TULIP formulation than is warranted by good historical or theological inquiry. We ought therefore to proceed with more skepticism toward TULIP as an alleged authentic exposition of Reformed theology than has characterized the Calvinist movement to date. We need to recover the big picture that was more evident to many of our forebears than it has been to us, that is, that everything of truly abiding value in Calvinism serves the interests of "our common Christianity."

Table 3.1. Expositions of the Points of Calvinism Traced Since 1900

Author/Title/Year	TULIP used?	Comments
Richard Mouw, *Calvinism in the Las Vegas Airport* (2004)	Yes	An apologetic approach is taken. The rough edges of some of the points are removed by a generous method of exposition. The supposition that the points actually represent Dordt is not challenged.
Robert Peterson and Michael Williams, *Why I Am Not an Arminian* (2004)	No	This book provides an exposition of critical differences separating Calvinist and Arminian positions. Not a defense of TULIP but an exploration of predestination, perseverance, human freedom, sinful inability, the operation of grace and the design of the atonement. An apologetic approach.

Airport; the exception is rooted in their standing astride the two worlds of Dutch and English-speaking Calvinism, so that they both know Dordt and more popular expressions of Calvinism in the English-speaking world.

Author/Title/Year	TULIP used?	Comments
James Boice and Philip Ryken, *The Doctrines of Grace* (2002)	Yes	An apologetic approach is taken. "Total" becomes "radical," "limited" becomes "particular," "irresistible" becomes "efficacious." Yet, the old supposition that these renamed points actually represent Dordt itself is maintained.
Timothy F. George, *Amazing Grace* (2002)	No	An apologetic approach for persons not previously familiar with or suspicious of Calvinist doctrines. A new acrostic is proposed: ROSES (radical depravity, overcoming grace, sovereign election, eternal life, singular or particular redemption).
Roger Nicole, *Standing Forth* (2002)	Yes	An apologetic approach. TULIP is said to be "now quite traditional." "Total" becomes "radical," "unconditional" becomes "sovereign," "limited" becomes "particular," "irresistible" becomes "effectual." "Limited" is denounced as "a complete misnomer."
R. C. Sproul, *Grace Unknown* (1997)	Yes	An apologetic approach. TULIP is endorsed, then modified. "Total" becomes "radical," "unconditional" becomes "sovereign," "limited" becomes "purpose-ful," "irresistible" becomes "effectual," and "perseverance become "preservation."
John R. DeWitt, *What Is the Reformed Faith?* (1981)	No	Apologetic. The significance of the five points is rapidly passed over in favor of five other overarching concerns.
Arthur C. Custance, *The Sovereignty of Grace* (1979)	Yes	Sovereign grace emphasis. Here, the points of TULIP are given a very unflinching exposition across 140 pages. Yet evidently, on p. 83, the author makes plain that he had viewed the actual Canons of Dordt.
Edwin Palmer, *Five Points of Calvinism* (1972)	Yes	Apologetic. Commences by distinguishing total depravity (which he affirms) from absolute depravity (which he affirms is the case only occasionally)
Jack Seaton, *The Five Points of Calvinism* (1970)	Yes	Sovereign grace emphasis. Seaton promptly goes to work to clarify what total depravity does not mean, etc. Yet he accepts uncritically that TULIP is conveying the message of Dordt to us.

Author/Title/Year	TULIP used?	Comments
Steele and Thomas, *Five Points of Calvinism* (1963)	Yes	Sovereign grace approach. The points are upheld according to the acronym, though "limited" and "particular" are used interchangeably. There is the *appearance*, but only the appearance, of a paraphrase of Dordt.
J. I. Packer, introductory essay to *Owen* (1959)	No	TULIP is named, but Packer does not use this framework. He argues that this framework is deficient.
Ben Warburton, *Calvinism* (1955)	No	Seems more U.K. than U.S. oriented. "Predestination," not unconditional election; "particular redemption," not limited atonement; "invincible," not irresistible grace, etc. Reminiscent of eighteenth- and nineteenth-century writers.
Loraine Boettner, *Reformed Doctrine of Predestination* (1932)	Yes	TULIP is introduced for the first time in a published book. Yet Boettner claims no originality in introducing it. It might be fairly inferred that he has found TULIP already in circulation. He will be less nuanced when, in 1983, he reiterates the points of TULIP in his pamphlet *The Reformed Faith*. Now, the cautions of 1932 that the Reformed faith is much larger than TULIP seem to have vanished.
B. B. Warfield, *Plan of Salvation* (1915) *Works*, vol. 5 (1929)	No	In his *Works* (p. 363) Warfield describes Dordt as reasserting the fundamental doctrines of "absolute predestination, particular redemption, total depravity, irresistible grace, and the perseverance of the saints." Here we have *three* elements of TULIP. It is possible that Warfield provided materials from which Boettner (1932) developed the scheme so familiar to us. From another perspective, Warfield merely reflects the diversity of definition that William Vail (n. 15) reported in 1913.

DISCUSSION QUESTIONS

1. If you are familiar with the acronym TULIP, can you remember

how you first encountered it? Was it from an individual whose judgment you trusted, a person whose judgment you questioned or from a recommended author?

2. Did you have an initial objection to the acronym? What was it? Do you still have the same objection?

3. Is your branch of the church supportive of, neutral toward or opposed to Calvinistic doctrines?

4. Have you observed positive benefits from the use of the acronym? Harmful effects?

5. If TULIP had never been invented, would it be good for someone to devise it now?

FURTHER READING

Descriptions of the Situation That Gave Rise to the Points of Calvinism
Sell, Alan F. *The Great Debate*. Grand Rapids: Baker, 1982.
DeJong, P. Y., ed. *Crisis in the Reformed Churches*. Grand Rapids: Reformed Fellowship, 1968.
Olson, Roger. *Arminian Theology: Myths and Realities*. Downers Grove, Ill.: InterVarsity Press, 2006.

Guides to the Points of Calvinism (see table 3.1 for a longer list)
Boice, James, and Philip Ryken. *The Doctrines of Grace*. Wheaton, Ill.: Crossway, 2002.
Mouw, Richard. *Calvinism in the Las Vegas Airport*. Grand Rapids: Zondervan, 2004.
Peterson, Robert, and Michael Williams. *Why I Am Not an Arminian*. Downers Grove, Ill.: InterVarsity Press, 2004.
Sproul, R. C. *Grace Unknown*. Grand Rapids: Baker, 1997.

George Whitefield, The Awakener

Image: http://faculty.polytechnic.org/gfeldmeth/lec.ga.html

MYTH FOUR

Calvinists Take a Dim View
of Revival and Awakening

As THE NINETEENTH CENTURY gave way to the twentieth, Christians in the Reformed theological tradition still regularly approved the
concept of spiritual awakening and revival. After all, reputable nineteenth-century historians of Christianity had argued that the Reformation of the sixteenth century had *itself* been a movement of European
spiritual awakening. And as the nineteenth century, in which they
wrote, had itself witnessed such events in connection with the year
1859 and the transatlantic ministry of D. L. Moody, these writers were
willing to suppose that what was happening in their own time had also
occurred in the sixteenth century. The Scottish church historian T. M.
Lindsay (1843-1914) accordingly wrote of the Reformation era in 1882:
"It was a genuine revival of religion, a fulfillment of the promise of the
outpouring of the Spirit of God upon his waiting church, and this religious movement springing up in these conditions took shape and force
from its surroundings."[1]

---

[1]T. M. Lindsay, *The Reformation: A Handbook* (1882; reprint, Edinburgh: Banner of Truth,
2006), p. 216. Lindsay addressed the same theme in his two-volume *History of the Reformation*
(Edinburgh: T & T Clark, 1906), 1:127-37. The concept of the Reformation as a movement of
spiritual awakening had been popularized earlier in the century by the evangelical Swiss histo-

And as the twentieth century dawned, we could find a highly similar approach taken by Williston Walker, whose oft-revised *A History of the Christian Church* is still consulted. The Yale historian set the career of Luther in a context of what he described as an "age of religious revival" that was already in progress before the revolt against Rome.[2]

Yet from the second half of the twentieth century to the present, particularly within North America, this welcoming perspective has been abandoned, and for three main reasons. First, this sympathetic stance has tended to evaporate among Calvinists because the movement of evangelical revival in the eighteenth century (the era of Whitefield, the Wesleys and Jonathan Edwards) is alleged to have promoted an unhealthy obsession with preaching on the need for spiritual rebirth or regeneration; this alleged obsession (never properly documented to date) is reckoned to have represented a departure from the proper balance. As well, such critics maintain that this concentrated preaching on the importance of rebirth was an inappropriate message for children raised in Christian families.[3]

Second, this formerly supportive outlook on revival has been challenged because of widespread reaction in the Presbyterian and Reformed constituency against the determination, manifested in the 1830s and especially associated with the career of Charles G. Finney, to carry out what might be called "improvements" on earlier ideas of revival. Whereas formerly such events of spiritual resurgence had been understood to come only periodically and according to a divine calendar hidden from us, Finney sought to optimize the likelihood of revival's occurrence *and* the certainty of its effects on many people.[4]

---

rian J. H. Merle D'Aubigné in his *History of the Reformation of the Sixteenth Century* (New York: Carter, 1846), 1:iii-v. One could find this perspective expressed as recently as 1968 by the Canadian historian W. Stanford Reid in his edited anthology *The Reformation: Revival or Revolution?* (New York: Holt, Rinehart & Winston, 1968), p. 2. His popular presentation of the same framework had appeared as "The Greatest Revival Since Pentecost, "*Christianity Today*, October 22, 1965, pp. 79-82.

[2]Williston Walker, *A History of the Christian Church* (New York: Scribner, 1918), pp. 332-37.

[3]See this complaint made already in 1940 by Lewis Bevans Schenck, *The Presbyterian Doctrine of the Children of the Covenant* (1940; reprint, Phillipsburg, N.J.: Presbyterian & Reformed, 2003), chap. 2.

[4]Note this emphasis in D. G. Hart, *Recovering Mother Kirk: The Case for Liturgy in the Reformed Tradition* (Grand Rapids: Baker, 2003), p. 208; D. G. Hart, "Jonathan Edwards and the Ori-

Finney's approach manifested itself in what were rightly termed "new measures." As part of a reaction against the unleashing of these ideas in the 1830s, our times have seen a three-way division of opinion among Christians in the Presbyterian and Reformed branches of the church.

There are some who are eager to champion pre-1830 conceptions of revival as perfectly viable for our time, while repudiating everything since the "new measures" (e.g., Iain Murray, Ronald E. Davies); others, who while acknowledging that there was a process of development (not without error) in thinking about revival since 1830, still see a general legitimate succession of these revival movements extending into the twentieth century (Richard Lovelace, Garth M. Rosell); and still others have repudiated the value of all such movements before or after 1830.[5] Some persons of this third view have been caught up in a revival of interest in the career and writings of one of the most trenchant Calvinist critics of that era of early-nineteenth-century Protestant revivalism, John W. Nevin (1803-1886).[6]

There is a third reason why the Presbyterian and Reformed branch of Christianity has learned to say less about revival, and it is that late-twentieth-century historians of Christianity have advanced a fresh understanding of the revivals of the eighteenth century. We have been encouraged, as not previously, to see the Christian leaders of that period as entrepreneurs, as impresarios, who learned the value of good publicity and used networks of influence to promote this movement in their time. It has been pointed out that Jonathan Edwards's *Narrative*

---

gins of Experimental Calvinism," in *The Legacy of Jonathan Edwards*, ed. D. G. Hart, Sean Michael Lucas and Stephen J. Nichols (Grand Rapids: Baker, 2003), p. 170; D. G. Hart and John Muether, *Seeking a Better Country* (Phillipsburg, N.J.: Presbyerian & Reformed, 2007), chap. 6.

[5]Representatives of the first approach are R. E. Davies, *I Will Pour Out My Spirit: A History and Theology of Revivals and Evangelical Awakenings* (Eastbourne, U.K.: Monarch, 1992); and Iain Murray, *Revival and Revivalism* (Edinburgh: Banner of Truth, 1994). Representatives of the second approach are Richard Lovelace, *Dynamics of Spiritual Life* (Downers Grove, Ill.: InterVarsity Press, 1979); and Garth M. Rosell, *The Surprising Work of God: Harold John Ockenga, Billy Graham, and the Rebirth of Evangelicalism* (Grand Rapids: Baker Academic, 2008). Representatives of the third approach are D. G. Hart, *Recovering Mother Kirk* (Grand Rapids: Baker, 2004); and *Seeking a Better Country* (Phillipsburg, N.J.: Presbyterian & Reformed, 2007).

[6]D. G. Hart, *John W. Nevin: A High Church Calvinist* (Phillipsburg, N.J.: Presbyterian & Reformed, 2005).

of Surprising Conversions (1737), when read in homes and from pulpits on both sides of the Atlantic, helped to build an expectation of what kind of awakening might soon transpire in distant communities. We now know that publicist William Seward, who traveled with George Whitefield, would write a hundred letters at a time to persons and newspapers in cities the evangelist would soon visit in order to raise expectations of what was to come. No one has portrayed these men as charlatans, but we have been encouraged to see them as willing to employ publicity and marketing methods to extend their movement.[7]

Personally, I am glad that this historical investigation has brought these significant factors to light; yet we must admit that one of the unforeseen consequences of the dissemination of this information is that the shine is off the Great Awakening apple, compared to former days. We are much less certain than in earlier times that this era provides a model to be emulated.[8] The principles that in fact distinguished it from the movements of the nineteenth century have tended to be obscured under this modern approach, which has made all these leaders from Edwards onward just so many employers of a template for revival.

Thus, we have witnessed a substantial (though not total) turning of tables. A century or more ago revival and awakening was regularly treated as integral to evangelical Protestant history. Writing in 1842 the Princeton graduate Charles Baird indicated—as he explained Christianity in America to European audiences—that regarding revivals:

> While differences exist as to what constitutes a well-conducted revival, all or nearly all, agree that such a revival is an inestimable blessing: so that he who should oppose himself to revivals *as such* would be regarded by most of our evangelical Christians as, *ipso facto*, an enemy to spiritual religion itself.[9]

---

[7]This approach is most pronounced in the volumes of Harry Stout, *The Divine Dramatist: George Whitefield and the Great Awakening* (Grand Rapids: Eerdmans, 1991); and of Frank Lambert, *Inventing the Great Awakening* (Princeton, N.J.: Princeton University Press, 1999). A more measured approach is provided in Thomas S. Kidd, *The Great Awakening* (New Haven, Conn.: Yale University Press, 2008).

[8]Stout, *George Whitefield*; and Lambert, *Inventing the Great Awakening*.

[9]Robert Baird, *Religion in America: Or an Account of the Origin, Relation to the State, and Present Condition of the Evangelical Churches in the United States* (1842; reprint, New York: Harper, 1856), p. 404. Baird (1798-1863) a Princeton Seminary graduate of 1822 was successively an

Today, by contrast, so many have adopted the view that revival is a dark secret, a part of our Reformed family history best kept in the closet. This chapter reexamines this phenomenon and asks, Is it right that Christians in the Reformed tradition now have so much difficulty affirming a proper place for revival and awakening? But this quest cannot go forward in a truly helpful way without certain clarifications being offered. Needed *first* is a clarification of terms, and *second* a clarification of chronological sequence. Let us take these in turn.

CLARIFICATION OF TERMS

The awkward initial fact is that when we take up the terms *revival*, *awakening*, *revivalist* and *revivalism*, we are employing terms that are plainly *not* as old as the Reformed expression of Protestant Christianity. Thus, for example, Lindsay, who in 1882 was happy to apply the term *revival* to the Reformation, was utilizing a term to describe these sixteenth-century movements for which there is no record of use in the English language until 1674, when the English Puritan John Owen used the term in his personal correspondence.[10] We *could* argue, therefore that *revival* terminology was unknown before that date, so that those who employ such language to describe prior occurrences are engaging in anachronism. Perhaps they are projecting backward in time the kind of occurrence that only happened at a later date? Yet I suspect that few would find such a criticism satisfying because we are aware that what could be called a "revival" could just as well be called something else—and was.

English independent ministers John Guyse and Isaac Watts used alternative terminology already familiar to them such as "plentiful effu-

---

agent for the American Bible Society, American Sunday School Union and (in France) the Foreign Evangelical Society. *Religion in America* originated as lectures written during a period of residence at Geneva and delivered to European audiences.

[10]While the *Oxford English Dictionary* attributes the first use of the noun *revival*, indicating "a general re-awakening of or in religion in a community or some part of one," to Cotton Mather's *Magnalia Christi Americana* in 1702, Owen's published correspondence demonstrates him using the terminology in July 1674 (see Peter Toon, ed. *The Correspondence of John Owen: 1616-1683* [London: James Clarke, 1970], p. 159). Owen urges his correspondent to "labour after spiritual revivals (sic)." I am indebted for this reference to the Rev. Daniel R. Hyde of Carlsbad, California through his February 15, 2010 post "John Owen on Revival" on the Meet the Puritans website <www.meetthepuritans.com/category/john-owen>.

sion of the Spirit" when they wrote a commendatory preface to the London edition of Jonathan Edwards's *Narrative of Surprising Conversions* at its 1737 publication.[11] There was a range of existing terminology available to late-seventeenth and early eighteenth-century writers, which included "further Reformation," "returning to God" and the "descent of a Spirit of converting grace."[12] Therefore, it was permissible for Lindsay and others to speak of "revival" occurring before 1674 because synonyms for that term were readily available and put to use. But we return to the question, What do the terms *revival, revivalist* and *revivalism* refer to?

Attempts have been made to define and distinguish these terms, right down to our time; plainly some are more helpful than others. It is important that we grasp both the gradual introduction of these terms and their shades of meaning. Two guides are available to help us: the *Oxford English Dictionary* (1928, rev. 1989) and *A Dictionary of American English on Historical Principles* (1938), which document actual use of terms across the centuries. The term *revival* (which both works record—incorrectly as it turns out—as first appearing in 1702) is described as "A general re-awakening of or in religion in a community or some part of one" (OED) and "A period of renewed interest in and devotion to religion" (DOAE). *That* is the eighteenth-century conception; the idea communicated involves both a movement and an elapse of time. However, the idea that "revival" involves an extended program or strategy of meetings belongs to the nineteenth century. The OED reports this by 1848, and the DOAE by the following year; then, but not before, it was possible to speak of a "series of revival meetings."

These series of meetings have leaders. The DOAE records the use of the term *revivalist* only after 1820; this is one who "conducts or takes part in a religious revival." The term does not emerge in print in Great Britain until sixty years later. *Revivalism* is equally a nineteenth-century item. A brief allusion in 1815 is followed by this usage in 1859: "hysteria in connection with revivalism is now commonly produced and propagated by

---

[11]I find the expression twice in the preface. See *A Narrative of Surprising Conversions* in the Jonathan Edwards anthology, *Jonathan Edwards on Revival* (Edinburgh: Banner of Truth, 1984), pp. 2, 4.

[12]W. J. Couper et al., *Scotland Saw His Glory: A History of Revivals in Scotland* (1918; reprint, Wheaton, Ill.: International Awakening, 1995), p. 9 n. 1.

man" (OED). By this point we have clearly moved beyond the notion of revival as spontaneous and surprising when it comes.

For lack of such historical anchors as these we currently find ourselves in a quandary of meaning. We have all heard or read of Whitefield, Edwards and Wesley being referred to as "revivalists," but the terminology implies something in the way of scheming and strategizing, which was far *less* true of them than their counterparts after 1830. We would be far better off to conceive of these individuals as evangelists, with Edwards being a pastor-evangelist and the others being itinerant evangelists.[13] We must at very least carry forward from this discussion the notion that, in the eighteenth century, *revival* and *awakening* are interchangeable concepts, with the primary emphasis being on the conversion of the unbelieving.

CLARIFICATION OF CHRONOLOGICAL OCCURRENCES

Bearing in mind the triple objection that has made it much less common today to hear Christians in the Reformed tradition warmly endorse the concept of "revival," it requires no manipulation of the evidence to demonstrate that these occurrences (even when described by terms current at the time) *were* periodic features of Reformed church life long before the Whitefield-Edwards-Wesley period. Once this is admitted, it will be seen that it is mistaken to trace the origin of these movements to the eighteenth century. It will be sufficient to give a series of examples in support of this contention prior to and subsequent to the classic period of the eighteenth century so closely associated with the names just provided.

---

[13]For a different approach to defining these terms, see Steve Latham, "God Came from Teman: Revival and Contemporary Revivalism," in *On Revival: A Critical Examination*, ed. Andrew Walker and Kristin Aune (Carlisle, U.K.: Paternoster, 2003), p. 172. Latham shows that there are six distinguishable layers of meaning connected to the term *revival* and urges us to be clear in spelling out which of these we intend. He lists (1) a spiritual quickening of the individual believer, (2) a deliberate meeting or campaign especially among Pentecostals to deepen the faith of believers and bring nonbelievers to faith, (3) an unplanned period of spiritual enlivening in the local church, quickening believers and bringing unbelievers to faith, (4) a regional experience of spiritual quickening and widespread conversions, e.g., the Welsh, Hebridean, East African and Indonesian revivals, (5) societal or cultural "awakenings," e.g., the transatlantic First and Second Awakenings, and (6) the possible reversal of secularization and "revival" of Christianity as such.

If, in reliance on the *Dictionary of American English* we adopt as a definition of *revival* "a period of renewed interest in and devotion to religion," it is not difficult to show that from the Reformation forward public preaching of the gospel with a view to the conversion of hearers was very common. It was, after all, the conception of the early Reformers (as with the Christian Renaissance humanists with whom they shared so many common convictions) that Western Europe in the sixteenth century was Christian in name only. While corruption of Christian teaching and morality may have extended widely among the clergy of the Western church, there was in the population at large a still more pervasive biblical ignorance, superstition confused with Christian practice, and lingering devotion to ideas and practices left over from old paganism.[14]

These raw Reformation realities are not sufficiently recognized now. Among those who take the view that the occurrence of revival/awakening was a novelty when it emerged in the 1730s, there is a supposition that almost instantly the churches of the Reformed tradition became fastidious, orderly and composed of rank-and-file people of deep Christian conviction. Admittedly (these theorists allow), this fastidiousness was temporarily set back by the immigration to the new world and to its western frontier.[15] Yet too much evidence points in the opposite direction. The Presbyterian and Reformed churches were, in many cases, churches "of the multitude" or territorial churches; they embraced populations that had not long before adhered to Roman Catholicism with greater or lesser fervor. Thus, in the early decades of Protestant history the pastoral challenge faced across Europe was to bring to *actual* Christian profession populations that were Christian only by cultural heritage.

We read of itinerant preaching in villages and markets, of hedge or field preachers, and of early Protestant "privy-kirks" meeting with the connivance of local authorities.[16] This European situation persisted

---

[14]Scott W. Hendrix, "Rerooting the Faith: The Reformation as Re-Christianization," *Church History* 69, no. 3 (2000): 558-77. Hendrix expands on this theme in his *Recultivating the Vineyard: The Reformation Agendas of Christianization* (Louisville, Ky.: Westminster John Knox, 2004).

[15]This approach is explicitly taken by Lewis Bevans Schenck, *The Presbyterian Doctrine of the Children of the Covenant* (Phillipsburg, N.J.: Presbyterian & Reformed, 2003), chap. 2.

[16]Note examples of this in Kenneth Hylson-Smith, *Christianity in England from Roman Times to the Reformation*, vol. 3, *1384-1558* (London: SCM, 2001), pp. 156-59; Carl Bangs, *Arminius:*

into the seventeenth century on account of the lingering shortage of Protestant clergy and of the accumulation of old superstition and ignorance. The movements we have come to call Puritanism or Second Reformation reflect a situation in which a territorial form of Christianity (which is now Protestant) is still treated with great indifference by much of the population, which despite its indifference is expected to attend church regularly.[17]

Thus, in his efforts to preserve the Christian character of Sunday as a day of rest and worship, a late-sixteenth-century Puritan minister of the Church of England, Nicholas Bound (d. 1613), took to task those who so preferred hunting to worshiping that they came to church not only with bows and arrows but also with their hunting falcons, tethered to their fists. He lamented the widespread practice of families bringing their dogs with them to divine service.[18] It was in just this setting that there unfolded the energetic pastoral, evangelistic and proclamation ministry of the Puritans, which one modern writer has taken the liberty to describe as "a movement of revival."[19] In such circumstances there were many occurrences of religious revival or awakening. We can identify two types.

Multitudes won to Christ in a compressed period. From this period,

---

A Study in the Dutch Reformation (Nashville: Abingdon, 1971), p. 93. On the Continent it is evident that two associates of John Calvin—Guillaume Farel and Pierre Viret—were renowned for their itinerant preaching, often before vast outdoor crowds. See Robert D. Linder, "Pierre Viret," in *Oxford Encyclopedia of the Reformation*, ed. Hans Hildebrand (Oxford: Oxford University Press, 1996), 4:237; and Frances Higman, "Guillaume Farel," in *Oxford Encyclopedia of the Reformation*, ed. Hans Hildebrand (Oxford: Oxford University Press, 1996), 2:99-100. See also John Knox, *A History of the Reformation in Scotland*, 2 vols. (New York: Philosophical Library, 1950), 1:148, 2:277-79. The functioning of the Scottish privy-kirks and their "mission to convert" is helpfully elaborated by James Kirk, *Patterns of Reform: Continuity and Change in the Reformation Kirk* (Edinburgh: T & T Clark, 1989), chap. 1.

[17]The term "Second Reformation" is used to describe efforts in Holland, similar to those of English Puritanism, to carry the Reformation further in national life.

[18]These helpful vignettes of sixteenth-century English church life are provided by John H. Primus, "Calvin and the Puritan Sabbath: A Comparative Study," in *Exploring the Heritage of John Calvin*, ed. David E. Holwerda (Grand Rapids: Eerdmans, 1976), pp. 53-55. Primus traces the development in Puritan thinking about the sabbath between the two editions of Bound's work, *The Doctrine of the Sabbath* (London, 1595) and *Sabbathum Veteris et Novi Testamenti* (London, 1606).

[19]J. I. Packer, "Puritanism as a Movement of Revival," in *Evangelical Quarterly* 52 (1980): 2-16, later appearing in the same author's *A Quest for Godliness: The Puritan Vision of the Christian Life* (Wheaton, Ill.: Crossway, 1994).

in which there was need for the grassroots implementation of Reformation principles parish by parish and house by house, have come down to us numerous reports of considerable "visitations" or "outlettings" of the Spirit of God in conjunction with the preaching of the Word. The first of these reports comes to us from the towns of Stewarton and Irvine, near Glasgow, where beginning in the year 1625 great numbers were won to Christ in connection with the preaching ministry of David Dickson (a biblical commentator of some renown):

> For a considerable time, few Sabbaths did pass without some evidently converted, or some convincing proofs of the power of God accompanying his word; yea, that many were so choked and taken by the heart, that through terror, the Spirit in such measure convincing them of sin, in hearing of the word, they have been made to fall over, and thus carried out of the church; who after proved most solid and lively Christians. . . . And truly this great spring-tide (as I may call it) of the gospel, was not of a short time, but for some years continuance; yea thus like a spreading moor-burn, the power of godliness did advance from one place to another.[20]

Another such report comes from Northern Ireland, to which many Scots migrated under what was called the "plantation" of Ulster, commencing in 1609. Presbyterian by heritage and uneasy with the current efforts of the Stuart dynasty to bring the Scottish Church into greater conformity with the Church of England, these immigrants were for a long time almost bereft of the ministry of settled ministers. For decades, concerned ministers in Scotland were deputed to spend summer months in the province of Ulster doing itinerant preaching, catechizing and the administration of the sacraments.

In this context occurred what came to be known as the "that remark-

---

[20]Robert Fleming, *The Fulfilling of the Scriptures* (Rotterdam: n.p., 1669), p. 185, quoted in John Gillies, *Historical Collections Relating to Remarkable Periods of the Success of the Gospel* (1754; reprint, Kelso: John Rutherfurd, 1845), p. 197. The editor of the 1845 edition, Horatius Bonar, estimates that this period of "spring-tide" endured from 1625-1630. These sixteenth-century incidents are alluded to by Leigh Eric Schmidt in *Holy Fairs: Scotland and the Making of American Revivalism*, 2nd ed. (Grand Rapids: Eerdmans, 1999), chap. 1; and Marilyn J. Westerkamp, *The Triumph of the Laity: Scots-Irish Piety and the Great Awakening* (New York: Oxford University Press, 1988), chaps. 1-2.

able work in the Six-Mile water," a region of county Antrim. Zealous evangelical ministers, encouraged to come over from Scotland, met astonishing success in their preaching in the year 1628. Often preaching in the open air in conjunction with twice-yearly Communion seasons (which drew large audiences of thousands, comprised of converted and unconverted) the preachers witnessed

> a bright and hot sun-blink of the gospel, yea (it) may with sobriety be said to have been one of the largest manifestations of the Spirit, and of the most solemn times of the down-pouring of the Spirit that almost since the days of the apostles hath been seen; where the power of God did sensibly accompany the word with an unusual motion upon the hearers, and a very great catch as to the conversion of souls to Christ.[21]

So great was the attraction to the preaching of the gospel in these settings that it was not unknown for hearers to travel thirty or forty miles.

Within five years there occurred the most notable event of this kind associated with Scotland in the seventeenth century, the outpouring of the Spirit at the Kirk of Shotts in 1630. In June of that year, once more in connection with a twice-yearly Communion season that featured both sermon and sacrament in the out-of-doors, the young preacher John Livingston delivered a sermon on a Monday "with a strange unusual motion on the hearers . . . of divers ranks; it was known that near five hundred had at that time a discernible change wrought on them, of whom most proved lively Christians afterwards."

That preacher, not yet twenty years old, later looked on it as "the day in all my life wherein I found most of the presence of God in preaching."[22] In the seventeenth century such events were not confined to Ulster and the southwest of Scotland; we read of them in the Western Isles of the Highlands in 1675 and 1724.[23] And all this in advance of the proper onset of events known in Britain as the Evangelical Revival and in North America as the Great Awakening.

---

[21]Fleming, *Fulfilling of the Scriptures*, p. 185, quoted in Gillies, *Historical Collections*, p. 206. The incident is also alluded to in J. I. Packer, *Quest for Godliness*, p. 47.

[22]*Fulfilling of the Scriptures*, p. 185, quoted in Gillies, *Historical Collections*, pp. 198-99. The incident is also remarked on by Schmidt, *Holy Fairs*, chap. 1.

[23]John MacInnes, *The Evangelical Movement in the Highlands of Scotland* (Aberdeen: University Press, 1951), pp. 154-56.

A sluggish church stirred to fresh vigor. We have alluded to two types of revival, or visitation of the Spirit, in the century or more preceding the better-known movements of the eighteenth century. The second of these has to do with the observable stirring of the church in a time of slackness. Of this, there is a shining example as early as 1596. In that year there were stirrings in the General Assembly of the Church of Scotland, the summoning of which was initially motivated by a sense of national peril in light of a feared Spanish naval invasion. The defeat of the naval Armada against England in 1588 had not exhausted the Spanish desire for conquest over these Protestant lands. Sensitive Scots were driven to reflect on how such an invasion might also represent a divine visitation against the national Church, which had seemed to relapse from an earlier zeal for godliness.

One of these, minister John Davidson of Prestonpans (1549-1604), stood up in the Scottish General Assembly meeting at Edinburgh in March 1596 in order to relay to the Assembly the sentiments of his own presbytery of Haddington that

> the chief and gross sins of all estates which procure this present wrath of God be agreed upon by name, severally, and acknowledged by this Assembly for the more easy provocation of the whole body of this realm to earnest repentance and speedy turning away from the sins foresaid.[24]

Davidson made it plain that there were failings to be confessed by the ministry, by the leaders of society and by the population at large. Charged by the Assembly to return to them with a detailed "catalogue of offenses" touching all classes named, he did so, and beginning with their own number the General Assembly heard a call to repentance from the practice of too-easy admission of unfit persons to the ministry, from the practice of disciplining only those persons in their congregations guilty of gross sins (neglecting to deal with the rest), of ministerial frivolity (dancing, card playing, gambling), sabbath breaking,

---

[24]The extended quotation of Davidson's address is provided in the account given by his contemporary David Calderwood in his *History of the Kirk of Scotland*, rev. ed. (1648; reprint, Edinburgh: Wodrow Society, 1844), 5:394-97.

drunkenness, and brawling. The chronicler of the event, who was present that day, records:

> There were such sighs and sobs, with shedding of tears among the most part . . . that the kirk resounded, so that the place might worthily have been called Bochim; for the like of that day was never seen in Scotland. . . . There have been many days of humiliation for present or imminent dangers, but the like for sin and defection was there never since the Reformation. After prayer and public confession . . . the moderator desired them to hold up their hands to testify their entering a new league with God. They held up their hands presently. Many were wonderfully moved at the sight of so many hands so readily held up.[25]

Young King James VI, who had been briefed on the proceedings, consented to be approached privately by a delegation of ministers regarding his own shortcomings. He was faulted (among other things) for a lack of prayer and Bible reading at meals, for absenting himself from weekly sermons and for permitting swearing in the palace. This same exercise of rebuke for and confession of sin was ordered to be repeated across the regional synods of the Scottish Church in that year.[26]

REVIVAL TRANSPOSED TO THE NEW WORLD

It is clear that the patterns already observed regarding spiritual awakening in Scotland and Ulster were concurrently a part of the seventeenth-century life of the early American colonies. This is the case partly because the middle colonies (New York, New Jersey, Pennsylvania, Maryland, Virginia) began to be populated by immigrants from Scotland and Ulster, who carried with them conceptions of the outpouring of the Spirit gained in their homelands. In fact, these Scots-Irish were but one of three identifiable constituencies making up the Protestant religious population of the eastern seaboard of the future United States. There were, in addition to the Scots-Irish, the

---

[25]Calderwood, *History of the Kirk of Scotland*, pp. 397-407.
[26]This is the account of another contemporary, John Row (1568-1646), *History of the Kirk of Scotland* (Edinburgh: Maitland Club, 1842), 1:39. Row treats this large-scale repentance as part of a national covenant renewal. He provides supporting documents in vol. 2, pp. 434-38.

English Puritan colonists of Massachusetts and Connecticut, and the European Pietists (Dutch and German) inhabiting New York, Pennsylvania and New Jersey.[27] If the Scots-Irish brought ideas and conceptions of current manifestations of the Holy Spirit's power with them, so did others.

We find that in colonial Massachusetts there had been sermons preached since 1674 against the spiritual complacency that could then be detected spreading in the colony. From that time onward bold preachers had called for an outpouring of the Holy Spirit in the churches and upon the society of Massachusetts. What emerged, in time, were many services of "covenant renewal," gatherings in which many congregations devoted themselves afresh to serve the Lord. Notable instances of these came at Old South Church, Boston, in 1680 and at Taunton, Massachusetts, in 1705. Young persons were most frequently found responsive to appeals for personal spiritual commitment, fulfilling parental pledges made on their behalf in infant baptism.[28] Perhaps it was to just such services as these that Jonathan Edwards referred when he sought to trace the antecedents of the awakening that dawned in his own community of Northampton in 1735. Edwards had found records of five "harvests" under the ministry of his grandfather Solomon Stoddard (d. 1728) in the town in the years 1678, 1683, 1695, 1711 and 1717; the harvests in the middle years brought the most conversions. Edwards too records the prevalence of responsive young people in these "harvests."[29]

The European Pietist emphasis was most seen in the middle colonies. It centered around but was not confined to the ministry of the Dutch immigrant minister Theodorus Frelinghuysen, which commenced in New Jersey in 1720. The thrust of Frelinghuysen's itinerant ministry was the absolute need for personal conversion and "heart-change"; this change was something he did not presume was the present possession of his Dutch Reformed hearers. Though his preaching

---

[27]These parallel constituencies are helpfully explained in Thomas S. Kidd, *The Great Awakening* (New Haven, Conn.: Yale University Press, 2007), pp. 24-39.

[28]Kidd, *Great Awakening*, p. 2.

[29]Jonathan Edwards, *A Narrative of Surprising Conversions* (1736), reprinted in *Jonathan Edwards on Revival* (Edinburgh: Banner of Truth, 1965), pp. 8-9.

ministry often brought protests and polarization of congregations, over time he prevailed. He also soon came into contact and collaboration with Scots-Irish evangelical Presbyterians in his region.[30] But to have come this far in our survey is to have observed sufficient evidence that the Reformed tradition did not need to wait until the first quarter of the eighteenth century to be exposed to movements of awakening and revival; these had been awaited, prayed for and tasted within this tradition, on both sides of the Atlantic, for at least a century and a quarter when the Great Awakening came.

THE GREAT AWAKENING AS A DIVISIVE ERA

As widespread and as venerable as this tradition of revival may have been in the various branches of the Reformed family, there is no disguising that, especially in its eighteenth-century American manifestations, revival proved to be a divisive force. We need both to note the details of this division and to go on to inquire about the reasons for it.

Contrary to popular understanding, there were *three* Presbyterian and Reformed responses to the occurrence of revival in the eighteenth century, rather than two. Clearly opposed to the movements that emerged in New Jersey in 1720, in Massachusetts in 1734, in Pennsylvania in 1739 and in South Carolina in 1740 were ministers who found the emphasis on personal spiritual regeneration and the sensible operations of the Holy Spirit to be unbalanced and dangerously subjectivist. Such observers were not content to see congregations polarized between those who had and had not experienced regeneration. In this category stood men such as Congregationalist Charles Chauncy of Boston and Episcopalian Alexander Garden of Charleston, South Carolina.

The diametric opposite to this position was presented in preachers who were, at least for a time, separatistic in their readiness to limit the number of believers to those who claimed to have undergone rebirth and could testify to it. Consistent with such principles as these, preach-

---

[30]Kidd, *Great Awakening*, pp. 24-29. The larger story of the transmission of European Pietism to the American colonies is related in W. R. Ward, *The Protestant Evangelical Awakening* (Cambridge: Cambridge University Press, 1992).

ers who did not proclaim the new birth were singled out for scorn; true believers were encouraged to shun their ministry. Actual separations within congregations emerged where this exclusive approach was urged by itinerant preachers such as James Davenport (1716-1757), Gilbert Tennent (1703-1764), Daniel Rogers (1692-1773) and—until he later thought better of it—the young George Whitefield (1714-1770).[31] Inherent in this strident position was an unwillingness to hear criticism of what was proclaimed or of any extreme behavior among those who listened and responded.

Between these two positions, each of which was known by its outspoken representatives, stood a great middle party, appropriately called "moderate."[32] The terminology is indicative not of a halting, temporizing outlook toward revival, but of a readiness to defend the authenticity of the awakening in the face of both of the extreme tendencies named. Moderates believed that skeptical commentators should be cautioned that they not utterly spurn something which was "of God"; radical enthusiast preachers needed to be cautioned to weigh their words in evaluating the erratic behaviors that characterized a good proportion of those who heard awakening sermons.

The impact on Presbyterians in the middle colonies. These three identifiable positions, affecting Protestantism generally, were transposed into two positions within colonial Presbyterianism. Persons clearly approximating the antirevivalist tendency we associate with Boston's Charles Chauncy were, in Presbyterian terms, known as "Old Side," a point of view which was especially rooted in the greater Philadelphia region. Conversely, persons clearly approximating the "separatist" or "radical" tendency were, in Presbyterian terms, known as "New Side"—a point of view associated especially with the region of New Jersey north of Trenton. Each of the two positions, New and Old, also contained persons of a moderating outlook who were aware of the limitations of the polarization.

---

[31]Kidd, *Great Awakening*, pp. 96-97.
[32]Kidd uses the terminology to describe the position of Jonathan Edwards, reflected in his 1741 essay *Distinguishing Marks of the Work of the Spirit of God* (ibid., p. 120). He employs the same language to describe the stance taken by the Whitefield ally Josiah Smith, of Charleston, South Carolina (see Kidd, *Great Awakening*, pp. 69-70).

For our purpose here, it is sufficient to note that the New Side was characterized by an aggressive advocacy of the current evangelical awakening and had its own sources of ministerial training in the "Log College" at Neshaminy Creek, Pennsylvania, and similar academy-style institutions.[33] Though the Presbyterian Synod of Philadelphia, meeting at Philadelphia in 1741, voted to remove this northern Presbytery of New Brunswick from the Synod, the momentum did not lie with the Old Siders. The New Side Presbytery of New Brunswick, which joined in 1745 with the Presbyteries of New York and Londonderry to form the Synod of New York, was expansionist in a way that the Old Side was not. The determination to itinerate into territories that Presbyterianism had not yet penetrated (such as Virginia and the Carolinas),[34] the success of the Log College in training young ministers, and the general affinity New Side shared with the wider movement of American revival meant that when, in 1758, the two streams agreed to reunite, the New Side predominated in pastors, churches and sentiments.[35]

In the West. Current scholarship reckons the American (first) Great Awakening as enduring into the 1780s.[36] As settlers left the Atlantic seaboard and crossed the Appalachians and Alleghenies to the Great Plains beyond, their settled religious life was disrupted; the migrants had bid farewell to familiar pastors and congregations. Yet in these new frontier situations there were still occurrences of religious awakening as pioneers gathered to hear itinerant ministers in large outdoor summer gatherings reminiscent of Scottish outdoor Communion seasons.[37] Yet this

---

[33]Leonard J. Trinterud lists similar schools at Fagg's Manor, Nottingham and Pequea (*The Forming of an American Tradition: A Re-examination of Colonial Presbyterianism* [Philadelphia: Westminster Press, 1949], p. 151).

[34]A good account of New Side evangelistic activity in the South in this period is provided by Ernest Trice Thompson, *Presbyterians in the South* (Richmond, Va.: John Knox Press, 1963), 1:52-66. The extended reach of the Log College at Neshaminy, Pennsylvania, is made explicit.

[35]D. J. Hart, "Old Side/New Side Schism and Reunion," in *Colonial Presbyterianism: Old Faith in a New Land*, ed. S. Donald Fortson III (Eugene, Ore.: Wipf & Stock, 2007), pp. 174-75. A more sympathetic account characterized by much greater statistical detail is provided by Trinterud, *Forming of an American Tradition*, chap. 9. In stressing the numerical strength of the New Side at the time of reunion in 1758, it must be admitted that this party was by then shorn of its separatistic tendencies.

[36]Kidd, *Great Awakening*, chap. 19.

[37]Schmidt, *Holy Fairs*, p. 60; Iain Murray, *Making and Marring of Revivalism*, chap. 4.

movement, now termed the "Great Revival," gave way to something about which opinion easily divided: the Cane Ridge phenomenon.

At this Kentucky site in August 1801 commenced a kind of awakening that fractured Presbyterian opinion for decades to come. While not exclusively Presbyterian, this summer gathering, which began as an extended Communion season and featured the involvement of some eighteen Presbyterian ministers and some twenty thousand persons, came to be associated with emotional and physical excesses of all kinds. Whereas movements of awakening in earlier decades had exercised a restraining influence on the behavior of those brought into distress under the preaching of the Word in these settings, at Cane Ridge it was as though this restraint was nonexistent. Reports circulated of listeners with the "jerks," listeners who "spun like tops" and a general disregard of the preaching of the Word. It was not long before Presbyterian observers who had been broadly supportive of the moderate tradition of revival, nearer the eastern seaboard, began to find fault with the unrestrained practices of the western frontier. They wrote not to denigrate revival movements but to highlight a declension of Christian discernment as to what was indeed Spirit-prompted and to protest against the marginalization of the ministry of the Word.[38] The centrifugal force of this movement sent some Presbyterians into the fledgling Disciples of Christ movement, others joined with the Shakers, while a good portion separated in 1810 to form the Cumberland Presbyterian movement. This breach was only partly closed with a Presbyterian reunion in 1910.

In the then-Northwest. Within decades similar centrifugal forces were at work in upstate New York and Ohio. The attorney-preacher Charles Grandison Finney, once converted to Christ in 1821, was tutored for the Presbyterian ministry by his pastor, George Gale

---

[38]Thomas Cleland, "Bodily Effects of Religious Excitements" (1834), reprinted in *Princeton vs. the New Divinity: Articles from the Princeton Review* (Edinburgh: Banner of Truth, 2001), chap. 8. Cleland wrote as one who had been an eyewitness of the events of 1801, and thereafter as a young minister serving in eastern Tennessee. Helpful overviews of the Cane Ridge revival are provided in Keith Hardman, *Seasons of Refreshing* (Grand Rapids: Baker, 1994), chap. 6; and D. G. Hart and John Muether, *Seeking a Better Country: 300 Years of American Presbyterianism* (Phillipsburg, N.J.: Presbyterian & Reformed, 2007), pp. 97-101.

(1789-1861), a Princeton graduate. Ordained by the local presbytery in spite of his stated reservations toward portions of the Westminster Confession of Faith, Finney rapidly became a sensation by his evangelistic preaching in rural towns and villages of upper New York. From such venues he moved to larger towns and cities ranging from Syracuse, Rome and Utica in the upper Hudson River region to Cleveland, Ohio, in the west, Boston in the east and New York City. His preaching campaigns were controversial, not because they replicated the emotional excesses for which Cane Ridge had become known (in fact, as an attorney he was quite fastidious) but because of "improvements" he introduced in connection with his meetings. Chief of these was the use of the "anxious bench," a front pew to which Finney summoned those who were ready to humble themselves before the congregation as a means of indicating their having come under a conviction of sin and a desire to seek salvation. Finney also employed the tactic of public denunciation from the pulpit and in prayer against prominent persons who were known to obstruct the success of his campaigns. In this respect at least, he resembled the radical separatists of the Great Awakening era.

Finney was not the first to publish a manual on revivals; that honor belonged to the circle of ministerial friends (many shared his Princeton connection) who collaborated with William B. Sprague (1795-1876), the Presbyterian minister of Albany, New York, in the 1832 volume *Lectures on Revivals of Religion*.[39] This volume, which was intended to distinguish between the longstanding moderate conception of revival traceable back to Jonathan Edwards's writings and the innovations Finney was known for, was in time followed by the latter's own *Lectures on Revival* (1835). This actual sequence is of greater importance than might first appear.

While it is quite well known that the theologians and alumni of Princeton were adamant in their opposition to Finney and his new measures, it deserves to be better known that in opposing Finney's innovations they were not opposing revival itself; for Princeton, the linear

---

[39]This important volume was republished in 1959 by Banner of Truth.

descendant of the old Log College at Neshaminy, Pennsylvania, had historically defended Jonathan Edwards's moderate position on revival.[40] The ensuing contest over *which* heritage of revival was to be transmitted forward in the Reformed tradition in America stimulated a considerable amount of writing. This was the context in which the aged Archibald Alexander (1772-1851) wrote his supportive history of *The Log College: Biographical Sketches of William Tennent and His Students* (1851), and his volume of reminiscences, which reflect on the pivotal importance of revival in his own early adulthood, *Thoughts on Religious Experience* (1841).[41] As in 1741 and 1801, religious revival—or at least divergent *approaches* taken to it—was a major contributing cause to another Presbyterian division. Now, opposition to the prevalence and acceptability of Finney's new measures and to a declining zeal for confessional orthodoxy found among Presbyterians in the American Northeast led to the Old School-New School Presbyterian division of 1837.[42]

WIDER SIGNIFICANCE

I began our consideration of this subject with the acknowledgment that general support for religious awakening and revival in the Presbyterian and Reformed tradition through the nineteenth century fell on hard times in the latter half of the twentieth. Of course there are additional developments in the history of religious revival since the mid-

---

[40]The Princeton opposition to Finney's published *Lectures* is epitomized by the essay of Albert B. Dod (1835) "On Revivals of Religion," reprinted in *Princeton Vs. the New Divinity: Articles from the Princeton Review* (Edinburgh: Banner of Truth, 2001), chap. 6. On Dod's larger contribution to this debate see also James Bratt, ed., *Antirevivalism in Antebellum America* (New Brunswick, N.J.: Rutgers University Press, 2006), chap. 2.

[41]This qualified Presbyterian support for religious awakenings is helpfully noted by James Bratt's *Antirevivalism in Antebellum America*, pp. 15-17. This volume provides additional excerpts of the writings of Albert B. Dod, noted in n. 35. A son of Archibald Alexander (the founding professor of Princeton Seminary in 1812), James W. Alexander, who himself taught briefly at Princeton in 1849-1851, explored the connection between John Livingston, the notable seventeenth-century preacher of Scotland, and the proper emphasis for contemporary religious revival in the essay "The Life and Times of John Livingston," *Biblical Repertory and Theological Review* 4 (1832): 428-50.

[42]The wider reasons for this division are helpfully explored in Hart and Muether, *Seeking a Better Country*, pp. 121-27. This chapter does not mean to imply that it was only the Presbyterian branch of the American Reformed family that experienced tension and polarization over religious revival. It is quite widely acknowledged that New England Congregationalism and the transplanted German Reformed Church similarly grappled with the question.

nineteenth century that could be identified as providing the reasons for this. But enough information has been provided here to support two major tenets:

1. There is an admirable history of religious awakening (both in the sense of the stirring of a lethargic church, and in the sense of the rousing of the unconverted) in the Reformed tradition extending back to the sixteenth century. Admittedly, this legacy once noted does *not* oblige us to seek its continuation now. But once this legacy is acknowledged to exist, it will serve to restrain both those who wish to treat it now as though it were some dark family secret best hushed up, and those who dismissively treat religious awakening as something utterly alien to this branch of the Christian family.

2. Since the eighteenth century the recurring flash points regarding religious revival within the Presbyterian and Reformed tradition have consistently included concerns over the propriety of treating bizarre behaviors as undoubted manifestations of the work of the Holy Spirit, (moderates have always insisted on treating this as at least an open question), on the propriety of any preaching that is denunciatory or abusive toward pastors or Christian leaders who have proved unenthusiastic in their support (preachers who transgress here have rightly been labeled separatist), and over the advisability of professional itinerant evangelists anchored to no particular congregation.

Thus there is a strong case requiring many Calvinists to reexamine their attitudes and prejudices on this issue. Currently, Calvinism has come to strike a very negative posture toward the history of religious revivals; these have come to be treated as "somebody else's problem." This approach ignores not only the material surveyed here up to mid-nineteenth century but a whole succession of fervent preachers in the Presbyterian and Reformed family whom God used as awakeners right into the twentieth century—persons from whose examples we ought to learn.

DISCUSSION QUESTIONS

1. Using a dictionary of church history, look up the following figures, all of whom lived and served in the period since 1900: Wilbur Chap-

man, Leighton Ford, John McNeil, W. P. Nicholson, Billy Sunday, David Patrick Thompson. What factor, besides being evangelists, binds them together?

2. Are there obvious factors that have dampened interest in promoting large-scale evangelical awakenings among the Presbyterian and Reformed churches and movements you have knowledge of?

3. Claimed "revivals" come and go; some are flashes in the pan. What is the last movement of spiritual revival about which you have a high degree of trust and confidence?

4. If, as this chapter asserts, the churches in the Reformed tradition have moved away from seeking and promoting awakening and revival, what price might they have paid in consequence?

FURTHER READING

Hardman, Keith. *Times of Refreshing: Evangelism and Revivals in America*. 1994; reprint, Eugene, Ore.: Wipf & Stock, 2007.

Kidd, Thomas S. *The Great Awakening*. Cambridge: Yale University Press, 2007.

Walker, Andrew, and Kristin Aune, eds. *On Revival: A Critical Examination*. Carlisle, U.K.: Paternoster, 2003.

PART TWO

Six Myths Non-Calvinists Should Not Be Circulating (But Are)

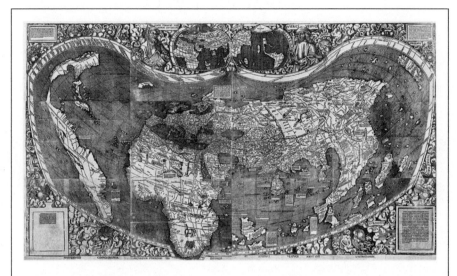

Map of the World, 1507, by Martin Waldseemüller

Image: Held by the Library of Congress. The only surviving copy of the 1507
world map by Martin Waldseemüller, purchased by the Library of Congress
and now on display in its Thomas Jefferson Building in Washington, D.C.

MYTH FIVE

Calvinism Is Largely Antimissionary

IN THE MID-TWENTIETH CENTURY one could readily find informed observers acknowledging the Calvinist tradition's major missionary contribution.[1] For example, in 1950 Norman Carr Sargant, a
British Methodist missionary to India, exploring the subject of "Calvinists, Arminians and Missions," maintained that these two expressions of Protestantism had served one another well with each goading
the other toward foreign missionary effort. From within his own Wes-
leyan-Arminian tradition, Sargant wrote, "To praise Arminianism and
to reproach Calvinism is the conventional judgement. In respect of
missions, however, rigid Calvinism and the warm Arminianism of the
Wesleys were in substance the same."[2]

Was this verdict simply an example of charity run wild? I would not
conclude this upon reading Carr Sargant's patient analysis, for he main-

[1]This chapter appeared in an earlier draft as "Calvinism and Missions: The Contested Relationship Revisited," *Themelios* 34, no. 1 (2009): 63-78.
[2]N. Carr Sargant, "Calvinism, Arminianism and Missions," *London Quarterly and Holborn Review* 176 (1951): 340-44. From the same era, note J. Van den Berg, "Calvin's Missionary Message: Some Remarks About the Relation Between Calvinism and Missions," *Evangelical Quarterly* 22 (1950): 174-87; and S. M. Zwemer, "Calvinism and the Missionary Enterprise,"
Theology Today 7 (1950): 206-21.

tained that the Calvinism of the period of the Great Awakening/Evangelical Revival was in fact only showing its true colors when it began to pursue foreign missions aggressively. The founding of the broadly Calvinist London Missionary Society (originally simply the "Missionary Society") in 1795 was in fact the linear descendent of a proposal of 1772 made at Trevecca, Wales, to send missionaries to pre-revolutionary America's settlers and aboriginals.[3] For his own Methodist tradition in the eighteenth century, Sargant claimed the honor *not* of pioneering Protestant foreign missions (for a distinctly Wesleyan missionary society did not arise until 1817)[4] but of demonstrating a pattern of domestic evangelistic activism, which served as a stimulus to foreign missions by Calvinists.[5] Moreover, Sargant was candid enough to acknowledge that whereas Calvinist missionaries in the early decades of that era had "gone to the heathen," his own theological tradition, Methodism, for too long specialized in sending preachers to places where nominal Christians were abundant, and in preaching conversion and holiness to these.[6]

THE REFORMED TRADITION HAS NEGLECTED WORLD MISSIONS AND EVANGELISM

More recently a different version of the story has been spread. Since the time Sargant wrote, churches standing in the Reformed theological tradition have regularly been suspected of constituting a "weak link" in support for world missions and evangelism. More than anything, Reformed theology's endorsement of the doctrine of predestination has been singled out as the reason for this; it has been reckoned by non-

[3]Sargant has used the Welsh event of 1772 not to mark an utter beginning for English-speaking Protestant foreign missions but to show how natural an expression this was of the spiritual fervor of the era we call the Great Awakening or Evangelical Revival. Later we will see several instances of Protestant missionary effort long before 1772.
[4]Some examples of Methodist foreign missions predated the erection of a formal Mission Society, notably the efforts of Thomas Coke (1747-1814).
[5]Carr's thesis is an interesting one. He believed that the danger (real or imagined) that Calvinism would serve the interests of antinomianism helped Calvinists focus on the need for missionary activism, an activism that would demonstrate that their beliefs did not result in indolence and indifference.
[6]Sargant, "Calvinism, Arminianism and Missions," p. 51. We will return to the question of Protestant missions in the eighteenth century and earlier. The point being established initially here is simply that twentieth-century judgments about Calvinism and missions have been subject to wide variation.

Calvinists to provide a kind of respectable subterfuge for lethargy in missions and evangelism. *After all* (Calvinists are alleged to think), *God will see to it that the proper number of elect persons are saved—irrespective of whether we are active as his agents.* This kind of suspicion was certainly in existence in 1959 when theologian J. I. Packer gave the university talks that eventually grew into his little book *Evangelism and the Sovereignty of God.* In it, Packer stated by way of preface:

> The aim of the discourse is to dispel the suspicion (current it seems in some quarters) that faith in the absolute sovereignty of God hinders a full recognition and acceptance of evangelistic responsibility and to show that, on the contrary, only this faith can give Christians the strength that they need to fulfill their evangelistic task.[7]

Something was in the wind. In 1960 William Richey Hogg, Methodist professor of missions and ecumenics, gave credibility to this kind of suspicion when he wrote (surveying Protestant missions since 1517) that from the era of the Synod of Dordt (1619) onward, "an extreme Calvinism . . . prevailed widely and worked effectively to throttle missionary endeavor."[8] Now, in the contemporary scene, it has become commonplace for this kind of second-guessing to go on. A reputable church historian of the Reformation period, the late William Estep, in 1997 called Calvinism "logically anti-missionary."[9] He viewed with alarm the late-twentieth-century resurgence of Calvinistic views and spoke with apprehensiveness about the likely diminution of missionary concern that would follow if this resurgence went unchecked in his own Baptist churches. Norman Geisler, a widely published evangelical theologian and apologist, insisted in 1999 that resurgent Calvinist views, which he termed "extreme" militated "against enthusiasm for missions and evangelism." Another evangelical writer, given to the writing of

---

[7] J. I. Packer, *Evangelism and the Sovereignty of God* (Downers Grove, Ill.: InterVarsity Press, 1961), p. 8.

[8] William Richey Hogg, "The Rise of Protestant Missionary Concern, 1517-1914," in *The Theology of Christian Mission*, ed. Gerald H. Anderson (New York: McGraw-Hill, 1961), p. 101. Hogg was alluding to the robust defense of the doctrine of unconditional election in this Synod, in the face of the challenge posed by Arminius and his followers. We will have reason to note, later, that strong advocates of foreign missions participated in the Synod of Dordt.

[9] William Estep, "Calvinizing Southern Baptists," in *Texas Baptist Standard*, March 26, 1997.

exposés, Dave Hunt, declared in 2002 that as regards world missions, men and women holding such views "bring the gospel to the world not *because* of their Calvinism, but only *in spite* of it."[10] Don Fanning of Liberty University has recently written, "Calvinism has undercut missionary and evangelistic efforts, especially hyper-Calvinism, which is merely the logical implication of the theology."[11] Yet, in addition to this recent upsurge of criticism, there remains the legacy of criticisms uttered centuries earlier.

THE ENTIRE REFORMATION MOVEMENT NEGLECTED MISSIONS

There is no disputing the fact that in the sixteenth century the European pacesetter in foreign missions was Roman Catholicism. The Portuguese vessels that plied the west coast of Africa had landed missionary priests at the mouth of the Congo River by 1491. Portuguese ships in the Indian Ocean soon landed missionary priests such as Francis Xavier (1506-1552) on India's west coast. Spanish missionary priests and friars (Franciscans, Dominicans and later Jesuits) were in Central and South America in the same decades along with waves of colonists.[12] Admittedly, early Protestantism would lag behind this pace for some decades; these facts and more beside have been regularly rehearsed.

A sense of proportion to the recounting of this tale would be restored, however, if it were admitted that there were contemporary Catholic observers who did not find these admitted missions advances to be everything that could be hoped for, given their symbiotic relationship with European conquest.[13] Bartolomé de las Casas (c. 1474-1566), who reached Spanish America in 1502, became after his own religious conversion in 1514, the foremost advocate of the rights of the aboriginal peoples of the conquered territories. These peoples were being deci-

[10]Norman Geisler, *Chosen But Free* (Minneapolis: Bethany House, 1999), p. 136. Dave Hunt, *What Love Is This? Calvinism's Misrepresentation of God* (Sisters, Ore.: Loyal, 2002), p. 29.
[11]Don Fanning, "Calvinism and Missions," *DigitalCommons@Liberty University*, 2009 <http://works.bepress.com/don_fanning/18>.
[12]I am indebted to the accounts provided by Justo González in his *The Story of Christianity*, vol. 1 (Peabody, Mass.: Prince, 2001), chaps. 35-36; and Stephen Neill, *A History of Christian Missions*, 2nd ed. (London: Penguin, 1990), chap. 6, for these remarks.
[13]We can acknowledge that conquest was not a feature of Portuguese commercial expansion in the same manner as it was for Spain.

mated by the introduction of disease and the imposition of forced labor. De las Casas, who was made colonial bishop of Chiapas, Mexico, complained to King Philip that under Spanish colonial rule, even aboriginals with proof of their freedom were likely to be abused and pressed into forced labor.[14]

The Christian humanist Desiderius Erasmus (1466-1536), who died a loyal Catholic, complained that Catholicism's missionary commitment was neither deep nor heartfelt. In the year before his death, he penned *On the Art of Preaching*, urging gospel preaching at home and abroad in order to claim the world for Christ; he observed that many of his European contemporaries were deploring

> the decay of the Christian religion (and saying) that the gospel message which once extended over the whole earth is now confined to the narrow limits of this land. Let those, then, to whom this is an unfeigned cause of grief, beseech Christ earnestly and continuously to send laborers into His harvest. . . . Everlasting God! How much ground there is in the world where the seed of the gospel has never yet been sown, or where there is a greater crop of tares than of wheat! Europe is the smallest quarter of the globe; Greece and Asia Minor the most fertile. . . . What shall I say of those who sail around unknown shores, and plunder and lay waste whole States without provocation? What name is given to such deeds? They are called victories. Even the heathen would not praise a victory over men against whom no war had been declared. . . . Christ orders us to pray the Lord of the harvest to send forth laborers, because the harvest is plenteous and the laborers are few. . . . But all offer various excuses. . . . There are thousands of the Franciscans who believe in Christ . . . and the Dominicans abound in equal numbers.[15]

---

[14]Bartolomé de las Casas, "Letter to King Philip II," in *Classics of Christian Missions*, ed. Francis M. DuBose (Nashville: Broadman & Holman, 1979), pp. 213-19.

[15]Erasmus's treatise of 1535 was published under the Latin title of *Ecclesiastes sive Concionator Evangelicus* (On the Art of Preaching) in four books. Only the first book was translated into English. Excerpts are available in Roland Bainton, *Erasmus of Christendom* (New York: Scribners, 1969), p. 324; and James Smith, *A Short History of Christian Missions*, 8th ed. (Edinburgh: T & T Clark, 1920), pp. 116-17. The attitudes of Erasmus and other Christian humanists toward the state of the unevangelized is helpfully explored by G. H. Williams in the essay "Erasmus and the Reformers on Non-Christian Religions and *Salus Extra Ecclesiam*," in *Action and Conviction in Early Modern Europe: Essays in Memory of E. H. Harbison*, ed. Theodore K. Rabb and Jerrold E. Seigel (Princeton, N.J.: Princeton University Press, 1969), pp. 319-70. The approach of Zwingli to the same question was explored by W. P. Stephens in "Zwingli and the

Erasmus did not accept that Catholicism's missionary response adequately reflected its resources; he did not either accept that evangelization at sword point was authentic. It would be beneficial if this more sober assessment of Catholic missions in the sixteenth century was noted at intervals.

The various expressions of early Protestantism rapidly had to face the criticism that for all their claimed zeal for the recovery of pure biblical teaching, they had very little to show in terms of conversions of non-Christian peoples. So far as we know, the first to raise the question about early Protestantism's failure to apply itself to missionary work was the Catholic theologian and controversialist Robert Bellarmine (1542-1621). Bellarmine believed that only the church that demonstrated missionary activity proved it stood truly linked to the original missionary apostles. Because Roman Catholicism's missionary activity was at this time indisputable and because this strongly supported its claim to stand in solidarity with the original missionary apostles, the question naturally arose, Had Protestantism any such evidence of its link with the apostles? It was a good question.

> In this one century the Catholics have converted many thousands of heathens in the new world. Every year a certain number of Jews are converted and baptized at Rome by Catholics who adhere in loyalty to the Bishop of Rome. . . . The Lutherans compare themselves to the apostles and the evangelists; yet though they have among them a very large number of Jews, and in Poland and Hungary have the Turks as their near neighbors, they have hardly converted so much as a handful.[16]

Bellarmine must have thought he had struck a bull's-eye with this criticism. Many Protestant writers since that time have accepted that he did, and winced. Having felt the sting of Bellarmine's seventeenth-century charge, they have tended to plead "no contest" and to accept it as settled that Luther, Zwingli, Calvin and their followers were stay-at-home Christians. The Protestant Reformers have in consequence tended to be portrayed as men who, if pressed for reasons, were ready to

Salvation of the Gentiles," in *The Bible, the Reformation and the Church: Essays in Honor of James Atkinson*, ed. W. P. Stephens (Sheffield, U.K.: Sheffield Academic Press, 1995), pp. 224-44.
[16]Robert Bellarmine, *Controversiae*, bk. 4, quoted in Neill, *History of Christian Missions*, p. 189.

provide contrived theological rationalizations for sending no missionaries to the horizons of their then-expanding world.[17] But the very readiness of many modern Protestant writers to plead guilty has left unexplored various factors which, because neglected, seriously cloud the question before us.

UNDENIABLE OBSTACLES TO PROTESTANT WORLD MISSIONS

Lack of access to the sea. In fact, a good number of mitigating factors can be put forward to explain why transoceanic missions were not a realistic option for Protestants in the earliest decades of the Reformation era; the respected historian of missions Kenneth Latourette provided six.[18] None were so weighty as the fact that, in the earliest decades of the Reformation, no Protestant domain had access to the sea, was a maritime power or had any immediate prospect of a seaborne empire.[19] Catholic Spain and Portugal, the acknowledged leaders among missionary-sending

---

[17]So, for example Gustav Warneck, *An Outline of the History of Christian Missions from the Reformation to the Present Time*, trans. George Robson, 3rd ed. (New York: Revell, 1901), pp. 8-12; Hogg, "Rise of Protestant Missionary Concern"; Neill, *History of Christian Missions;* David F. Wright, "The Great Commission and the Ministry of the Word: Reflections Historical and Contemporary on Relations and Priorities," *Scottish Bulletin of Evangelical Theology* 25, no. 2 (2007): 132-57. Especially in the late sixteenth century was there an appeal to the idea that, in keeping with the Pauline statement of Colossians 1:23 (the gospel has been heard by every creature under heaven), there had already been a universal gospel proclamation. Nations now in heathen darkness *could* on this understanding be reckoned as having already rejected the gospel. For the association of this idea with Calvin's successor, Theodore Beza, and second-generation Lutheran theologian Johan Gerhard, as well as Protestant opposition to this view, led by Adrian Saravia, see Neill, *History of Christian Missions*, pp. 189-90.

[18]Kenneth Scott Latourette, *History of the Expansion of Christianity* (London: Eyre & Spottiswoode, 1944), 3:25-30. The six are (1) Early Protestantism was preoccupied with its own consolidation. (2) Some early Protestants disavowed the application of the great commission to their age. (3) Interconfessional religious wars encouraged a survival mentality among Protestants. (4) Protestant governments that supervised early Protestantism lacked missionary interest. (5) Protestantism lacked the monastic workforce that supported Catholic missionary effort. (6) Early Protestant territories lacked contact with non-Christian peoples—a factor that did not change until the seventeenth century.

[19]Here Latourette's *History* followed Warneck, *Outline of the History of Christian Missions*, p. 8. See also Neill, *History of Christian Mission,* p. 188. Contemporary historian Glenn Sunshine has revived this significant argument in his essay "Protestant Missions in the Sixteenth Century," in *The Great Commission: Evangelicals and the History of World Missions,* ed. Martin Klauber and Scott Manetsch (Nashville: B & H, 2008), p. 14. Andrew Walls, in his "The Eighteenth Century Protestant Missionary Awakening," helpfully speaks of the "new Iberian maritime consciousness" (see *Christian Missions and the Enlightenment,* ed. Brian Stanley [Grand Rapids: Eerdmans, 2001], p. 28).

regions at this time, had all these. For lack of one or more of these, whole Catholic nations of Europe (such as Poland and Hungary) evidenced no more foreign missionary concern at that time than did Lutheran Saxony or the Zurich of Zwingli. There were also Catholic seagoing nations such as France, adjacent to Spain and Portugal, which initially failed to share the level of missionary concern shown in those neighboring nations.[20] Therefore, it was not the case that every Catholic territory, across the board, uniformly recognized foreign missionary obligation whereas no Protestant territory did.

Factors beyond access to the sea. Moreover, those seagoing Catholic regions of Europe which did demonstrate missionary concern abroad did so through the combined interest of monarchs (such as Ferdinand and Isabella of Spain), of willing navigators (such as Christopher Columbus) and concerned monks within their kingdoms. It is important to acknowledge these important constituent factors, rather than to simply attribute early European overseas missionary concern to Catholicism as a system. The Catholic Church, considered corporately as an institution, only took steps to coordinate foreign mission in the post-Columbus era in 1622 when Pope Gregory XV established at Rome the "Sacred Congregation for the Propagation of the Faith."[21] When Protestant missionary concern emerged beginning in the second half of the sixteenth century (and we will see that it made a small beginning then), it would need to proceed without the sponsorship of heads of state to succeed in capturing the imagination of pastors and people at the parish or regional level, to find missionary workers (as monasticism had been abolished in Protestant regions) and to gather funding. There were no ocean-going navigators standing by ready to help. Yet in spite of these obstacles, most of which were completely beyond the control of the early Protestants, missionary beginnings were not so long in coming as is widely believed.

PROTESTANT MISSION BEGAN IN REGIONS NEIGHBORING HOME

Looking back from this distance of time, during which global missions

---

[20]Latourette, *History*, 3:27.
[21]The importance of this milestone in Catholic missions is helpfully described in Neill, *History of Christian Mission*, p. 152.

have been now conducted on a very large scale over five centuries, we find it easy to draw a clear distinction between such long-distance, overseas missionary efforts and missions carried out nearer to home. But why draw such a distinction? In the sixteenth century, missions nearer home were customarily carried out under circumstances as perilous and against opposition as fierce as might have been encountered in some remote place, far from European civilization.

A closer look at early Protestant "regional" mission near to home shows how widespread this reality was.[22] The fact is that Reformation cities such as Geneva, Lausanne, Emden, Zurich and Basel were like hubs. From them streamed out many hundreds of persons who—often after finding a safe haven from persecution in a particular city of the Reformation—returned to their home regions with the theological and pastoral training required to fit them for work as pastors and evangelists. They went in response to appeals from cells of evangelical believers in France, the Low Countries (today's Belgium and the Netherlands), north Italy and regions of the Alps. Particularly in France there is evidence of a determination to build networks of congregations, systematically, across the kingdom.[23] From Geneva alone (by no means the only sending center) more than two hundred preachers were sent out during the fifteen-year period 1555-1570. The sober fact is that many were arrested, imprisoned and executed before they ever reached the destinations they had set out for.[24] Others served faithfully where they were

---

[22]It is fascinating to see this conception of home mission used to describe the early effort of European Protestantism utilized by historian of missions George Smith in a work originating in 1884. See his *A Short History of Christian Mission*, 8th ed. (Edinburgh: T & T Clark, 1920), p. 110.

[23]W. Stanford Reid, "Calvin's Geneva: A Missionary Centre," in *Reformed Theological Review* 42 (1983): 69.

[24]The big picture of this training of refugees in Reformation cities so that they might return as missionaries is well described by William Monter, *Calvin's Geneva* (New York: Wiley, 1967), pp. 134-35, who spoke of 120 sent out from that city alone between 1555 and 1572; and Graeme Murdock, *Beyond Calvin: The Intellectual, Political and Cultural World of Europe's Reformed Churches* (New York: Palgrave Macmillan, 2004), pp. 34-35. Murdock speaks of more than 200 missionary preachers returned to France from Geneva, Lausanne and Neuchatel between the mid-1550s and 1570. Further light, especially on Geneva's role in this, is provided by Robert M. Kingdon, *Geneva and the Consolidation of the French Protestant Movement 1564-1572* (Madison: University of Wisconsin Press, 1967), pp. 30-36; Philip Edgecumbe Hughes, "John Calvin as a Director of Missions," in *The Heritage of John Calvin*, ed. John Bratt (Grand Rapids: Eerdmans, 1973), pp. 140-54; Reid, "Calvin's Geneva," pp. 65-73.

called, and saw Protestant congregations take root and flourish.

Detailed information about European Protestant home missions has now been available from various historians for at least half a century. Yet, by itself, it has not tended to convince naysayers that this Protestant missionary work deserved to be equated with going to the jungles of Central America or the west coast of India (places where Catholic missionaries were present in numbers by the mid-sixteenth century); yet it ought to have done so for multiple reasons.

The Protestant Reformers saw Europe as imperfectly Christianized. It is interesting to reflect on how, much earlier than the decisive year of 1517 (when Luther nailed his theses to the Wittenberg church door), advocates of reform had wished to spur European Christianity beyond its complacency, low biblical literacy and poor appropriation of a biblical morality. Preaching in the vernacular? Scriptures in the common tongue? Rebukes of the church for its accumulation of wealth and land? We can find all these in the ministry of the Waldensians of Piedmont in the twelfth century, among the followers of John Wyclif—the Lollards in fourteenth-century England—the Hussites of Bohemia or the followers of Savonarola in fifteenth-century Florence.

In Luther's time these were the concerns of Erasmus and the Christian humanists—that trans-European movement of scholars who were determined to turn the fruits of Renaissance learning in the ancient languages toward the project of the purification of Christianity. Erasmus's edition of the Greek New Testament, printed at Paris in 1516, became the foundation on which would stand vernacular translations in German, English, French and Dutch. Erasmus, just as surely as the translators of those vernacular versions, had it as his ambition that ploughboys and milkmaids would be able to read the Holy Scriptures for themselves.

In the mind of European Christians concerned for the restoration of scriptural Christianity, the nonavailability of the Bible in the language of the people had been the mother of confusion in doctrine, in morals and in the wielding of ecclesiastical power. Traces of earlier pagan religion—the veneration of places, groves, annual days and feasts—had never been adequately rooted out. A good portion of Europe's professed Christians considered Christianity to consist in the mere observance of set days and reverencing of certain places and objects. In consequence too much that passed for Christianity in Europe was deplorably substandard. The Reformation historian Scott Hendrix has described the mind of those concerned for the restoration of Christianity; he observed: "The veneration and intercession of saints contained a mixture of superstitious, folkloric, and Christian elements; the same can be said for prayers, pilgrimages, indulgences, and other types of medieval piety."[25]

Thus, advocates of reform genuinely expected that the recovery of a purer Christianity was the prerequisite for the expansion of Christianity *within* Europe as well as beyond it. And this is why, from Wittenberg, Basel, Strasbourg, Lausanne and Geneva, missionary preachers went in all directions.[26] That they encountered opposition (often of a brutal sort) in their advocacy of the purification of Christianity was demonstration enough that what passed for European Christendom was very often bound in thick darkness. With such a mindset in place, we should not be surprised that when given the opportunity to look beyond Europe, early Protestants (Calvinists among them) would seize opportunities to take the gospel abroad.

EARLY PROTESTANT TRANSOCEANIC MISSION: WHO WOULD GO?

In the illuminating essay "The European Missionary Awakening in Its European Context," Andrew Walls highlighted how the elimination of the monastic orders in Protestant territories served also to eliminate the labor force that, in Catholic lands, had been the first to go abroad in service of the gospel. Filling this gap would require Protestants not

---

[25]Scott Hendrix, *Recultivating the Vineyard: The Reformation Agendas of Christianization* (Louisville, Ky.: Westminster/John Knox Press, 2004), p. 17.

[26]It is the primary purpose of this essay to demonstrate that Reformed theology was not without missionary concern. It could be argued in parallel form that the Lutheran influence of Wittenberg was expressed in the preaching of reform and the provision of vernacular Scriptures in Denmark, Sweden, Iceland, Finland, Poland, Moravia and Hungary. See Paul E. Pierson, "The Reformation and Mission," in *Evangelical Dictionary of World Missions*, ed. A. Scott Moreau (Grand Rapids: Baker, 2000), pp. 813-14.

simply Christians of the mainstream but of the enthusiast variety.[27] But, from where would they come?

The Genevan Calvinist mission to Brazil. For reasons previously outlined, landlocked Geneva was unlikely to launch transoceanic mission initiatives of the kind we associate with Spain and Portugal. However, when Geneva's neighbor France gradually grew alert to the potentialities of transoceanic navigation, that nation focused (among other sites) on the coast of Brazil; in France's doing so, a door of opportunity was opened for Geneva. A colonizing expedition was led by one Nicholas de Villegagnon.[28] A shortage of willing colonists on the initial voyage, which departed from Havre de Grace in July 1555, meant that the door would be opened also to French Protestants to join the expedition in the following year. The Genevan church was asked to provide French-speaking ministers and some colonists to join the expedition.[29] The missionary possibilities were clear to the leaders of the Genevan church. Contemporary chronicler (and participant in the expedition) Jean de Léry recorded that "upon . . . hearing this news, the church of Geneva at once gave thanks to God for the extension of the reign of Jesus Christ in a country so distant and likewise so foreign and among a nation entirely without the knowledge of the true God."[30]

The church was further helped in deciding to support the matter when it received correspondence from Gaspard de Coligny, who was

---

[27]Walls, "Eighteenth Century Protestant Missionary Awakening," p. 24. Walls goes on (pp. 30-31) to demonstrate that this "want" in Protestantism was ultimately supplied by European Christians of the Pietist variety.

[28]Some details about Villegagnon are provided in G. Baez-Camargo, "The Earliest Protestant Missionary Venture in Latin America," *Church History* 21 (1952): 135; and Amy Glassner Gordon, "The First Protestant Missionary Effort: Why Did It Fail?" *International Bulletin of Missionary Research* 8 (1984): 12-13.

[29]It is important to note that the expedition, conceived of originally as an all-Catholic enterprise, entailed the sending of no missionary priests—or priests of any kind.

[30]Jean de Léry, *Journal de Bord de Jean de Léry en la Terre de Brésil 1557, presénté et commenté par M. R. Mayeux* (Paris, 1957), quoted in R. Pierce Beaver, "The Genevan Mission to Brazil," in *The Heritage of John Calvin*, ed. John Bratt (Grand Rapids: Eerdmans, 1973), p. 61. Portions of the de Léry journal appeared in English as "Journey to the Land of Brazil, 1557," in Joannes Boemus, *The Manners, Lawes, and Customes of All Nations, Collected out of the Best Writers*, trans. Ed Aston (London: G. Eld, 1611), pp. 483-502. I am indebted to Boston University and Gordon-Conwell Theological Seminary Th.D. student Travis Myers for pointing me to the Boemus volume, which is accessible through Early English Books Online.

Admiral of France and a known Protestant sympathizer.[31] Two ministers, Pierre Richier and Guillaume Chartier, were commissioned to go in the company of carpenters, a leatherworker, a cutler and a tailor. As a part of a group of three hundred, they reached the island colony (now called Fort Coligny) in March 1557.[32]

Villegagnon, the colonial governor, had determined that the colony should establish itself on an island off the Brazil coast. It lacked both sources of fresh water and native inhabitants. Since interaction with the natives was the key to obtaining adequate food supplies and to any missionary possibilities, this island location seemed very disadvantageous. Interaction with the Indian population, when it came, proved difficult; the Genevan pastors were initially taken aback at the barbarism of the people they now met. But they adopted the long-term strategy of placing boys from the colony among the Indians so that, with time, they would have the services of bilingual translators.[33] One of the colonists, the chronicler de Léry, spent extensive time among the onshore native population and wrote up extensive observations about their manners, customs and religious ideas. His work has been termed an attempt at missionary ethnography.[34]

Religious differences soon surfaced; Villegagnon seems to have been unprepared for the degree of religious diversity that the arrival of the Francophone Protestants represented, and in consequence disputes broke out about Catholic-Protestant doctrinal differences. The governor made it his business to hinder the ability of the Genevan Calvinists to proselytize among the at least nominally Catholic French colonists. In the course of time Villegagnon exiled the Genevan pastors to the mainland, where their exposure to the Indian population continued until the time when they and other Genevans were forcibly returned by the governor to France. At best, we can say that the short interlude of missionary opportunity among the natives of Brazil provided the Geneva contingent with a seedbed for further thinking and reflecting

---

[31]De Coligny was responsible for French naval and maritime ventures.
[32]Beaver, "Genevan Mission," p. 62.
[33]Ibid., p. 64.
[34]Gordon, "First Protestant Missionary Effort," p. 14.

about crosscultural mission.[35] In fairness, we should be able to grant that the Genevans seized this modest missionary opportunity when it was offered to them.

John Eliot's ministry among Massachusetts Native Americans. There is no disguising that among the English interested in developing their own seaborne empire, there was more talk about missions to native peoples encountered in foreign territories than there was any systematic plan of carrying the gospel to those peoples when they were actually encountered.[36] More intense interest may have been generated for the cause in old England rather than new.[37] The discrepancy between aim and actuality was obvious enough in Massachusetts. John Winthrop, original governor of the colony, had promoted emigration there by listing first among reasons for locating there the prospective missionary opportunities: "It will be a service to the church of great consequence to carry the gospel into those parts of the world, to help on the coming of the fullness of the gentiles and to raise a bulwark against the kingdom of anti-Christ which the Jesuits labor to rear up in those parts."[38]

Yet the settlers who responded to such reasoning were, on arrival, preoccupied with their own safety and sustenance, rather than the spiritual needs of the native population. Moreover, they had no prior experience with those outside their country to guide them in intercultural questions. The governing General Court of Massachusetts, however, persisted in its attempt to stir up interest in evangelization of the na-

---

[35]Ibid., p. 16.

[36]This is a point made most effectively by Henry M. Knapp, "The Character of Puritan Missions: The Motivation, Methodology and Effectiveness of the Puritan Evangelization of the Native Americans in New England," *Journal of Presbyterian History* 76 (1998): 113.

[37]This is the sober assessment of R. Pierce Beaver, "American Missionary Motivation Before the Revolution," *Church History* 31 (1962): 216. The point is made with new force in the excellent essay of Jon Hinkson, "Missions Among Puritans and Pietists," in *The Great Commission: Evangelicals and the History of World Missions*, Martin I. Klauber and Scott M. Manetsch (Nashville: B & H, 2008), pp. 224-25. See also the treatment of this problem in J. A. de Jong, *As the Waters Cover the Sea: Millennial Expectations in the Rise of Anglo-American Missions 1640-1810* (Kampen, Netherlands: J. H. Kok, 1970), pp. 31-33.

[38]"Reasons to Be Considered for Justifieinge the Undertakinge of the Intended Plantation in New England," in R. Winthrop, *Life and Letters of John Winthrop* (Boston: Little, Brown, 1864), 1:309-11, quoted in *The Past Speaks: Sources and Problems in English History*, ed. Lacey Baldwin Smith, 2nd ed. (Lexington, Mass.: Heath, 1993), p. 411. It is interesting to note Winthrop's awareness of Jesuit missionary activity in the New World.

tives in the 1644-1645 period.[39] This provided the context in which John Eliot (1604-1690), Puritan minister at Roxbury, Massachusetts, began in 1646 prolonged efforts to evangelize them. He never left his Roxbury pastorate, but began to go every two weeks to preach among the natives and to catechize their children.

It was not long before his missionary work came to the attention of sympathetic persons in England. The Parliament of England sanctioned the creation of the "Society for the Propagation of the Gospel in New England";[40] over time £12,000 was gathered for the support of this ministry. By 1652 Eliot and his associates saw the first signs of faith; by 1659 eight adults were ready to make formal professions of faith. Eliot and those assisting him took seriously the need to communicate in the language of the nearby Indians. They soon gained the ability to preach in it (variously termed Algonquian or Moheecan), and subsequently produced a catechism by 1653, select Psalms in translation by 1658 and a complete Bible by 1663.[41]

Eliot's New England ministry was not only significant in demonstrating an early Calvinist attempt to carry out the Great Commission (admittedly without extensive support from other colonists) but in its methods, which were in some ways eclectic and in other ways distinctly Protestant. Eliot's method of gathering an eventual 3,600 persons into what were called "Praying Towns" (all-Native American Christian settlements) approximated to some degree the tendency in Catholic missions to Central America and the American Southwest, to gather those willing to accept instruction in the Christian faith into stable communi-

---

[39]Note the helpful discussion of the only gradual pursuit of native evangelization by the Massachusetts Bay Colony in Richard W. Cogley, *John Eliot's Mission to the Indians Before King Philip's War* (Cambridge, Mass.: Harvard University Press, 1999), chaps. 1-2.

[40]It would appear that the action of the Long Parliament in 1649 was the *first* action by a Protestant legislature to assist the carrying out of foreign missionary activity. Jon Hinkson, "Missions Among Puritans and Pietists," terms it "the oldest English Protestant Missionary Society." Surviving archival records of Eliot's ministry were analyzed by Sidney H. Rooy, *The Theology of Missions in the Puritan Tradition* (Grand Rapids: Eerdmans, 1965), chap. 3; and de Jong, *As the Waters Cover the Sea*, pp. 67-78. The seventeenth-century tracts published by Eliot for the purpose of advocating missions to the Indians and progress observed there have been edited by Michael Clark and republished by Praeger in 2003.

[41]These details regarding Eliot are provided by P. C-H. Lim in the *Biographical Dictionary of Evangelicals*, ed. Timothy Larsen (Downers Grove, Ill.: InterVarsity Press, 2003), p. 206.

ties in which trades could be learned, crops cultivated and education provided.[42] These methods were persisted in until the terrible disruption
brought about in "King Philip's War" of 1675-1677; this colonist-native
conflict had converts and their communities caught in the crossfire and
held suspect by both sides. Happily, a parallel ministry to native people
was carried out on the Massachusetts island Martha's Vineyard by
Thomas Mayhew (c. 1620-1657) and, after his untimely death at sea, by
his own father and descendants; it was untouched by King Philip's War.
By the early eighteenth century some 1,600 Native Americans professing
Christianity were worshiping in their own churches on this one island.[43]

    In relation to other Protestant mission efforts of the seventeenth
century, we find Eliot's work setting the pace in early production of
vernacular Scriptures, in training indigenous Christian leaders in
Scripture and doctrine, and the rapid elevation of native persons into
positions of Christian leadership. The first native pastor was ready for
ordination by 1683, less than forty years from the time Eliot had commenced his biweekly Native American ministry. Though rural Massachusetts would have been considered somewhat on the fringe of European civilization, the Christian world would take note of what Eliot
and his successors had accomplished.

    German church historian Ernst Benz has shown how information
about the late John Eliot's Native American ministry in Massachusetts
was mediated by the prominent Boston minister Cotton Mather (1663-
1728) to his Halle (Germany) contact, Lutheran Pietist leader August
Hermann Francke (1663-1727). Through Francke this information was
communicated to the German Pietist missionaries Bartholomaeus
Ziegenbalg (1682-1719) and Heinrich Plutschau (1678-1747), who had
accepted missionary appointments to South India from the King of
Denmark in 1705. Missions news from South India eventually reached
Mather in Massachusetts via a network extending through Halle and
London.[44] In Tranquebar (the region of South India where Denmark's

---

[42]R. W. Cogley reports that members of the Roxbury congregation taught carpentry and agri-
    culture to the Indians, as well as providing them with medical care ("John Eliot's Puritan
    Ministry," *Fides et Historia* 31 [1999]: 9).
[43]Hinkson, "Missions Among Puritans and Pietists," pp. 31, 39.
[44]Ernst Benz, "Pietist and Puritan Sources of Early Protestant World Missions," *Church History*

colony was situated) the ministry led by Ziegenbalg and Plutschau produced a Tamil-language New Testament by 1714, and their successors
produced an entire Bible of high quality by 1796. An Indian pastor was
ordained by 1733; fourteen in all would be set aside for ministry in the
mission's first century.[45]

The significance of these accomplishments in New England and
South India are best appreciated when comparisons are drawn. Nearly
three centuries would pass between the time Catholic missions to the
Americas began and the ordination of its first native clergy in 1794.[46]
An even greater lapse of time separated the onset of Catholic mission-
ary effort in the Americas and the availability of vernacular Scriptures
in these regions. These finally were made available when James (Diego)
Thomson (1788-1854), the peripatetic agent of the British and Foreign
Bible Society, entered Argentina in 1818 and subsequently set up Bible
distribution networks in that country, Chile, Peru, Colombia and
Mexico.[47] Here we may see the natural outworking of the European
Reformation (and also Calvinist) principle of re-Christianization: if, in
Europe vernacular proclamation, vernacular Scriptures and vernacular
liturgy were requisite because intelligent, heartfelt worship required
them, why would the same principle not apply in non-European
lands?[48]

Dutch Reformed missionaries to Southeast Asia. Returning to the
early decades of the seventeenth century, and concurrent with the Puritan experiment in the New World, Holland was, after 1590, gradually

---

20 (1951): 31-33. The basic details about the Danish-Halle mission are supplied in Neill, *History of Christian Missions*, pp. 194-98. Ronald E. Davies has shown that another important
purveyor of transoceanic missions news in this era was the Scot Robert Millar (1672-1752).
See Ronald E. Davies, "Robert Millar—An Eighteenth Century Scottish Latourette," *Evangelical Quarterly* 42 (1990): 143-56. Tales of John Eliot's ministry and the Tranquebar missionaries were circulated in mid-eighteenth century also by the Scottish minister John Gillies
(1712-1796) in his *Historical Collections Relating to Remarkable Periods of the Success of the Gospel*,
rev. Horatius Bonar (1754; reprint, Kelso, U.K.: J. Rutherfurd, 1845).

[45]Neill, *History of Christian Missions*, pp. 195-96.

[46]Cogley, "John Eliot's Puritan Ministry," p. 10 n. 10. By contrast, Catholic missions efforts
commenced in Central America shortly after 1500 and yet ordained no native persons before
1794. See Neill, *A History of Christian Mission*, p. 150.

[47]Stephen Sywulka, "Thomson, James 'Diego,'" in *Evangelical Dictionary of World Missions*, ed.
Scott Moreau (Grand Rapids: Baker, 2000), pp. 959-60.

[48]Hendrix, *Recultivating the Vineyard*, pp. 172-73.

extending its reach into Southeast Asian territories earlier reckoned as the trading domains of Portugal. This Dutch incursion had the double effect of curtailing further Roman Catholic missionary work in those regions and opening the door to missionary work of the Protestant and Reformed type. The trading concern that represented Holland's interest in the region, the Dutch East India Company, was obliged by concerned Dutch Reformed believers (and it was this constituency which most heavily supported the monopolistic trading company) to take some steps to prepare a missionary force for Southeast Asia. A seminary was established at Leyden for the purpose of training workers who would minister to the needs of the trading company's employees and commence the presentation of the gospel to the native population. These, when they proceeded to that region, had some success in gathering and baptizing a large number who professed the Christian faith. A vernacular New Testament was produced in Malay by 1668 along with catechetical materials.[49]

Mission historians such as Neill have indicated the ways in which this initial Reformed missionary effort to Southeast Asia left much to be desired. As the missionaries, who were actually employed by the trading company, received economic incentives relative to the numbers baptized, there was a willful inflation of the numbers reckoned to be enfolded in the church.[50] But for our present purposes, it is sufficient to note that contrary to the kind of aspersions that have been cast in the past half-century, Dutch Calvinism, far from being hostile to foreign missions or second-guessing the need for it (in light of acceptance of the doctrine of divine election), was in fact congenial toward it. Research has demonstrated the presence in the Synod of Dordt (1618-1619)—a synod alleged to have restrained missionary labor because of its support for the doctrine of election—of advocates of foreign missionary work, such as Gisbertus Voetius, and of language in the Canons of Dordt, which was supportive of the missionary task.[51] The sizeable Protestant

---

[49]Jan Jongeneel, "The Missiology of Gisbertus Voetius: The First Comprehensive Protestant Theology of Missions," *Calvin Theological Journal* 26 (1991): 72. Jongeneel reports that a single Gospel, *Matthew*, had been available in translation from 1629.

[50]Neill, *History of Christian Missions*, p. 191.

[51]On the Synod, note the interpretation offered by Hogg in 1960 without any corroborating

population of Indonesia today is a witness to Dutch missionary activity carried on almost without a break until that nation withdrew from its former colony in 1947. Comparable missionary progress had been achieved under Dutch instrumentality in Ceylon (now Sri Lanka).

The American mission to Indians under David Brainerd. The era of the 1730s was one of heightened spiritual vitality in regions of Western Europe, Britain and British territories in North America.[52] Christians and churches in the Reformed tradition were by no means the only branch of Christianity quickened during this period. It is certain that the surge of missionary activism associated with Count Ludwig von Zinzendorf (1700-1760) and the Church of the United Brethren (commonly known as the Moravian Church) was the foremost direct expression, for missions, of the zeal engendered in this period of spiritual awakening. Yet it was not the *only* such expression, and here, since it is our purpose to highlight chiefly the missionary activity proper to the Reformed or Calvinist tradition, we focus on the most illustrious missionary career in this stream of Christianity in the first half of the eighteenth century. David Brainerd (1718-1747), himself a convert of the Great Awakening, was appointed, with his brother John, to work among the Native Americans of western Massachusetts under the auspices of a society that was a kind of successor to the Society for the Propagation of the Gospel in New England.[53] This was the Scottish Society for the Propagation of Christian Knowledge, which existed to evangelize the Highlands of Scotland, and to send ministers among Scots' emigrant communities abroad as well as among unevangelized native peoples.[54]

---

evidence ("Rise of Protestant Missionary Concern," p. 3). On Voetius, see James Tanis, "Reformed Pietism and Protestant Missions," *Harvard Theological Review* 67 (1974): 71-73. Jongeneel reports that Voetius's own belief in the doctrine of election was the guiding principle of his missions theology (see "The Missiology of Gisbertus Voetius," n. 49). On the Canons of Dordt, see Anthony Hoekema, "The Missionary Focus of the Canons of Dordt," *Calvin Theological Journal* 7 (1972): 209-20.

[52]The literature on this era is vast; the one major work bridging all geographic regions is that of W. R. Ward, *The Protestant Evangelical Awakening* (Cambridge: Cambridge University Press, 1992).

[53]Timothy George, "The Evangelical Revival and the Missionary Awakening," in *The Great Commission: Evangelicals and the History of World Missions*, ed. Martin Klauber and Scott Manetsch (Nashville: B & H, 2008), p. 47.

[54]The Society had origins in Edinburgh extending back to 1709, the year it was founded by royal charter. Details are supplied in the article by D. E. Meek, "Scottish S.P.C.K.," in *Scottish*

Brainerd's initial years in western Massachusetts preaching among the Housatonic people were not especially heartening. But when, in August 1745, he preached among the Delaware Native Americans of New Jersey, he saw something entirely different: assembled crowds of native people visibly affected by his preaching about the love of God shown in the suffering of Jesus Christ. Brainerd was observing developments highly analogous to events unfolding under the preaching ministry of the Moravians: ordinary hearers were enabled to respond to the message of the cross simply proclaimed. Traditionally, it had been understood that there had to be a clearing of the ground for the preaching of the gospel, consisting of a defense of theism, miracle and revelation. Now, Brainerd believed that he witnessed such methodology being made unnecessary by an almost immediate working of the Holy Spirit, employing only the essentials of the gospel message.

As surely as Eliot's labors had been reported in London, Halle and Tranquebar (India), the reputation of Brainerd spread abroad, primarily through the posthumous publication of his diary and *An Account of the Life of the Late Reverend David Brainerd*, the latter composed by Jonathan Edwards in 1749.[55]

William Carey, father of modern missions. I began this inquiry by noting that a dispassionate Methodist researcher, Norman Carr Sargant, had found special significance in a conference regarding world missions held by Welsh Calvinistic Methodists in 1772. Here there was evidence of the quickening of missionary interest, four decades into that era of evangelical awakening. The transatlantic circulation of literature, such as the *Life of David Brainerd*, was certainly part of the blend of influences, which helped forward this quickening of interest. William

---

Dictionary of Church History & Theology, ed. Nigel M. de S. Cameron (Downers Grove, Ill.: InterVarsity Press, 1993), pp. 761-62. An English counterpart, the SPCK had existed since 1698. Important details about the Scottish SPCK have been provided by Donald MacLean in "Scottish Calvinism and Foreign Missions," *Records of the Scottish Church History Society* VI (1938): 5-7. See also F. V. Mills, "The Society in Scotland for the Propagation of Christian Knowledge in British North America," *Church History* 63, no. 1 (1994): 15-30.

[55]Hinkson, "Missions Among Puritans and Pietists," pp. 32-33. Edwards, who would have become father-in-law to Brainerd had not premature death from tuberculosis intervened first for Brainerd, himself served the mission to the Native Americans of western Massachusetts when he fell from favor with his Northampton congregation (see George Marsden, "Jonathan Edwards as Missionary," *Journal of Presbyterian History* 81 [2003]: 5-17).

Carey, the English Calvinistic Baptist, who first helped promote the foundation of the Baptist Missionary Society in 1792,[56] is reported to have been able to quote sections of that work from memory.[57]

As Carey first promoted the need for a missionary society (only later volunteering to go himself) he encountered opposition. A Baptist minister, John Ryland Sr. (1723-1792), on hearing Carey advocate a mission to the heathen is reported to have reminded him that "when God pleases to convert the heathen, he will do it without you."[58] Here was a recurrence of an idea, at least as old as Ulrich Zwingli, that God, in considering the fallen heathen, was at liberty to bestow mercy on them irrespective of their inability to hear and respond to the claims of Christ and the gospel.[59] But in spite of what polemical writers have tried to "wring" from the episode (e.g., that opposition from such a quarter as Ryland's requires us to accept that Carey held a position antithetical to that of the avowedly Calvinist Ryland),[60] it is difficult to shirk the conclusion that Carey, as surely as Brainerd, Mayhew and Eliot before him, was a Calvinist convinced that God uses means.[61]

The outline and the significance of Carey's mission to India have often been described. Here, three things can be stressed. First, we must grasp how, given the rise in missionary zeal across Britain in that century of spiritual awakening, Carey and his cause were taken up and

---

[56]Brian Stanley indicates that the society was originally designated "The Particular-Baptist Society for Propagating the Gospel Among the Heathen" (see "Baptist Missionary Society," in *Evangelical Dictionary of World Missions*, p. 110). The original term *particular* indicated that these were Baptists held to the concept of "definite" or "particular" atonement; this is a Calvinist distinction.

[57]George, "Evangelical Revival," p. 47. George similarly demonstrates that Henry Martyn, the young Church of England chaplain to India, influenced so much by Carey's example, was just as definitely influenced by Brainerd's life and example.

[58]The account is provided in ibid., p. 50.

[59]Cf. the essay of W. P. Stephens, "Zwingli and the Salvation of the Gentiles," in *The Bible, the Reformation and the Church: Essays in Honor of James Atkinson*, ed. W. P. Stephens (Sheffield, U.K.: Sheffield Academic Press, 1995), pp. 224-44. Stephens shows that Zwingli's attitude was one reasonably common among sixteenth-century Christian humanists, who were excessively deferential to the great minds of classical antiquity, and who were willing to assume their inclusion among the elect on the basis of their close approximation to revealed truth.

[60]In fact, the very line of reasoning followed by a polemicist such as William Estep; see note 9 of this chapter.

[61]On the contested nature of the Rylands-Carey exchange, note the comments of Thomas J. Nettles in his "Baptists and World Missions," in *The Great Commission*, pp. 90-91.

endorsed by evangelical Calvinists of all stripes. His contemporary Andrew Fuller (1754-1815), who traveled on behalf of the nascent mission society after its launch (and after Carey's departure for India), recorded the almost-universal welcome extended to him in a wide range of churches, across denominational boundaries; believers within the broadly Calvinist tradition and beyond it gladly contributed their gifts to a cause now dear to their hearts also.[62] Carey was both a symptom of and focus for the surge in missionary zeal as the evangelical Protestant public took up the cause of world mission to a degree not previously found.

Second, the record of Carey's ministry in India sounds some now-familiar notes of post-Reformation Protestant missions that we have already observed in New England and Southeast Asia: preaching in the vernacular, Scriptures in the vernacular and an indigenous ministry prepared with urgency. To stress this takes nothing away from Carey's extraordinary abilities as a self-taught linguist and translator; it is only to note that the priorities and strategies he pursued were very often those identified also by Protestant missionaries before him.

Third, we can note that Carey, and the mission society whose creation he advocated, was a part of what Andrew Walls has aptly called "the fortunate subversion of the church."[63] Having acknowledged earlier that Protestantism would be as reliant on a type of enthusiast to prosecute the actual task of world missions as Catholicism had been on members of the monastic orders, we must now acknowledge that as the broadly Calvinist Protestant world more actively embraced the cause of world missions, the societies that stood at the vanguard of this movement were not (with the exception of the Moravians) the *direct* instruments of the churches of the Reformation; they were *voluntary* societies made up of likeminded persons drawn from those churches and united for a common purpose. It was true of Carey's sponsoring Baptist society; it would be even more the case for the Missionary Society founded at London in 1795 (later known as the London Missionary Society),

---

[62]J. W. Morris, *Memoir of the Life and Writings of Andrew Fuller* (London: n.p., 1816), pp. 145-47.
[63]See Andrew Walls, "Missionary Societies and the Fortunate Subversion of the Church," *Evangelical Quarterly* 60 (1988): 141-55.

which provided a vehicle for the missionary aspirations of zealous Christians found in Anglican, Presbyterian and Congregational/ Independent churches. The one who takes the time to sample the biographies of the earliest leaders of the London Missionary Society assembled by John Morison as *Fathers and Founders of the London Missionary Society* (1844) will be struck again and again at their combined zeal for Calvinism and missions.[64]

In emulation of these British developments, similar voluntary missions societies were begun in short order by concerned believers within Scotland at Glasgow and Edinburgh (1796) and in connection with the Reformation churches of the Continent in Amsterdam (1797), Basel (1815) and Paris (1822). Though the London society had welcomed Church of England involvement, by 1812 a similar voluntary society serving, but not controlled by, the Church of England was begun as the Church Missionary Society. The example of Carey and the Baptist Mission extended across the Atlantic, for another voluntary society— the American Board of Commissioners for Foreign Mission (Congregationalist)—was commenced in 1812 in support of missions efforts in India. The element of subversion Walls spoke of would require a leavening work over time, for it was only decades later that the various denominations that the early enthusiastic supporters of mission were drawn from committed themselves corporately to the ecclesiastical support of the missionary cause.[65]

CONCLUSION

This chapter has not attempted to rewrite the history of Protestant missions but only to draw attention to underrepresented parts of that story.

---

[64]John Morison, *Fathers and Founders of the London Missionary Society: A Jubilee Memorial Including a Sketch of the Origin and Progress of the Institution* (London: Fisher, 1844). Ten of the thirty-six leading ministers involved in the origination of the LMS were Scottish Presbyterians serving expatriate Scots in England, while others served Congregational/independent or Calvinistic Methodist churches in London and the south of England. The evangelical Calvinism of the early LMS is also helpfully detailed by Johannes Van den Berg, *Constrained by Jesus' Love* (Kampen, Netherlands: J. H. Kok, 1956).

[65]In broad terms the decade of 1820s witnessed denominations in the Reformed tradition, on both sides of the Atlantic, authorizing the setting up of foreign missions agencies reckoned as expressions of their corporate life.

Required is a fresh acknowledgment of both the temporal priority of Catholic transoceanic mission in the age of the European voyages of discovery, begun a half-millennium ago, and the unfortunate combination of military conquest and colonial domination with those early missionary efforts. Also required is the acknowledgment that we do not lack early and regular examples of Protestant missionary effort (with Calvinists very prominent in them) as Protestant regions of Europe gradually gained oceanic access in the late sixteenth and early seventeenth centuries. Those oceanic accesses brought first Geneva, then the Netherlands and in turn the New England Puritans to embrace missionary opportunity.

In the eighteenth century, Lutheran Pietists as well as German Moravians joined this Protestant world missions effort. All this effort preceded the epoch marked by the departure of William Carey for India in 1793. The reader who has devoured Carey's seminal booklet *An Inquiry into the Obligations of Christians to Use Means for the Conversion of the Heathens* (1792) will know that Carey had made it his business to devour all the previous Protestant missions history, including that of Calvinists, he could lay hold of.[66] In light of this prehistory, we may only with qualification go on describing Carey as "the father of modern missions."[67] The fervor for missions work laid bare by the transdenominational outpouring of support for Carey and the Baptist Mission Society clearly brought much nearer the founding of the London Missionary Society; this differed from the Baptist Society, not over Calvinism (with which both were in harmony) but only the administration of the baptismal ordinance given by Christ. The passing of this missionary torch to new, likeminded societies on the Continent and in America in the decades following fills out this undertold story of how evangelical zeal combined with Calvinist theology provided the underpinnings of a vast proportion (never the whole, of course) of Protestant missionary expansion in what Latourette so

---

[66]A facsimile edition of Carey's *Inquiry* was published in 1961 (London: Carey Kingsgate). It is now also accessible in the 2005 volume of Daniel Webber, *William Carey and the Missionary Vision* (Edinburgh: Banner of Truth, 2005).

[67]See A. Morgan Derham, "Carey, William," in *New International Dictionary of the Christian Church*, ed. J. D. Douglas (Grand Rapids: Zondervan, 1974), p. 192.

wisely called "the great century" of missionary expansion.

It seemed so obvious at the end of the nineteenth century that Calvinism and missions had been good partners that few felt pressed to document the full extent of it. One who did, from within the Presbyterian and Reformed constituency, claimed at century's end that of the world's Protestant missionary force, a full 25 percent were recruited from that family of churches.[68] Had Congregationalists, Anglicans and Baptists (whose missionaries also extensively shared this theological outlook) been added to this accounting, an already impressive figure would have swelled drastically. It is good to be reminded just how many household names from that great era of missionary expansion were both sent out by agencies upholding and serving within a Calvinistic framework. A dictionary of biography would rapidly make this plain regarding Robert Morrison (1782-1834), who translated the Bible into Chinese by 1818; Robert Moffat (1795-1883) and son-in-law David Livingstone (1813-73), who gave themselves to South and Central Africa; and a host of others.

Late-twentieth-century prognosticators about an assumed dampening effect of Calvinism on missions have therefore made their pronouncements rashly. Alarmist statements, made in these last decades in the face of the current resurgence of interest in Reformed theology, surely ought to give way to more careful assessments if missions history is to be trusted. If it is true that *all* branches of the Christian family might have done more for missions, then it is also true that this branch has been "in missionary harness" as long as any expression of Protestantism.

DISCUSSION QUESTIONS

1. How many of these names (all of Presbyterian or Reformed missionaries) can you identify? Use a dictionary of church history or world missions to identify at least three who were previously unknown to you.

    19th century: Alexander Duff, Donald Fraser, John Geddie, Jonathan and Rosalind Goforth, Adoniram Judson, David Livingstone,

---

[68]The claim is made by Scottish church historian T. M. Lindsay (1843-1914) in the Glasgow 1896 General Council Meeting of the Reformed and Presbyterian Alliance, quoted by S. M. Zwemer, "Calvinism and Missionary Enterprise," *Theology Today* 7 (1950): 215.

Robert Moffat, Samuel A. Moffett, Robert Morrison, John L. Nevius, John G. Paton, John Philip, A.T. Pierson, John Scudder, Mary Slessor, Johannes Van der Kemp, John Williams.

20th century: J. H. Bavinck, William Borden, David Bosch, Bruce Hunt, Hendrik Kraemer, Samuel Hugh Moffett, Lesslie Newbigin, J. H. Oldham, Ida Scudder, Robert E. Speer, Johanna Veenstra, Johannes Verkuyl, Samuel Zwemer.

2. Samuel Zwemer, himself a long-term missionary to the Middle East, contended in 1950 that missionaries in the Calvinist branch of Protestantism had, up to that time, been especially oriented to the Muslim world. Is there any obvious explanation for this? Would the generalization he drew be as fitting now, as in 1950?

3. If you have ever heard someone excuse a neglect of evangelism and missions by pointing to God's sovereignty in such matters, how did you respond then? How would you respond now?

FURTHER READING

Anderson, Gerald H., ed. *The Theology of the Christian Mission.* New York: McGraw-Hill, 1961.

Klauber, Martin I., and Scott M. Manetsch, eds. *The Great Commission: Evangelicals and the History of World Missions.* Nashville: Broadman & Holman, 2008.

Moreau, Scott, ed. *Evangelical Dictionary of World Missions.* Grand Rapids: Baker, 2000.

Neill, Stephen. *A History of Christian Missions.* Vol. 6 of The Penguin History of the Church. 2nd ed. London: Penguin, 1986.

Stanley, Brian. *The Bible and the Flag: Protestant Missions and British Imperialism in the Nineteenth and Twentieth Centuries.* Nottingham, U.K.: Inter-Varsity Press, 1990.

———, ed. *Christian Missions and the Enlightenment.* Grand Rapids: Eerdmans, 2001.

Webber, Daniel. *William Carey and the Missionary Vision.* Edinburgh: Banner of Truth, 2005.

Moses with the Ten Commandments, Philippe de Champaigne, 1649
Image: Held by the Hermitage, St. Petersburg

MYTH SIX

Calvinism Promotes Antinomianism

IF IT WERE POSSIBLE FOR US TO TIME travel backward to early Reformation Europe, we would be confronted with a bewildering array of moral ambiguities related to the institution of marriage; the examples would cross ecclesiastical boundaries. Exhibit one involves Philip of Hesse (1504-1567), a German prince who strongly supported the Protestant cause. Acting under parental pressure, Philip had married while still very young to Christina, daughter of the Duke of Saxony. Philip found his first wife to be unattractive and sickly, and began to contemplate taking a second—a course of action to which his first wife apparently gave consent! But even a prince could not keep two wives without the concurrence of the Christian leaders of the day. Martin Bucer of Strasbourg was contacted first, in the hope that he could favorably influence the Wittenberg Reformers Luther and Melanchthon.

Bucer, who was already known for his progressive views on the question of divorce and remarriage, tried to balance two chief concerns: bigamy *had* been practiced by biblical patriarchs such as Jacob, and Philip was seeking support for a bigamous marriage as a more wholesome alternative to his own past adulterous conduct.[1] Philip let it be

---

[1]Hastings Eels, *The Attitude of Martin Bucer Towards the Bigamy of Philip of Hesse* (New Haven, Conn.: Yale University Press, 1922), chap. 2. It is worth noting that it was Bucer's strong rec-

known that he was prepared to seek sanction for such bigamy from Charles (the Holy Roman Emperor, who opposed the young Protestant movement) and the pope, should the Protestant Reformers not side with him. Bucer lamely supported this proposal and agreed to commend it in a visit to Wittenberg. In secret correspondence with Philip, Luther and Melanchthon conceded that bigamy was at least preferable to divorce. The prince eventually took the second wife in 1540, with both Bucer and Melanchthon present to witness the ceremony.

Predictably, the news got out. Of course, Europeans were much more interested in the fact that bigamy had been committed with the complicity of these Protestant leaders (who were in fact "holding their noses") than in understanding the military and diplomatic pressures they had been put under to lend some kind of approval.[2] It is easy to imagine how the mishandling of this ethical and pastoral case was used to bring discredit on the young Protestant movement. Didn't it appear to suggest that obedience to the law of God (in this case the commandment against adultery and infidelity) was somehow negotiable for the one who had faith (which Philip no doubt claimed he had)?[3]

We shift to exhibit two: in the same period, Henry VIII of England was *also* seeking a second marriage while his first was intact. In 1509 Henry had married Catherine (1485-1536), widow to his older brother, Arthur; she was his senior by six years. Catherine was a Spanish princess, the youngest daughter of Ferdinand and Isabella of Spain. Now early on Henry developed a "wandering eye" for the ladies. Catherine gave him a daughter (Mary) but no sons who survived; Henry, both for

---

ommendation that this bigamy ought to be kept strictly secret lest it cause scandal among the common population. In 1539 Philip would not so much as admit that he already had in view the woman he aimed to take as a second wife.

[2]The incident is reported and explained in detail in ibid., chaps. 3-4; Lewis W. Spitz, *The Renaissance and Reformation Movements*, 2nd ed. (St. Louis: Concordia, 1987), 2:366-67; and Hans W. Hillerbrand, *The Division of Christendom: Christianity in the Sixteenth Century* (Louisville, Ky.: Westminster John Knox, 2007), pp. 187-88. See also William J. Wright, "Philip of Hesse," in *Oxford Encyclopedia of the Reformation* (New York: Oxford University Press, 1996), 3:262-63.

[3]See Ex 20:14 and its parallel, Deut 5:18. If it be suggested with regard to the case of Philip and others named here that bigamy or polygamy is still a form of marriage, it is well to remember both that Old Testament narratives regularly show that strife and inequity followed such irregular marriages and that the New Testament standard is raised higher for the Christian leader in such passages as 1 Tim 3:2 and Tit 1:6.

dynastic and egotistical reasons, was determined to move on.

Henry's first marriage had required the securing of a papal ruling (called a dispensation), which permitted him to do something considered irregular: marry his widowed sister-in-law.[4] Two decades later the king attempted (without success) to secure from the papacy a *second* ruling that would acknowledge that the first marriage ought never to have been entered into (and thus, because invalid, leave him free to remarry). But the pope of the day, Clement VII, had two reasons for declining Henry's request: *first* there were solid theological grounds for viewing the original decision as warranted; *second,* the nephew of Henry's wife, Catherine, was Charles V, the current Holy Roman Emperor. And the armies of Charles just then had Rome surrounded, even as the papal negotiations with the English continued at a glacial pace!

Henry VIII had his own theological advisers who pressed the case for annulment or divorce at Rome; among them were the leaders of the then-nascent Protestant movement in England. Early English Protestantism as a movement was committed (for quite distinct and valid reasons) to seeking a limitation of papal authority. Pope Clement VII, on the other hand, realizing that the wider stakes for the papacy and for Europe were very high, found a way to let King Henry know that under these circumstances, he might find a way out of his intractable dilemma by bigamy.[5] Again, moral ambiguity.

Finally, we shift to exhibit three. We now zero in on the events in Münster, Westphalia, in 1534-1535. To this city had gravitated many hundreds of early Anabaptists who had been led to expect the imminent end of the world. They had leaders who encouraged them in this direction: Jan Matthys (an Amsterdam baker), Bernard Rothmann

---

[4]The admittedly difficult ethical case had long been understood to involve the bringing into harmony of two Old Testament Scriptures which seemed at variance: Lev 20:21 (which was reckoned to forbid a man's marrying his brother's wife) and Deut 25:5-6 (which seemed to urge a man's marriage to his brother's widow in the interest of raising up heirs). The Leviticus passage was considered to establish the norm, which could only be lifted by papal dispensation; this had indeed been secured in time for the first marriage in 1509.

[5]An exhaustive treatment of Henry's divorce negotiations with Rome is provided in J. J. Scarisbrick, *Henry VIII* (London: Eyre Methuen, 1986), chaps. 7-8. Note especially pp. 197-98. The hint from the papacy regarding a possible resolution through bigamy is also related in Spitz, *Renaissance and Reformation Movements*, p. 386.

(earlier a Lutheran minister) and Jan Bockelson (a tailor of Leiden). At Münster the Anabaptists declared the establishment of a "new Jerusalem," with Bockelson filling the role of King David. As female followers outnumbered males, Bockelson determined to take fifteen wives. Polygamy began to be practiced. Then, citizens who were not sympathetic toward this revolutionary society were driven out of Münster by force. Among the exiles was the prince-bishop of the city, who subsequently organized an armed invasion force embracing both Catholics and Protestants. Münster was retaken and all the Anabaptist leaders were put to the sword. In short order Münster's name came to be associated with wild excess, extremism and moral laxity. Again, moral excess.[6]

The Subsequent Fallout

While each of these three incidents we have glimpsed involve the compromise of marriage and the violation of the moral law, symbolic value has been attached supremely to the first example. The fact is that both Lutheran and Reformed leaders were drawn into Philip's scheme to secure a religious cover for his wrong desire. Philip, who managed the situation to his own advantage, was one who claimed to have Christian faith. It is not surprising that when European Roman Catholic bishops and cardinals met to give their considered response to the danger posed by the young Protestant movement in the sessions of the Council of Trent (1545-1563) that this apparent tendency of Protestantism to relax the necessity of obedience to God's moral law was singled out for comment. In the Council's treatment of the doctrine of justification, came this warning:

> CANON XVIII.—If any one saith, that the commandments of God are, even for one that is justified and constituted in grace, impossible to keep; let him be anathema.
>
> CANON XIX.—If any one saith, that nothing besides faith is commanded in the Gospel; that other things are indifferent, neither com-

---

[6]The basic details are supplied in Spitz, *Renaissance and Reformation Movements*, 2:401-4; and Hillerbrand, *Division of Christendom*, pp. 119-23.

manded nor prohibited, but free; or, that the ten commandments nowise appertain to Christians; let him be anathema.

CANON XX.—If any one saith, that the man who is justified and how perfect soever, is not bound to observe the commandments of God and of the Church, but only to believe; as if indeed the Gospel were a bare and absolute promise of eternal life, without the condition of observing the commandments; let him be anathema.

CANON XXI.—If any one saith, that Christ Jesus was given of God to men, as a redeemer in whom to trust, and not also as a legislator whom to obey; let him be anathema.[7]

This Roman concern *seemed* to score a direct hit. True, the Council of Trent might have acknowledged that violations of God's laws could be found on Catholicism's own doorstep. There had, after all, been that confidential papal advice to England's Henry VIII; there were also the many lapses from the pledged celibacy required of Catholic leaders! Yet what of these Protestants who seemed to accommodate this violation of divine law even as they propounded their principle of salvation by faith? If such prominent leaders in the Protestant movement could seem to connive at a prince's immorality, what then?

ANTINOMIANISM: A RECURRING WRONG TURN

That may have been the perception, but in point of fact there is nothing about the opening decades of the Protestant era that should make us especially associate it with the problem of antinomianism. (Though the terminology itself was first employed then by Luther to critique an opponent.)[8] Antinomianism, a notion entailing "rejection of the moral law as a relevant part of the Christian's experience" in light of our free justification before God is an erroneous conception that has appeared at intervals ever since the apostolic era.[9]

Lest confusion arise, we need to acknowledge that antinomianism is

---

[7]"Sixth Session," *Canons and Decrees of the Council of Trent*, trans. and ed. J. Waterworth (London: Dolman, 1848), pp. 46-47.
[8]Hugh J. Blair, "Antinomianism," in *New International Dictionary of the Christian Church*, ed. J. D. Douglas (Grand Rapids: Zondervan, 1974), p. 48.
[9]Ibid.

of two types. First, there are honest Christians who, while living uprightly, take the precepts of the gospel (rather than the laws of Sinai) as their guide for living. If such upright persons are called "antinomian," it is not because they are lawless but because they do not grant that the life of the Christian should be governed by law.[10] More objectionable, however, is the second variety of antinomianism: this is the opinion that one who is professedly Christian is free from any obligation to uphold the laws of God. Persons of this character already appear late in the New Testament period; Paul seems to refer to persons of this cast of mind when he speaks of those who reasoned that we should "go on sinning so that grace may increase" (Rom 6:1). And among them also are the persons called the Nicolaitans (Rev 2:6, 15).

Why is this charge still being made? If *any* Protestants are currently suspected of this latter tendency, it is those in the Calvinist or Reformed tradition. Such Christians are suspected of encouraging antinomianism by onlookers who draw inferences from two doctrines Calvinists actually hold. The doctrines are in fact two alluded to in previous portions of this book: predestination to life and the final perseverance of believers. The faultfinding argument works along these lines: "If I believed in unconditional predestination as you Calvinists do, why would I not conclude that I could live however I pleased in the expectation that my decreed salvation would be unaffected?" Or, to put it another way, "According to Calvinists, salvation is decreed for the elect without respect to their works; why then should any (mis)behavior of the elect be feared to undermine final salvation?" It is easy to find variations of these protests continued from the sixteenth century until our own time.

Jacob Arminius claimed to detect this tendency among some Calvinist writers of his own era.[11] While not attributing the sentiment to

---

[10]John Agricola, a contemporary of Luther, was a champion of this point of view. He did not think that it was the laws of Sinai so much as the promises of the gospel that moved sinners to repent. Yet no one charged Agricola with brazen immorality. On Agricola see Steffen Kjeldgaard-Pedersen, "Agricola, Johann," in *Oxford Encyclopedia of the Reformation*, 1:10. Additional details are provided in F. Bente, *Historical Introductions to the Book of Concord* (St. Louis: Concordia, 1965), pp. 161-63.

[11]Objections of this kind were raised as early as the era of Jacob Arminius (1560-1609). See his "Declaration of Sentiments," in *The Writings of James Arminius* (Grand Rapids: Baker, 1977), 1:230-31.

all of Reformed persuasion, the German church historian J. L. von Mosheim (1694-1755) reported evidence of such errant thinking among some Calvinists of the seventeenth century when he compiled his *Institutes of Ecclesiastical History* (1726). Similarly, when writing a century later, two English church historians, David Bogue and James Bennett, traced the reemergence of such ideas among a fringe of the eighteenth-century Calvinist movement.[12] In our own time American Norman Geisler has claimed to locate this antinomian tendency in those whom he terms "extreme Calvinists."[13]

With what frequency has this alleged antinomianism shown itself? Notwithstanding surmises that this tendency "comes with the territory" of Reformed theology, it is not difficult to show that leading Reformers denounced the attitudes and behaviors of persons who, while claiming to be Christian, lived at cross-purposes with God's moral law disclosed in the Ten Commandments. Though not in the first edition of his *Institutes of the Christian Religion* (1536), certainly by the second edition of 1539 John Calvin warned against:

> Certain ignorant persons . . . (who) rashly cast out the whole of Moses, and bid farewell to the two tables of the Law. For they think it obviously alien to Christians to hold to a doctrine that contains the "dispensation of death" [II Cor 3:7]. Banish this wicked thought from our minds! For Moses has admirably taught that the law, which among sinners can engender nothing but death, ought among the saints to have a better and more excellent use.[14]

---

[12]J. L Mosheim, *Institutes of Ecclesiastical History* (1726; reprint, New York: Stanford, 1857), 3:423-24. David Bogue and James Bennett, *A History of Dissenters from the Revolution to 1838* (1838; reprint, Stoke on Trent, U.K.: Tentmaker, 2000), 2:215, 3:236.

[13]Geisler argues, "Extreme Calvinism leads logically (if not practically) to personal irresponsibility: if our actions are good actions, they are such only because God has programmed us to do good; if evil, then we cannot help it because we are sinners by nature and God has not given us the desire to do good" (Norman Geisler, *Chosen But Free* [Minneapolis: Bethany House, 1999], p. 132).

[14]John Calvin, *Institutes of the Christian Religion*, 2.7.13. The textual apparatus of the 1559 *Library of Christian Classics* edition (which is used) indicates that this material came to be inserted by 1539. The editor of the *Institutes* indicates that Calvin had in view here two kinds of persons: actual moral libertines who, claiming to be Christians lived dissolutely, and others, led by the Lutheran Agricola, who taught that the Christian is not any longer under the jurisdiction of the law.

Calvin is condemning certain contemporary persons outside the broad Swiss Reformed movement who have moved beyond God's laws. In his condemnation Calvin is representative of Reformed theology's upholding of the principle that God's moral law, announced at Mount Sinai, has *three* uses. The law of God, as a disclosure of God's holy will, first pinpoints sin in humans; it further restrains sin in society (which could be even more violent and unjust than it is). Finally, for the Christian believer the law of God serves as an indication of what a just and holy life ought to resemble; it models godliness.[15] If persons associated with Calvinism were or are observed to ignore or disregard God's laws, what are we to make of them? Can such persons, in spite of their disregard of the kind of caution Calvin supplied, fairly be said to represent the actual intention of Reformed theology? And yet this is, in essence, what certain critics would have us accept as true.

However, we need to acknowledge that these critics would have gained no traction in raising their complaints if there were not *some* seeming evidence of the antinomian tendency in the Calvinist movement. Let us consider a variety of these examples of antinomianism, asking what mainstream Calvinism says about them.

ANTINOMIANISM: THE MOTIONS OF THE SPIRIT OVER THE LAW

Puritan England. At intervals since the year 1600, Protestantism has had to contend with groups and individuals who took this stance. These were of the view that the inward promptings of the Holy Spirit, who is resident within the Christian believer, make it unnecessary to rely on the laws of God as a guide to conduct or as helps to sanctification.[16] This was an approach which, while it emerged among some branches of

---

[15]The conception of the law's three uses was hammered out within Lutheranism before it was expressed by Reformed theology, though the order or sequence of the three ideas differs in the two traditions. Karl-Heinze Zur Mohlen, in an article "Law," in *Oxford Encyclopedia of the Reformation* credits Philip Melanchthon with first introducing the conception of the law's "three uses" in 1523. Lutheranism since that time has not uniformly upheld Melanchthon's conception.

[16]J. I. Packer terms this type of antinomianism "Spirit-centered." See his *Concise Theology* (Wheaton, Ill.: Tyndale House, 2001), p. 178.

the Reformed tradition, was also found in Quakerism.[17] In the early decades of the seventeenth century, this approach was characteristic of the teaching and writing of English ministers John Eaton (1575-1630), John Saltmarsh (1612-1647) and Tobias Crisp (1600-1643).[18] It may be said in empathy toward these individuals that they found themselves in reaction against the growth of a then-current Puritan emphasis on protracted conviction of sin prior to conversion, and punctilious obedience to the commandments subsequent to conversion as a means of verifying one's status among the saved; this seemed to these critics to make the gospel just the "new law." The converts of Puritan ministers were indeed encouraged to consider their obedience as a litmus test indicative of their election and progress in grace.[19] This very circumspect Puritan emphasis was focused on a determination to ensure that true Christian believers would appear distinctive against the backdrop of a comprehensive national church, which was in many respects lax and defective.

The reaction against Puritan self-examination had not to do with alleged ill effects of predestination; this doctrine the antinomians affirmed as assuredly as did the Puritans.[20] In their protest Eaton, Saltmarsh and Crisp appealed to the early Martin Luther as a champion of their insistence that salvation in Christ is freely given without preconditions and is freely enjoyed without introspection.[21] Yet the "remedy" provided by the antinomians may well have been worse than the "disease" they sought to eradicate. In contrast to the Puritan emphasis on steps preparatory to conversion, they taught a justification of elect sinners from all eternity; for them, conversion only en-

---

[17]On this subject, the standard guide is that of Geoffrey Nuttall, *The Holy Spirit in Puritan Faith and Experience* (Oxford: Basil Blackwell, 1947).

[18]See the extremely helpful chapter 10, "John Eaton and the Antinomian First Wave," in T. D. Bozeman, *The Precisionist Strain: Disciplinary Religion and Antinomian Backlash in Puritanism to 1638* (Chapel Hill: University of North Carolina Press, 2004). On Saltmarsh, see Leo F. Solt, "John Saltmarsh: New Model Army Chaplain," *Journal of Ecclesiastical History* 2 (1951): 69-80.

[19]Tim Cooper, "The Antinomians Redeemed: Removing Some of the 'Radical' from Mid-Seventeenth-Century English Religion," *Journal of Religious History* 24, no. 3 (2000): 247-62.

[20]Bozeman adds "most shared selectively in Puritanism's bibliocentric, evangelical, conversionist and predestinarian emphases, its hostility to Arminianism, its search for a higher life beyond the tepid norms and forms of the official church . . . " (*Precisionist Strain*, p. 207).

[21]J. Wayne Baker, "Sola fide, Sola Gratia: The Battle for Luther in Seventeenth-Century England," *Sixteenth Century Journal* 16 (1985): 115-33.

tailed a sinner's awakening to a state of affairs already in existence. In contrast to the Puritan emphasis on the need for periodic self-examination, they taught that since Christ had kept the law for believers, "what they actually do makes no difference, provided that they keep believing."[22]

The early decades of the seventeenth century were a perilous time to be proclaiming such a message since the great national fear in England was that the country would lapse into utter lawlessness. There had yet to follow the serious misrule of King Charles I, subsequent civil war, the arrest and execution of the king, and the transition to the Protectorate of Oliver Cromwell. Whatever the antinomians meant, they were construed as propagating a message that relaxed moral obligation and encouraged a kind of passivity. Increasingly, they were called before ecclesiastical authorities and made to answer for their imprudent teaching.

Mainstream Reformed theology addressed these conceptions both in formal documents and in published treatises. As for the former, the Westminster Confession of Faith (1646) insisted in its chapter "Of the Law of God":

> The moral law of God doth for ever bind all, as well justified persons as others, to the obedience thereof; and that not only in regard of the matter contained in it, but also in respect of the authority of God the Creator, who gave it. Neither doth Christ, in the Gospel, any way dissolve but much strengthens this obligation.[23]

Prominent pastor-theologians also weighed in to counter the influence of Eaton, Saltmarsh and Crisp. Samuel Rutherford (1600-1661) addressed this menacing point of view in his *A Survey of the Antichrist* (1648),[24] while John Flavel (d. 1691) dealt with the same point of view (when it revived late in the century) in his *A Succinct and Seasonable*

[22]Packer, *Concise Theology*, p. 170
[23]Westminster Confession of Faith, 19.5.
[24]Samuel Rutherford works to overassociate his English antinomian contemporaries with a range of Christian deviants such as the Anabaptist citizens of Münster in 1535 and the Familists, or Family of Love, associated with the Dutch city of Emden, c. 1540 (see Rutherford's *A Survey of the Antichrist* [London: Andrew Crooke, 1648]).

Discourse on the Occasions of Mental Errors (1691).[25] Among antinomianism's erroneous tenets, he listed these:

- Justification is an immanent and eternal act of God.

- Justification by faith is but a manifestation of what God has already done.

- It is wrong for Christians to examine themselves as to whether they are in the faith.

- As all sin has been pardoned, confession of sin is not necessary.

- God never sees the sin in believers.

- At no time does God ever punish the elect.

- On the cross, Christ became as sinful as we are, and now the elect are as righteous as he is.

- Christians should not worry about sin in their lives, for these can do them no harm.

- Christians are not to rely on signs and marks of grace in their lives as helps to an assurance of salvation.[26]

In the same decades of the seventeenth century a variety of antinomian groups was springing up in England's American colonies. Writers such as the Scot Samuel Rutherford, aware of these troubles in Massachusetts, believed them to be all of one piece with what he found in his English contemporaries, Eaton, Crisp and Saltmarsh.[27] It was little to be wondered at, since the early settlers of New England had very often been under the influence of these English authors and preachers prior to their relocation across the Atlantic.

Puritan New England. The pastoral environment was radically al-

---

[25]I am indebted to the discussion of the antinomian threat in Peter Toon's *The Emergence of Hyper-Calvinism in English Nonconformity* (London: Olive Tree, 1967), p. 28, and the same author's *Puritans and Calvinism* (Swengel, Penn.: Reiner, 1975), chap. 6.

[26]John Flavel, "A Succinct and Seasonable Discourse on the Occasions of Mental Errors," in *Works of John Flavel* (1691; reprint, Edinburgh: Banner of Truth, 1968), 3:555-57. The helpful summary is provided by Toon, *Emergence of Hyper-Calvinism*, p. 30.

[27]Samuel Rutherford, *A Survey of the Antichrist* (London: Andrew Crooke, 1648), p. 188. Flavel shows a similar awareness of New England antinomianism ("Succinct and Seasonable Discourse," 3:557).

tered for the Puritan pastors and people who crossed to Massachusetts. In old England the challenge they faced was that of helping to distinguish true believers and to emphasize true Christian living within the comprehensive Church of England, which embraced a multitude of citizens, many of whom were no more than nominal believers. By crossing the Atlantic, however, this Puritanism was transformed from being one wing of the English national church to being the establishment in the new territory. Only pastors and people identified with the Puritan expression of Christianity were admitted to the colony. And yet, nevertheless, antinomianism reared its head there, as surely as in the old setting. Perhaps *this* is further indication that the Reformed expression of Christianity nurtures this standoffishness toward God's moral laws?

At the center of the New England expression of the movement stood a pastor, John Cotton (1584-1652), who crossed the Atlantic to Massachusetts in 1633. While Cotton was not clearly identified with the antinomian movement while in England, he began to show his sympathies for this approach to both Christian living and the need for assurance of faith for the Christian in his Boston pastorate.[28] A Christian woman, Anne Hutchinson (1591-1643), who had frequently come under Cotton's preaching ministry in old England, emigrated with her husband to Massachusetts soon after Cotton. In Boston she took Cotton's ideas further than did the preacher himself. In a sermon discussion group she hosted in her own home, she denounced regional pastors who stressed the conventional role of the moral law for the Christian as "legal." As she claimed to have assurance of her salvation by direct promptings from heaven, she disparaged careful walking in the laws of God as the way forward in gaining assurance of salvation. As in old England, such teaching was construed both as implying a kind of familiarity with God not promised to ordinary believers and as threatening upright living.[29]

---

[28]Reformed theology allowed that a Christian could grow in assurance of faith, in part, as he or she observed an advance or growth in grace characterized by happy obedience to the laws of God. Antinomians denied this use of the law and claimed that Christians had assurance of their acceptance before God *directly* by the inner working of the Holy Spirit. Obedience to the moral law was more or less irrelevant in the assurance question.

[29]Bozeman, *Precisionist Strain*, chap. 14; David D. Hall, *The Antinomian Controversy: 1636-1638* (Middletown, Conn.: Wesleyan University Press, 1968), pp. 4-23.

It was only with difficulty that John Cotton extricated himself from the inquiry of a synod of the colony's churches; he eventually gave sufficient satisfaction to their stated concerns that no further action was taken against him. However, Anne Hutchinson was eventually banished from Massachusetts and took up residence in what would become Rhode Island. Another emigrant pastor associated with the antinomian emphasis, John Wheelwright (1592-1679), was also banished from the colony in 1637; he relocated to New Hampshire. In face of questions about his soundness from both sides of the Atlantic, it was with some difficulty that John Cotton eventually rehabilitated his reputation. By 1648, while denying that he had ever truly been antinomian, he could write:

> the errors of Antinomianism and Familism stirring in the country and condemned in the synod at Newton were not more dangerous than the old Montanism. I confess the Familism afterwards broached by Mr. Gorton and his followers (was) the same which Calvin refuteth (in his *Instructio Adversus Libertinos*). . . . Both of them overthrow all principles and foundations of Christian religion.[30]

As in old England, all that can properly be said is that these expressions of antinomianism arose within a Reformed or Calvinist context, and that in this context antinomianism was repudiated as an aberration.

Georgian Britain. This is not the end of the story, however, for in the eighteenth century we stumble upon fresh allegations of antinomianism—but now, not from within the Calvinist movement but rather from outside it. It is apparent that the republication in 1690 of the *Collected Works* of Tobias Crisp, an antinomian writer of the early seventeenth century, set in circulation throughout the first half of the next century ideas that were unsound in tendency.[31]

Crisp's ideas, once recirculated, helped to fuel what is called the "high Calvinist" tendency among Congregationalists and Baptists in

---

[30]John Cotton, *The Way of the Congregational Churches Cleared* (1648), in Hall, *Antinomian Controversy*, pp. 397-98. The Samuel Gorton referred to by Cotton was banished from Massachusetts in 1644.

[31]See the prior allusion to Tobias Crisp on p. 159. For the negative influence of his republished works see Toon, *Influence of Hyper-Calvinism*, pp. 28, 49.

England. High Calvinism, even if it did not disparage the role of the moral law in the life of the Christian believer, certainly extended the reach of ideas such as justification from eternity, the dependence on secret promptings of the Holy Spirit to provide assurance of salvation, and the inconsequentiality of sin in the life of the Christian.[32]

In addition to the clearly negative criticism directed toward this tendency by responsible orthodox English Presbyterians and Congregationalists such as Daniel Williams (1643-1716), there was soon added the voice of John Wesley (1703-1791) and his lieutenant, the Anglican minister of Madeley, John Fletcher (1729-1785). While the two were careful to designate high Calvinism rather than all Calvinism as the seedbed of antinomian excess, Wesley's denunciations alarmed the entire English Calvinist community and contributed to what is now called the "Minutes Controversy" of 1770.[33]

John Fletcher, who functioned as the "apologist" for Wesley's approach to the antinomian danger, defended Wesley's utterances by writing:

> I could not help seeing that it was only to guard them and their hearers against Antinomian principles and practices, which spread like wild fire in some of his [i.e., Wesley's] societies; where persons who spoke in the most glorious manner of Christ, and their interest in his complete salvation, have been found living in the greatest immoralities, or indulging the most unchristian tempers.[34]

It is important to note that at this date in the final third of the eighteenth century, the leaders of the Wesleyan movement showed an awareness not only of the recirculating antinomianism of Crisp (from the preceding century) within Protestant Nonconformity, but as well in

---

[32]Toon helpfully describes this tendency (*Emergence of Hyper-Calvinism*, pp. 57-68).

[33]In the 1770 annual conference of the Wesleyan movement, Wesley made remarks, later circulated in printed minutes, in which he warned that in the past Wesleyans "had leaned too much towards Calvinism." He now advocated instead an emphasis that required that professed Christian faith not be considered genuine if isolated from obedience and works of love. Yet he was construed as advocating works righteousness. The best available treatment of this controversy is provided by Patrick Streiff, *Reluctant Saint? A Theological Biography of Fletcher of Madeley* (Peterborough, U.K.: Epworth, 2001), chap. 12.

[34]John Fletcher, *Checks to Antinomianism: First Book* (1771; reprint, London: Hill & Eaton, 1899), letter two.

the Moravian movement, which the Wesleyan movement had been informally allied with. Further, we detect the penetration of these views into the collected "societies" (we would call them "cell groups") in which Wesley's own followers met for fellowship and teaching. Recent investigations have made plain just how regularly the charge of antinomianism was leveled at Wesley and his movement by external critics, and just how great was the notoriety of certain secondary leaders of the Wesleyan movement whose lives came to be associated with debauchery and marital infidelity.[35] John Wesley's own brother-in-law, Westley Hall, while not the only example of this duplicity (he actually advocated polygamy and attempted to practice it serially), was certainly the most notorious of these.

The Wesleyan protest therefore had had real, rather than imaginary grounds for concern; yet the problem was internal to, as well as external to, the Wesleyan movement. Nonconformist Calvinists did not so effectively rebuke the antinomian tendencies of high Calvinism in the balance of the century. Particularly those branches of British Nonconformity that lacked access to higher education tended to keep alive the old seventeenth-century notions (justification from eternity, the non-necessity of the confession of present sin, the nonnecessity of self-examination) that had been linked with the antinomianism of that age. It is only fair to point out that certain Nonconformists held these views *without* neglecting the role of the Ten Commandments for the Christian's life.[36] Perhaps the most sensational late-eighteenth-century exponent of this cluster of views was William Huntington (1745-1813), the pastor of London's Providence Chapel.[37]

---

[35]Two recent treatments of the Wesleyan movement in the eighteenth century deal discerningly with this question. See W. Stephen Gunter, *The Limits of Love Divine: John Wesley's Response to Antinomianism and Enthusiasm* (Nashville: Abingdon, 1989), see especially chap. XII; also Patrick Streiff, *Reluctant Saint?*, chaps. 12, 13. It becomes apparent, especially in Gunter's fine study, that the Methodist movement would have been alleged to be antinomian in tendency by its critics simply on account of its preaching a message of justification by faith alone; that there were also some notorious moral hypocrites associated with the movement only served to convince some people of the actual tendency of Methodist teaching.

[36]On the passage of this high Calvinism through the eighteenth century and the factors that gave it its peculiar stamp, see Toon, *Influence of Hyper-Calvinism*, chap. 5, esp. pp. 146-52.

[37]J. H. Y. Briggs, "Huntington, William," in *Blackwell Dictionary of Evangelical Biography: 1730-1860*, ed. Donald M. Lewis (Oxford: Blackwell, 1995), 1:586.

And if it were to be supposed that this tendency was limited to England in this period, we find in the example of the Swiss Calvinist preacher César Malan (1787-1864) ample proof that these tendencies knew no international boundaries. Malan, who often preached in Britain, was simultaneously a high Calvinist and a fervent evangelist, yet those who listened closely to his evangelistic sermons observed the notes we have identified already: the justification of the sinner was a present, preexisting reality, only waiting to be acknowledged in faith; the gospel invitation need not require heartfelt repentance, only faith; the enjoyment of Christian assurance entailed no self-examination to locate evidences of progress in grace, but only taking to heart the promise of 1 John 5:1 that whoever affirms that Jesus is God's Son is born of God. Malan, no less than Huntington, was often censured for articulating this untenable position.[38]

Getting perspective. It is important to reflect on what has and has not emerged in this two-century overview of evangelical and Reformed history. We find no moral license advocated on the basis of the predestinarian doctrine known to be associated with Calvinism; we find only a tendency in some Calvinists of extreme views to so grossly exaggerate the ineradicable position of Christian believers that the practical obligation to obey God's laws inside the Christian life has been underemphasized. Mainstream Calvinism has generally been the first to point out this imbalance; it finds in this tendency to antinomianism a perversion of something very valuable, that is, the true fact that the person who is "in Christ" *has* a new position and a new nature. When there have been criticisms of the presence of this tendency within Calvinism by outsiders such as Wesleyans, Wesleyans have generally recognized that their own nonpredestinarian movement has also afforded some fertile ground for the sprouting of this antinomian error.

---

[38]Malan's career is sketched by John B. Roney, "Malan, César," in *Blackwell Dictionary of Evangelical Biography*, 2:736, and his theological views plumbed by Kenneth J. Stewart, *Restoring the Reformation: British Evangelicalism and the Francophone 'Réveil' 1816-1849* (Carlisle, U.K: Paternoster, 2006), pp. 207-12.

THE CONTEMPORARY SCENE

This chapter began with the acknowledgment of three notorious cases of marital unfaithfulness from the sixteenth century. Each took place within a distinct expression of Christianity (Lutheran-Calvinist, Catholic and Anabaptist), and yet there has grown up the strong prejudice that one subgroup of these—the Reformed Protestant—is *especially* prone to foster this kind of disobedience. We have found very little evidence to support this prejudice. When dispassionately considered, the evidence points in a quite different direction: that the tendency to disregard the moral law of God has been present far too often in a whole range of branches of Christianity.

We find a depressing amount of evidence of this antinomian tendency at the present time. It is fascinating to reflect on (if loud reports in the Christian and public press are to be taken as representative) the epidemic entailing: the misuse of charitable donations by registered Christian charities and of some Christian institutions by the Christian leaders who preside over them; the abuse of young children by Christian leaders, both Protestant and Catholic; far too many cases of marital infidelity among Christian leaders and their loyal followers; and the staggering evidence that Christians—driven by the covetous desire to acquire—are staggering under unsustainable debt obligations. And we must all face up to the fact that we have been pressed by our culture, which prides itself on doing business 24/7, to embrace views about the Christian day of rest and worship that are so accommodating as to be pathetic.

Is the usual suspect, predestination, to blame for this epidemic? Hardly! The epidemic I am alluding to has affected Christians who hold a whole range of opinions about that doctrine. The root of our problem is that we have ceased to love God supremely; God's law reflects his holiness and purity, and lack of respect for his laws is an expression of lack of reverence for him. We have not only loved God too little, we have gone on loving this world order inordinately (see Ex 20:3; Mt 22:37; 1 Jn 2:15-17). How did our Christian civilization descend to such a level?

This has happened for more than one reason. The secular spirit of our age has urged us to adopt the attitude that there are no fixed moral absolutes and that we can, at best, be guided by love in making moral choices.[39] The growing trend toward religious pluralism works to discount moral absolutes taught by any particular scriptures (be they Hebrew, Hindu, Islamic or Christian) in favor of some less-defined consensus view of morality.

Moreover, within Christian churches there has been a strong tendency, across the twentieth century and into the twenty-first, to treat the Ten Commandments as having primary application to the Old Testament people of God, the people of Israel. In churches influenced by this teaching, there has been a reluctance to go beyond pointing to the ways the commandments of Sinai are woven into the New Testament Scriptures. Christians in these settings, as well as in seeker-friendly churches, will probably never have heard the Ten Commandments recited in a worship service or made the subject of a series of teaching sermons; it is somehow calculated that this is *not* the emphasis that is needed for our time, when people's greatest need is to find Christ.

While the secularist and pluralist attitudes *openly* repudiate the abiding value of the Ten Commandments, the latter two (neglecting the gospel for theological reasons and neglecting the gospel for pragmatic reasons, both of which are Christians' attitudes) involve a *practical* discounting (by utter deemphasis) of the abiding role of God's laws. This latter kind of calculation mistakenly supposes that human sinfulness can be identified and the attractiveness of taking Jesus Christ as Savior can be highlighted without reference to God's absolute standards of goodness. If the reader recognizes the antinomian tendency as alive and well today, this question may be fitting: What ongoing place do the Ten Commandments themselves or the endorsements of them given in the New Testament have in popular teaching about Christian living, and in the worship life of the church? In posing this question it must also be stressed that the Christian must depend on the resources of the indwelling Holy Spirit for help in observing the commands. But with that acknowledged, is it not the case that steadily fewer professed

---

[39]Joseph Fletcher, *Situation Ethics* (Philadelphia: Westminster Press, 1966).

Christians can even name the Commandments and that many pastors have never preached sermons on them?

It will seem ironic to some readers that this chapter, having begun with a view to exploring whether the Reformed tradition might perhaps encourage antinomianism more than any other version of Christianity, now ends by urging the opposite. The Reformed theological tradition by its doctrinal confessions and catechisms,[40] its pattern of worship (which has generally, in the past, entailed a reading of the Ten Commandments or some summary of them in connection with a corporate confession of sin),[41] and its pulpit ministry has assuredly paid as much heed to the law of God as any expression of the Christian faith. If the Reformed theological tradition stays true to its historic bearings on this question, it may actually offer a helping hand to many beleaguered Christians in other streams of Christianity who are looking for a way out of our current antinomian malaise.

DISCUSSION QUESTIONS

1. You probably didn't call it "antinomianism," but did you ever have a serious discussion about the problem of prominent Christians breaking the Ten Commandments? If so, what did you identify as the underlying problem?

2. This chapter has argued that there is no cause-and-effect relationship between Calvinism and disregard of God's laws. If that idea can be set aside, what do you point to instead as contributing to the pervasive disregard of the Ten Commandments today?

3. Sometimes, over past centuries, advocates of the antinomian tendency have tried to justify their point of view by complaining about a kind of hair-splitting Christian legalism, which they wish to avoid. Is this argument being repeated today?

---

[40]I refer here to the Westminster Confession of Faith and Catechisms, the Belgic and French Confessions of Faith, the Thirty-Nine Articles of the Church of England, and the Heidelberg Catechism.

[41]The commandments are recorded in Ex 20 and Deut 5; they are summarized by Christ at Mt 22:34-40.

FURTHER READING

Davidman, Joy. *Smoke on the Mountain: An Interpretation of the Ten Commandments*. Philadelphia: Westminster Press, 1954.

Packer, J. I. *Growing in Christ*. Wheaton, Ill.: Crossway, 2008.

Schaeffer, Edith. *Ten Things Parents Must Teach Their Children*. Grand Rapids: Raven's Ridge, 1994.

Wallace, Ronald S. *Ten Commandments: A Study of Ethical Freedom*. Grand Rapids: Eerdmans, 1965.

Watson, Thomas. *The Ten Commandments*. 1692. Reprint, London: Banner of Truth, 1965.

Antique Justice—or Theocracy?
Image: Clipart.com

MYTH SEVEN

Calvinism Leads to Theocracy

The-oc-ra-cy. **1.** Government of a state by the immediate direction or administration of God; hence, the exercise of political authority by priests as representing the Deity. **2.** The state thus governed, as the Hebrew commonwealth before it became a kingdom.

—*Webster's Revised Unabridged Dictionary*

WHILE THE TERM *THEOCRACY* IS frequently bandied about in modern culture, it is never used in an approving sense. In Western nations such as the United States, there are many who fear the political aspirations of conservative Christians; these are alleged to have nothing less than the establishment of a theocracy as their objective. What that theocracy would specifically entail we are left to imagine. We also hear it suggested that certain Middle Eastern societies are theocracies; in such societies religious leaders stand above elected political officials and offer either religious affirmation or censure for the way the government and public life are conducted. Yet these two scenarios are hardly identical.

In the first, what apprehensive persons fear is not the conduct of the nation's affairs by members of the Christian clergy (of whatever stripe) but the quite distinguishable scenario of the conduct of a nation's affairs by any persons in a way that is openly informed by the Christian Scriptures and Christian moral precepts. Because it is surmised this would happen in a way that would jeopardize the existence and opinions of those of other faiths or no faith, strenuous opposition is judged to be appropriate. On this reckoning, theocracy is implied to be the opposite of cultural pluralism. This is quite a reach from the term's historical meaning.

What of the second situation? In it, there is quite clearly a demonstration of what happens to a society where religious leaders stand above all other officials and citizens, either lending legitimacy by their commendation or withholding it by their censure. This present-day phenomenon, traces of which can be found in our news broadcasts and daily newspapers, seems to conform quite well to the historical definition of theocracy. It is not what we would wish for. But our question is not whether theocracy now exists in certain Middle Eastern countries but whether the Christian church, and in particular the Protestant church since the Reformation, advocated or achieved theocracy in similar terms. Many would suspect this to be the case.

THEOCRACY IN THE CHRISTIAN TRADITION

Through the fifteenth century. The fact of the matter is that for centuries at a time one expression of Christianity *did* demonstrate some theocratic tendencies in the Mediterranean and Western world. This was Western Christianity, the figurehead of which came to be the bishop of Rome. Gradually, after the relocation of the capital of the empire from Rome to Constantinople in A.D. 330, and still more rapidly after Rome was successively sacked by Visigoths in 410 and abandoned as a Western regional imperial capital in 476, the bishop of Rome came to be reckoned the chief citizen of that city and of the former Western dominions that the empire (now headquartered at Constantinople) had formerly ruled from Rome. Through the affirmation by successive bishops of Rome that their city's Christian movement had gained something intangible through past association with both the apostles Peter and Paul (who were accepted to have met their deaths there), and the vacuum effect created by the withdrawal of the emperor eastward across the Balkans to Constantinople, exalted claims were made claiming superiority for Rome's bishop over both the whole Mediterranean church and temporal rulers in the former Western empire. These claims amount to what could be properly termed *papal theocracy*, that is, a determination to seize supremacy of a jurisdiction. In a letter addressed to Emperor Anastasius at Constantinople, Pope Gelasius I wrote from Rome in A.D. 494:

> There are two powers, august Emperor, by which this world is chiefly ruled, namely, the sacred authority of the priests and the royal power. Of these, that of the priests is the more weighty, since they have to render an account for even the kings of men in the divine judgment. You are also aware, dear son, that while you are permitted honorably to rule over human kind, yet in things divine you bow your head humbly before the leaders of the clergy and await from their hands the means of your salvation. In the reception and proper disposition of the heavenly mysteries you recognize that you should be subordinate rather than superior to the religious order, and that in these matters you depend on their judgment rather than wish to force them to follow your will.[1]

Such a claim to the precedence for spiritual leaders over their political counterparts presupposed two things. *First*, it presupposed the existence of a civilization that had given an increasingly honored place to the Christian church since the cessation of persecution in A.D. 313; without this now-traditional deference to Christianity, the bishop of Rome could never have presumed to issue such instructions as these.[2] *Second*, it presupposed sustained reflection by Christian thinkers on the meaning of certain Scriptures bearing on the relationship of Jesus Christ to the political order of the world. One such Scripture was

---

[1]Gelasius I, "Gelasius on Spiritual and Temporal Power," in *Readings in European History*, ed. J. H. Robinson (Boston: Ginn, 1905), pp. 72-73. Pope Gelasius's opinion reflected in this document demonstrates how the self-conception of the papacy had developed over the period since 330, when the bishop of Rome had ceased to exist in the immediate shadow of the emperor.

[2]Geoffrey Barraclough reports that even as he articulated this theory of papal-imperial relations, Gelasius had the backing of the Goth leader Theodoric, now in control of the Italian peninsula (*The Medieval Papacy* [London: Thames & Hudson, 1968], p. 28).

Revelation 1:5, in which Jesus Christ is described as "ruler of the kings of the earth." Now if Jesus Christ is claimed to have such a role, and if (as Roman Christianity claimed) his chief representative on earth was the Christian bishop of that city, then the question could legitimately be posed as to *how* Christ's rule over earthly rulers ought to be demonstrated. Gelasius believed he knew the answer to this question: earthly rulers ought to yield to the superior authority of Christ's representative on earth at Rome. Successive bishops of Rome pressed this claim very hard.

Two ironies attach themselves to this claim advanced by successive bishops of Rome. On the one hand, the counterpart of the bishop of Rome at Constantinople, the patriarch of that newer imperial capital, made no such claim—proximate as he was to the seat of imperial power. No, at Constantinople, there was an understanding that the power of the emperor and the power of the church were coordinate. The Christian emperor had a responsibility to seek the welfare of the church, as of his empire as a whole; deference was paid by the patriarch to the emperor on whose kindness and support the well-being of the Greek-speaking churches was understood to depend. It was a rare thing for Orthodox patriarchs to attempt to remind the emperor of the limits of his power.[3] On the other hand, history would show that the grand claims to jurisdictional superiority advanced by the bishops of Rome were exaggerated and lacking in bite. In the year 756, the current bishop of Rome, Stephen II, found himself besieged by invaders from the north; these were the Lombards, whose leaders cared not a whit for Stephen's claim to outrank them in God's sight. When appeals for help to Constantinople met deaf ears, the Roman bishop was delivered from the Lombards by the military intervention of Pepin III, the Frankish king. Pepin the conqueror then formally bestowed territories in northeast Italy upon the Roman bishop; they became known as the Papal States. In this era was forged the celebrated "Donation of Constantine," a document which alleged that after a miraculous cure from leprosy, the first Christian emperor had given to Rome's bishop his Lateran palace

---

[3]Joan Hussey, *The Orthodox Church in the Byzantine Empire* (Oxford: Oxford University Press, 1986), pp. 301-2.

and jurisdiction over all his Western territories.[4] This document, shown in 1440 by the Italian scholar Valla to be fictitious, aimed to make it appear that the papacy's aspiration to supremacy over Western rulers and territories were aspirations provided for by Constantine's action.[5]

Such claims of jurisdiction over Western Europe and its temporal rulers were held in check by Emperor Charlemagne, who clearly believed that the bishop of Rome was his dependent. Yet subsequently the bishops of Rome successfully worked to make the right of Charlemagne's descendants to rule appear to be dependent on papal blessing. One such bishop, Nicholas I, who presided at Rome from 858 to 867, claimed not only to be able to sanction those who aspired to rule but to intervene against those who ruled unjustly.[6] Yet the claim of Roman bishops to jurisdictional supremacy over earthly rulers was one that could only be made good with the military might provided by supportive temporal rulers. If under threat and lacking this backup, Rome's claims of superiority had no plausibility and went unheeded.

In a period commencing with the election of the monk Hildebrand as Pope Gregory VII in 1073, these claims of supreme jurisdiction in the West—even over temporal rulers—were reasserted. Sparks flew, with the particular bone of contention being the question of whether kings and emperors *or* the bishop of Rome had the right to nominate local bishops. While, considered in the abstract, this right of nomination might seem fitting for the bishop at Rome; kings and emperors professing Christianity had increasingly taken this role upon themselves since their barbarian peoples' acceptance of Christian baptism and instruction brought with it a need for the rapid religious organization of territorial life. If Roman popes could exert claims in support of *papal* theocracy, kings and emperors—following Charlemagne—could claim to exercise a *royal* theocracy on behalf of the church in their ter-

---

[4] The text of the "Donation of Constantine" is available in Henry Bettenson and Chris Maunder, eds., *Documents of the Christian Church*, 3rd ed. (New York: Oxford University Press, 1999), pp. 107-10.

[5] See major excerpts of Valla's treatise on the falsity of the Donation of Constantine in G. R. Elton, ed., *Renaissance and Reformation: 1300-1648*, 3rd ed. (New York: Macmillan, 1976), pp. 58-61.

[6] Barraclough, *Medieval Papacy*, p. 58.

ritories.[7] After all, Rome did not very easily exert its authority on the frontiers of northern and western Europe in the pre-A.D. 1000 era characterized by poor and slow communication.

But after 1073 this changed because an active pope, Gregory VII, began to reassert traditional papal claims of supremacy, which had recently gone underenunciated. We could say that this bishop of Rome won the battle (in the particular contest with German emperor Henry IV over the issue of the right to nominate bishops) and yet, over time, lost the war (the attempt to establish the supremacy of spiritual authority over temporal). Having threatened to excommunicate Henry IV for his intrusion into a matter the pope reserved for himself (and such an excommunication would have incited his subjects to rebel against him), he justified his doing so with this line of reasoning:

> Shall not an authority founded by laymen [i.e., monarchy]—even those who do not know God,—be subject to that authority which the providence of God Almighty has for his own honor established and in his mercy given to the world? Who does not know that kings and leaders are sprung from men who were ignorant of God, who by pride, robbery, perfidy, murders . . . have striven with blind cupidity and intolerable presumption to dominate over their equals, that is, over mankind?[8]

The zenith had not yet been reached, however, in this Roman attempt to hold supreme power. This would occur during the pontificate of a successor to Gregory, Innocent III, who in 1198 depicted the relations of pope and emperor thus:

> The Creator of the universe set up two great luminaries in the firmament of heaven; the greater light to rule the day, the lesser light to rule the night. In the same way for the firmament of the universal Church, which is spoken of as heaven, he appointed two great dignities, the greater to bear rule over souls (these being, as it were, days), the lesser to bear rule over bodies (those being, as it were, nights). The dignities are the pontifical authority and the royal power. Furthermore the moon

---

[7]This helpful terminology is supplied by Robert Walton, *Zwingli's Theocracy* (Toronto: University of Toronto Press, 1967), p. 18.

[8]Gregory VII, "Gregory VII's Letter to the Bishop of Metz," in *Documents of the Christian Church*, p. 116.

derives her light from the sun, and is in truth inferior to the sun in both size and quality. . . . In the same way the royal power derives its dignity from the pontifical authority.[9]

This was the zenith because over time the legitimate ambitions of Europe's rising nation states, such as France and England, worked to curtail papal power. An unlimited exercise of power by the bishop of Rome involving his questioning of the legitimacy of rule of monarchs and heads of state was no longer considered tenable.[10] Such presumption had its origin in a day when the former Roman Empire in the West lay in shambles. By the fifteenth century it was becoming clear that the assertive rising nations and the major cities of Europe that had the status of "Imperial City" within the Holy Roman Empire would no longer tolerate this kind of papal pretension. In their view this pretended supremacy of Rome had led to presumption and decay in the church and clergy across Europe. After approximately one thousand years in which European nations favorable to Christianity had shown varying degrees of deference toward the claimed authority of the successive bishops of Rome, the notion of papal theocracy—the superiority of spiritual to political authority—had largely expired. Still-Catholic European governments believed it was time for the temporal authorities (which Rome had long claimed to trump) to have a hand in rectifying the church's glaring accumulated woes.

After the birth of Protestantism. When the Protestant Reformation commenced, did Protestantism in general and Calvinism in particular only reassert the theocratic tendencies which Roman Christianity had exhibited in the period up through the fifteenth century? We shall find that the answer is both no and yes. The answer must be no inasmuch as the Western European Christendom over which the medieval papacy had formerly held sway had already given way to a Europe in which smaller political units, still holding to the Catholic faith, would vie

---

[9]Innocent III, "The Moon and the Sun" (1198), in *Documents of the Christian Church*, p. 123.
[10]An example of this far-reaching wielding of this power was Innocent III's deposing of the English King John in 1209 and his invitation to the king of France to invade England with the papal blessing. See "The Pope's Interdict on England," in *Documents of the Christian Church*, p. 178.

with one another for European supremacy while reminding the bishop of Rome of his reduced ability to intervene across their boundaries.[11] The Reformation movements wanted no papal attempts to claim jurisdictional supremacy. These movements, as they arose, accepted this emergent conception of national or regional political sovereignty and the right of that political authority to supervise the direction of the church. Working with the assumption that the surrounding society (political leadership included) was a Christian entity, a *corpus Christianum*, they accepted the appropriateness of national or regional political authority superintending the affairs of the church.[12] In its own way, this understanding that political sovereignty properly extended into the supervision of the church represented a resurgence of the older royal theocracy idea, which the papal sovereignty had struggled against for so long.

Because of the Protestant movement's recognition of the legitimacy of the exercise of political authority in matters touching the church, the main streams of the Reformation (Lutheran, Reformed, Anglican, but not Anabaptist) are termed *magisterial*.[13] Therefore, no one can credibly argue that the mainstream Reformation promoted theocratic arrangements of a kind analogous to the old papal variety; in virtually every territory of Europe that embraced the Reformation, clergy served a "territorial" church over which the governing authority had extensive jurisdictional claims. One might say that the state was the paymaster of

---

[11]This limitation of papal power by a rising nation-state found its classic expression in the "Pragmatic Sanction of Bourges" of 1438, issued under King Charles VII of France. Excerpts may be viewed in G. R. Elton, ed., *Renaissance and Reformation: 1300-1648*, 3rd ed. (New York: Macmillan, 1976), pp. 22-23.

[12]Walton, *Zwingli's Theocracy*, p. 28. Not very far in the background of this altered conception of the role of the nation-state in superintending the affairs of the church was the treatise of the conciliarist Marsiglio of Padua (1275-1342), *Defensor Pacis* (1324). I have consulted the portion of *Defensor* excerpted in Elton's *Renaissance and Reformation*, pp. 5-7. Marsiglio explicitly insisted on the competence of territorial rulers to determine a candidate's fitness for ecclesiastical office (*Defensor Pacis*, 2.17.15).

[13]Timothy F. George credits the late George H. Williams with having originated the term *magisterial* and describes it thus: "All the mainline reformers carried out their reformatory work in alliance with and undergirded by the coercive power of the magistrate, whether it be prince, town council, or . . . the monarch himself" (Timothy F. George, *Theology of the Reformers* [Nashville: Broadman, 1988], p. 98).

the Reformation church.[14] This is the "no" part of the equation.

And yet, having said this, we are still left to deal with the very widespread impression that the Reformation churches and their clergy *did* exert influence in their societies, influences which went *some* distance toward filling out the picture described in the definition of theocracy introduced at the start of this chapter: "Government of a state by the immediate direction or administration of God, hence, the exercise of political authority by priests as representing the Deity." Yet what kind of theocracy could be erected in a setting where reform was introduced by and regulated by Christian *civil* authorities who were not themselves members of the clergy? Our quest now leads us away from the older Roman concern for ultimate jurisdictional supremacy to the distinct concern for the right ordering of the church and the supervision of Christian morals. It is at this level that modern persons strongly suspect that the Reformation movements definitely nurtured theocracy. Let us consider three case studies.

Zurich. Zwingli, the leading reformer of Zurich, had come to that city in 1519 to serve as priest in the great Munster, a church formerly attached to a Benedictine monastery. From the pulpit of this church he commenced a reform program that emphasized the consecutive exposition of entire biblical books, commencing with the Gospel of Matthew. His allegiance to the jurisdiction of Rome and the papacy diminished by degrees; in 1520 he resigned a pension he had been receiving from the papacy, and by October 1522 he resigned his position as priest. The reform-minded city council became his sole employer; he was now given responsibility for pressing forward with a preaching program in the entire city.[15] Zwingli was content, in keeping with this employment relationship under the city fathers, not to press the reform program beyond a pace they could approve. It was they, not he, who authorized religious change; so, when restrictions were introduced regarding any further use of religious images in churches and the celebration of the

---

[14]Of course, the exception to this generalization were the Anabaptist movements, which, in principle, rejected both any jurisdictional role for the state over the church and any conception of the church dictating to society at large.

[15]George, *Theology of the Reformers*, p. 114.

Roman Mass, these restrictions were first deliberated by the civic authorities.

Followers of Zwingli, wanting to challenge the lingering old medieval dietary laws (which insisted that fish replace meat in Friday diets) defied these regulations by enjoying sausages on that day. Zwingli, who supported this change, was content to watch and did not share in the meal; he appealed to the city fathers to abolish these old dietary restrictions and published a sermon on the subject. To be sure, the city fathers' eventual decisions were informed by the teaching of Zwingli, but the pace of change was determined not by the church itself but by the Christian civic government.[16] When Zwingli had entered and won handily two public disputations with the regional Roman authorities, it was the city fathers who decreed that the remaining Catholic clergy in their city should now throw their weight behind the reform program Zwingli had championed.

The church of Zurich, having undergone this reform, which effectively ended Roman jurisdiction in the city, existed thereafter as a kind of department of the total Christian civic life administered by the city. The monitoring of public morals as well as disciplinary excommunication from this church was a civic rather than purely ecclesiastical matter. Under Roman Christianity, consistorial courts had held offenders accountable; after reform came, such responsibilities were added to the duties of the city magistrates. Zurich's pattern of reform set the standard for other German-speaking Swiss cantons. At Zurich, Zwingli and his colleagues were what might be called theological advisers to a magisterial theocracy.[17]

Geneva: Satellite of Bern. One of the German-speaking Swiss cantons that followed the lead of Zurich was Bern. As Zwingli's influence had been determinative in the other canton, so at Bern a significant preparatory influence was exerted as early as the year 1523 by the

[16]Lewis W. Spitz, *The Renaissance and Reformation Movements* (St. Louis: Concordia, 1987), 2:385.

[17]Robert C. Walton, "Zurich," in *Oxford Encyclopedia of the Reformation*, ed. Hans Hillerbrand (Oxford: Oxford University Press, 1996), 4:314. Note also the helpful survey of the coordinate roles of church and political authority in Alister McGrath, *Reformation Thought*, 2nd ed. (Oxford: Basil Blackwell, 1993), chap. 10.

preacher Berchtold Haller (c. 1492-1536). The early 1520s were a period when the cantonal government promoted church reform along Erasmian lines; this was not originally anti-Roman. After a 1528 public disputation authorized by the city government, this canton officially embraced the Reformation. Delegates of other Swiss cantons had been invited to this disputation; one of them, Zwingli of Zurich, played a very prominent part by preaching a public sermon attacking the Roman Mass and the use of religious images in churches. At this point Bern's reform became another instance of magisterial Reformation, with the pace and extent of further religious change firmly in the hands of the city fathers.[18] As in Zurich, so in Bern the reprimanding of public sin and any excommunication of the impenitent from the church became the duty of the city magistrates. As a further indication of the overarching supervision of the Reformation movement in Bern, there is the fact (noted earlier) that the city fathers placed controls on the preaching and debating of the doctrine of predestination, so eager were they to prevent public dissension in their young Reformation.[19]

After that disputation, and with Bern's support, Guillaume Farel (1489-1565) and Pierre Viret (1511-1571) began to preach first in the Bernese but French-speaking region adjacent to Lake Geneva known as the Pays de Vaud, and then in 1532 beyond the canton's boundary, at Geneva. They rapidly gained the approbation of the city fathers. Without this activity of Farel and Viret in promoting the cause of the reform and the military backing received from Bern, it is extremely unlikely that Geneva's city government would have acted as they did to embrace the Reformation in 1535. The pattern of reform being followed in Geneva, from the time in 1535 when the prince-bishop of governing Savoy was declared to have no more jurisdiction over the city, was none other than the Bernese model. Bern assisted Geneva religiously and militarily against its foe as part of a larger plan to exclude the longstanding reach of Savoy into the region of Switzerland west of Lake Geneva. Geneva would be extremely dependent for the next forty years on a

---

[18]Heinrich Richard Schmidt, "Bern," in *Oxford Encyclopedia of the Reformation*, 1:144.
[19]See the discussion of Bern as an example of a Reformation city that was not zealously predestinarian in chap. 2.

military alliance offered by Bern. Though not geographically part of
Bernese territory, the little republic of Geneva was nevertheless a satellite of the other city and canton.[20]

John Calvin, at his arrival in Geneva in July 1536 as a refugee in
flight, was prevailed on by the quasi-agent of Bern, Farel, to join him
in the work of implementing the new religious Reformation there. The
two, Farel and Calvin, were in consequence in the employment of the
city fathers, and their labors for Reformation were surely a matter mon-
itored and superintended by the Genevan government, as had been the
ministry of Haller at Bern and of Zwingli at Zurich. This too was a
magisterial reformation; it was also an expression of what in earlier
times was known as princely theocracy, with the role of the prince assumed by the city government. At Geneva, as surely as in the other
Swiss centers, this princely theocracy would extend into both the ordering of the church's affairs and the control of public morals.

Consequently, this princely theocracy resulted in the termination of
the employment of both Farel and Calvin in April 1538; they were
given exactly seventy-two hours to vacate the city.[21] The duo had come
to reflect deeply enough on the Zurich- and Bern-style civic Reformation to have developed certain reservations about it. They did not approve of Bern's insistence that Geneva, so dependent on Bernese might
for its own defense, keep up the traditional religious festivals of Christ-
mas, Easter and Pentecost, which the Geneva Reformers associated
with old Roman practice. They objected also to the notion that the
disciplining and (as necessary) removal of wayward persons from
the church was *not* the church's internal business, but the business of the
city fathers. When they made their disapproval public, they were re-
buffed with the summons to depart. Until 1538, therefore, we may say
that Farel and Calvin took that the kind of princely theocracy on display in Geneva was of a kind which was infringing on the actual prerogatives of the church as Christ intended it.

From Calvin's return to Geneva (from Strasbourg) in 1541 forward

---

[20]William Monter, *Calvin's Geneva* (New York: John Wiley, 1967), p. 64.
[21]John T. McNeill, *The History and Character of Calvinism* (New York: Oxford University Press, 1954), p. 153.

to the middle of the following decade, the large question awaiting satisfactory resolution was that of: how could this princely theocracy the city fathers were determined to wield be modified to provide for a greater freedom of action by the pastors and officers of the church? Calvin only returned to Geneva from his Strasbourg exile when assurances were given that he could present counterproposals to how the affairs of the church vis-à-vis the state could be handled more harmoniously. His proposal, to which appointed delegates of the city government also made a contribution, was put forward as *Draft Ecclesiastical Ordinances*.[22]

On the contested question of whether Bern's preferences for celebrating certain days in the Christian year should be honored, Calvin gained ground. Further, the liturgical forms required for congregations in Bernese territory would now no longer be mandatory in Geneva. Regarding the enhancing of the Geneva church's ability to govern its own members, headway was made in establishing an order of elders (something Calvin had observed firsthand at Strasbourg); yet in this matter the Geneva council was able to insist that *it* would select the elders from the male population of the city and name one of that number (not a minister) to chair this consistory (composed of these elders along with the city ministers).[23] In 1541 there was no rapid resolution in the church's favor of Calvin's determination to see the church have an independent right to excommunicate the wayward; the city government continued (like its Bern counterpart) to insist that this was its own prerogative. Only much later, in 1555, did this same consistory secure the unquestioned right to determine this matter itself.[24]

While Calvin and his ministerial colleagues were making these incremental gains in the direction of a less-encumbered exercise of churchly authority in these matters, they remained to a surprising degree subject to the supervision and admonition of the council who em-

---

[22]The "Ordinances" are available in English translation in J. K. S. Reid, ed., *Calvin's Theological Treatises* (London: SCM Press, 1954), pp. 56-72.

[23]Geneva's city fathers eventually ceded their selection of elders and allowed the congregations to choose them in 1560 (G. D. Henderson, *The Scottish Ruling Elder* [London: James Clarke, 1935], p. 29).

[24]Monter, *Calvin's Geneva*, p. 138.

ployed them. Any Genevan minister could be required to answer to the city government for what were considered to be intemperate remarks made in the pulpit; Calvin was called on the carpet for this numerous times.[25] When Calvin and his colleagues unilaterally decided to forbid parents in the canton from giving their infants birth names associated with various medieval saints formerly honored in the region, there were scenes and uproars in the church services, and the ministers had to answer to the city government. This situation was exacerbated by the fact that the Company of Pastors, to which all clergy belonged, was with one exception composed of French refugees—of which Calvin is the most obvious example.[26] The many Genevan families who took umbrage at these restrictions viewed the pastors with the same disdain as they did the thousands of other French refugees who had recently made their city so crowded. It is significant that Calvin himself was not granted Genevan citizenship until 1559; from his first arrival there in 1536 until 1559, he had the same civic status as that of other French refugees: merely *habitant* (resident).[27] And should we need further reminder that the Geneva pastors did not comprise a kind of patrician class, untouchable in the exercise of their prerogatives, a number of these colleagues of Calvin were forced to demit their ministries when the city government discovered in them serious moral failings that undermined their ability to serve further in the pastoral office.[28]

Do such details warrant us in supposing that Calvin and the company of pastors were treated shoddily by the city fathers? Such a judgment is as unfounded as one of the opposite tendency, that is, to suppose that Calvin and his ministerial fellows were always deferred to by an uncritical government. In fact, there is good reason to believe that the Genevan government generally stood by Calvin and his colleagues when they were attacked without warrant. Thus, when in 1551, Jerome Bolsec publicly derided Calvin's teachings about predestination, the

---

[25]William G. Naphy, *Calvin and the Consolidation of the Genevan Reformation* (Louisville, Ky.: Westminster John Knox, 2003), pp. 159-60.

[26]Ibid., pp. 143-53.

[27]Wulfert de Greef, *The Writings of John Calvin: An Introductory Guide* (Grand Rapids: Baker, 1993), p. 42.

[28]Naphy, *Calvin and the Consolidation of the Genevan Reformation*, pp. 57-79.

chief of police (who was present on the occasion) arrested Bolsec for creating a public disturbance. Eventually, the council of Geneva—after taking advice from other Swiss Protestant cantons—banished Bolsec; this is even more noteworthy because the other cantons consulted did not themselves necessarily endorse every detail of Calvin's view on this doctrine. And Calvin, while vindicated in this particular instance, was chagrined at the fact that the backing of the other cantons on the question itself was somewhat lame.[29]

In the still-more-notorious case of Michael Servetus, executed at Geneva in 1553 for heresy, the situation is admittedly more complex. It is safe to say that there is no incident associated with Calvin's career at Geneva that is alleged to demonstrate more clearly how this Reformer held the city in an iron grip and bent it to do his bidding.[30] We know that the arrest, trial and execution of Servetus at Geneva in 1553 was the sorry culmination of a strange relationship that had existed between Servetus, a Spaniard and Calvin since at least 1546. Since that time there had been correspondence with Calvin; there had been the exchange of parts of book manuscripts in the margins of which each faulted the other's views. Servetus, who dabbled in theology while engaged in work as a physician, held that early Christianity had rapidly declined from its original simplicity. He opposed the baptism of infants as an unwarranted innovation and, most significantly of all, denied the equality of Jesus Christ, the Son of God, with the Father.[31]

Servetus had by the dissemination of such views in person and in print gained a notoriety in both Strasbourg and Basel as well as France. A Genevan known to Calvin, Guillaume de Trie, disclosed in correspondence to a cousin at Vienne (a French Catholic city not far downstream on the Loire from Geneva) that his city was harboring this man (living under an assumed name) who deserved to be considered danger-

---

[29]Monter, *Calvin's Geneva*, pp. 128-31. De Greef, *Writings of Calvin*, pp. 118-21.

[30]So, for instance, even the respected late historian Roland Bainton claimed that "John Calvin was responsible for the execution of Michael Servetus" (*The Travail of Religious Liberty* [Philadelphia: Westminster, 1951], p. 55).

[31]For a sampling of Servetus's actual views, see Lewis W. Spitz, ed. *The Protestant Reformation: Major Documents* (St. Louis: Concordia, 1997), pp. 102-5. Correspondence relative to his trial is reproduced in Clyde Manschreck, ed., *A History of Christianity* (Englewood Cliffs, N.J.: Prentice-Hall, 1964), pp. 96-99.

ous. In corroboration de Trie passed on to his cousin incriminating documents (which had certainly passed through Calvin's hands) that at their arrival in Vienne hastened Servetus's arrest and examination by the Inquisition. From Vienne, Servetus escaped his confinement in June 1553; his frustrated captors burned him in effigy. For reasons that are not clear, Servetus, the fugitive, appeared in a church service in Geneva in August of the same year; there, he was recognized and arrested. Catholic Vienne, learning that Reformed Geneva had its prisoner, requested his extradition so that an existing legal proceeding against him could continue. Servetus himself implored his new captors that he be allowed to remain under Genevan jurisdiction.[32]

We should clarify Calvin's role in this—to the point of the arrest and confinement of Servetus. He had certainly furnished incriminating evidence, through de Trie, to the Catholic authorities at Vienne; he had also furnished to the Geneva city officials—at their request— elaboration of the seriousness of the errors of Servetus. Contrary to popular impressions, the leading city authorities in that year of 1553 were still of a mind that Calvin and his French ministerial colleagues had brought disruption and division to their city; Calvin was no favorite of theirs. A mere two years later the complexion of the city government would shift in the direction of radical sympathy for Calvin, but now—at the time of the Servetus trial—the council had no motivation to flatter their Reformer by agreeing to charges for which they had no sufficient grounds. Indeed, they would not even heed Calvin's plea that the death penalty (for which concurrence had been provided by the other Protestant cantons) not be inflicted by burning. Calvin visited the imprisoned Servetus prior to his execution date, but there was no turning. Farel, Calvin's old colleague then visiting Geneva, accompanied Servetus to his execution—reasoning with him to turn him from his error as they went. Servetus would not forsake his Arianism—the denial of the equality of the Son with the Father. As the Servetus biographer Bainton records it, Servetus met his death praying, "Jesus, son of the Eternal God, have mercy on me"; even in

---

[32]De Greef, *Writings of Calvin*, pp. 174-75; Monter, *Calvin's Geneva*, p. 155.

this withholding an affirmation of eternality to the Son.[33]

What kind of theocracy was this? Certainly not a priestly theocracy. As William Monter has wisely written:

> Calvin's Geneva was indeed a theocracy. This does not imply that she was governed by her clergy; it means rather that Geneva was in theory governed by God through a balance of spiritual and secular powers, through clergy and magistrates acting in harmony. In the sixteenth century, the intimate association of ecclesiastical and the secular government of a community was generally assumed to be both natural and desirable. Furthermore, the sphere of secular government was almost without exception the wider of the two. Geneva scarcely constitutes an exception to this rule.[34]

This being so, care must be taken not to take incidents such as the trial and execution of Servetus as furnishing some esoteric clue to the general tenor of life at Geneva. We might do the same with the information that Geneva forbade gambling, prosecuted dancing and frowned on card playing. At one point, the Company of Pastors advocated the installation of desk Bibles in the city's taverns in the hope that it would promote biblical literacy and spiritual conversation; the practice was discontinued after poor results.[35] Geneva, despite the hue and cry raised by persons determined to depict it as extreme, was—by the standards of the time—rather enlightened. Monter concludes:

> Many accounts of Calvin's Geneva, wishing to illustrate the unbelievable severity of her justice point to a five-year span in which 58 people were executed and 76 banished. Yet all the crimes for which capital sentence was pronounced were also punishable by death in the famous *Constitutio Criminalis Carolina* promulgated earlier in the reign of Charles V by the Diet of Regensburg in 1532. Thirty-eight of Geneva's executions were for witchcraft or for spreading the plague, which the *Carolina* punished with hideous tortures and executions. Among those banished, 27 were tainted with sorcery or with spreading the plague, and 53 were foreigners; banishing foreigners was among the commonest

---

[33]Bainton, *Travail of Religious Liberty*, p. 94.
[34]Monter, *Calvin's Geneva*, p. 144.
[35]Naphy, *Calvin and the Consolidation of the Genevan Reformation*, pp. 30-31.

tactics of any European government in this age. No one was ever executed in Geneva for blasphemy or for disobedience to his parents.[36]

It is important to acknowledge that Geneva was a city-republic of about ten thousand when John Calvin first took up residence there in 1536; even by 1589 the population had only risen to thirteen thousand.[37] We have seen that Geneva took ideas about the godly rule of a Protestant city first displayed in Zurich and then mediated through Bern before adapting these in ways unique to its own situation. The result was a princely theocracy with an eventual enlarged role for independent action by the church. What would happen when these ideas were mediated not to another city or canton but a compact nation?[38]

Scotland. It is not necessary to suppose either that Scotland was determined to be a kind of clone of Geneva, regarding the best way to implement godly rule, or that no other European center of Reformation had anything to contribute to the way the Protestant Reformation was adapted to this nation. We have already acknowledged that, both in terms of the leading personnel of this Reformation and the theological loyalties they brought to their work, diversity was a factor in Scotland's age of Reformation.[39]

It is most plain that the national Reformation enacted into law in Scotland in 1560 conformed to the magisterial pattern we have observed at Zurich, Bern and Geneva. The religious jurisdiction of the bishop of Rome was ended, all former legislation banning Protestant activity was abrogated and new prohibitions outlawing Catholic acts of ministry were introduced by legislation endorsed by a Scottish parliament assembled in August 1560.[40] In this basic legislation, which was

---

[36]Monter, *Calvin's Geneva*, pp. 152-53.

[37]Ibid., p. 2. Calvin had passed away in 1564.

[38]We here pass over the mediation of Swiss ideas of godly rule or theocracy to France and the Spanish Netherlands because the Reformed tradition was not embraced by entire political units but by religious minorities within these countries. Under such political circumstances, the charge of theocracy through the dominance of a single expression of Christianity finds less place.

[39]See myth 1, "One Man (Calvin) and One City (Geneva) Is Determinative," and myth 2, "Calvin's View of Predestination Must Be Ours."

[40]See the documents "1560: Acts of the Reformation Parliament," in *Scottish Historical Documents*, ed. Gordon Donaldson (1970; reprint, Glasgow: Neil Wilson, 1997), pp. 124-26.

aimed at providing a legal basis for the transformation of the existing form of institutional Christianity from Roman to Reformed, we do not find spelled out clear indications of how (if at all) the magisterial model will be implemented; the adaptations emerged in the following months. By January 1561 the appearance of the "First Book of Discipline" indicated that the application of principles from canton to nation had required considerable improvisation. Still more detailed plans were articulated in a "Second Book of Discipline," issued in 1581.

It is apparent that the Scottish plan, adapting Swiss models to a larger geographic terrain, needed to be creative.[41] Not only is the work of disciplining wayward Christians not left to public legal officials (as at Zurich and Bern), it is not left either to a body of individuals chosen by those public officials (as at Geneva). In Scotland, ruling elders were chosen by the congregations from which they hailed and in which they would assist the minister in tending to the spiritual welfare of the people. Very often, ruling elders would be selected from among the professional classes represented in a congregation. In Scotland, ministers or pastors were not employed by the governing authority (as both Zwingli and Calvin were) and assigned to certain congregations, but they were nominated or called (invited) to serve particular congregations, which supported their material welfare by their gifts and by the revenues derived from church lands. In addition, needy churches without pastors were assisted by appointed persons (readers) authorized to read the Scriptures and offer prayers but who, despite the terrible shortage of pastors, were judged not yet adequately prepared to join the ranks of ministers. As there were, in the opening decades of the Scottish church, vast regions where no minister was settled, superintendents were appointed by the General Assembly to provide overarching pastoral oversight over these areas while the acute pastoral shortage endured.

Evidence of this kind strongly suggests that the theocratic ideal of a

---

[41]There is strong reason to believe that those who drafted the two Books of Discipline were conversant not only with Genevan practice but also with the way the French Reformed churches adapted Genevan pastoral oversight practices in their more geographically diffuse situation. See Henderson, *Scottish Ruling Elder*, pp. 32, 37.

godly society underwent development in Scotland, which led the Reformed church to assert a right to exercise a coordinate authority *alongside* the national Christian government rather than as an expression of national Christian government. Whether that national government was the parliament, a monarch or a regent standing in place of a youthful monarch, the Reformed Kirk did not see itself simply as the entire nation "at prayer," or the entire nation considered in its spiritual aspect. The two jurisdictions overlapped but were not coextensive. By the 1580s, and especially as the boy-king James VI began to exert himself in national affairs, he could be reminded by the Reformed Kirk that there were "two kings and two kingdoms" in Scotland. He, James, was king of one of these jurisdictions, but in the other jurisdiction, the church of Jesus Christ, James was only an ordinary subject. This, at least, was how the Calvinists saw matters.[42]

There is strong reason to doubt that this was an acceptable view of things to King James, who as he matured to manhood came to think less and less of a church that understood itself to have an independent authority parallel to his own, and also that considered that its representatives had the right to meet and confer in large assemblies that were devoted to the consideration of multiple aspects of national life. James could press his will on the Scottish parliament but not the Scottish church. Little wonder then that James was eager to attempt to influence the policies of the Kirk by reviving the defunct, pre-Reformation office of bishop. His extended attempt to reinstate what in medieval times would have appropriately been termed a *princely* theocracy was a recipe for decades of strife.

The leaders of the Reformed Church of Scotland were not anti-monarchical; they were instead pursuing a *different* theocratic ideal—one in which the prince's voice and concerns had no more weight in the deliberations of the church than those of any other person. The Christian church was, in their minds, an independent sphere of jurisdiction *within* the political entity known as Scotland. After all, the mandate

---

[42]Gordon Donaldson, *The Scottish Reformation* (Cambridge: Cambridge University Press, 1960), p. 186; Ian B. Cowan, *The Scottish Reformation* (London: Weidenfeld & Nicholson, 1982), p. 124.

for Reformation had not come from the monarch (in 1560 Scotland lacked a resident monarch) but from the parliament. It was not for nothing that critics of this Reformed aspiration for ecclesiastical independence saw parallels with Catholic thought of the Middle Ages and labeled this Scottish aspiration "Hildebrandine" (after the medieval Pope Hildebrand, or Gregory VII, who had opposed Emperor Henry IV). But it would be fairer to typify it not as Hildebrandine (for that aimed at spiritual supremacy over the political order) but as a further adaptation of a Genevan understanding of the role of the church in relation to the state when that Genevan state was a republic rather than a monarchy.

It is sufficient to say that King James (and eventually his son, Charles I) took less kindly to this demand than did the governing council of Geneva in Calvin's last years. The Genevan Christian state could more readily relinquish some of its more pastoral duties to the church because its comprehensive control of its church and people was still virtually complete. The Scottish monarchy, by contrast, had been obliged to accept a parliamentary Reformation settlement that awarded to the Reformed church a far greater range of self-government than Geneva ever granted, and they made it their purpose to try to recover some of that prerogative for the crown.

Meanwhile, at the level of the church parish, it was the elders and ministers of the church who scrutinized the behavior of parishioners in ways that went beyond the requirements of local magistrates. Magistrates concerned themselves with violations of the laws of the land and violations of the peace involving theft, robbery, property and contracts; Kirk sessions (comprised of a minister and elders) looked to see godliness lived out in those who professed to be Christian. Slander, gossip, questions of marital fidelity, fornication, drunkenness, swearing, gambling—these were the vices which the Scottish Reformed Church attempted to root out among parishioners.[43] This community moral scrutiny had gone on prior to the onset of Reform, but generally by members of the Roman clergy; now, with the election of elders within

---

[43]Henderson provides a very even-handed description of this work across three post-Reformation centuries ("Kirk Session Discipline," *Scottish Ruling Elder*, chap. 4).

local congregations, the scrutiny was exercised by nonministerial community members.

CONCLUSION

The Western world has now not known theocracy of *any* kind for centuries. Europe and the Mediterranean world, when they experienced theocracy in its various expressions, were civilizations that accepted without question the idea that a nation or culture could have only one religion and one expression of that one religion. This was the idea of the unitary society. But this idea has been in retreat since the Enlightenment era advanced the idea of religious toleration; in consequence it is now accepted as a given that not only different expressions of Christianity but differing great religions may coexist in a single society. It is fair to say that the real danger of theocracy (in any oppressive sense of the term) in the modern world is not associated with countries that have been the strongholds of Christianity, [44] but instead with those (of more than one kind) that resist both the idea of the coexistence of distinct religions and its counterpart, the idea of the freedom to depart from one religion in order to embrace another. If we want to show moral indignation at intolerance or at the denial of basic human rights, the latter kind of regimes, rather than Reformation Europe, ought to be the focus of our concern.

---

[44]It needs to be acknowledged that within the United States, beginning in the 1970s, the Christian Reconstruction or theonomy movement emerged. Motivated by a concern that the nation was drifting rapidly from its earlier Christian moorings, Reconstruction proposed that Old Testament judicial (as well as moral) law, because reflective of the unchanging holy character of God, must be upheld by leaders and law courts. According to this view the New Testament, describing such officials as "ordained by God" (Rom 13:1) implies that nothing less than God's laws could be their standard. Such views were expounded at length by R. J. Rushdoony in his *The Institutes of Biblical Law*, 3 vols. (Nutley, N.J.: Craig Press, 1973), and popularized by his disciple Greg Bahnsen, *Theonomy in Christian Ethics*, 2nd ed. (Phillipsburg, N.J.: Presbyterian & Reformed, 1984). Two main symposia weighed the claims of theonomy: Gary Scott Smith, ed., *God and Politics: Four Views on the Reformation of Civil Government* (Phillipsburg, N.J.: Presbyterian & Reformed, 1989); and William S. Barker and W. Robert Godfrey, eds., *Theonomy: A Reformed Critique* (Grand Rapids: Zondervan, 1990). In the opinion of this writer, theonomy or Christian Reconstruction did not accurately interpret the New Testament development of Old Testament judicial law or the Reformation-era stance on the applicability of Old Testament judicial law to the Christian era. It might be said that theonomy was theocratic in tendency in that it would have installed religious leaders as the arbiters of the propriety of government policy and judicial ruling.

DISCUSSION QUESTIONS

1. If you periodically hear Calvin's Geneva being held up as the paragon of an oppressive regulation of life and morals, what alternate ways are there of explaining the popularity of this idea? For instance, it may well be that we know far less about *other* sixteenth-century cities. Other possibilities?

2. Geneva in Calvin's day was an extremely popular place for religious refugees and theological students to flock to. The first group, at least, wanted freedom from the harassment they had found at home. Why is this so counterintuitive to the idea of oppressive Geneva?

3. No sixteenth-century European city (Catholic or Protestant) was tolerant of anti-Christian heresy, and extremely few permitted more than one expression of Christianity inside their boundaries. About what time did the complete freedom of religion (or the freedom to be nonreligious), which we today associate with a civilized country, emerge?

FURTHER READING

Kingdon, Robert M. *Geneva and the Consolidation of the French Protestant Movement*. Madison: University of Wisconsin Press, 1967.

McGrath, Alister. *Reformation Thought*. 2nd edition. Oxford: Blackwell, 1993.

Monter, William. *Calvin's Geneva*. New York: John Wiley, 1967.

Naphy, William G. *Calvin and the Consolidation of the Genevan Reformation*. Louisville, Ky.: Westminster John Knox, 2003.

Walton, Robert. *Zwingli's Theocracy*. Toronto: University of Toronto Press, 1967.

Dutch Calvinist Iconoclasm, 1566 from an engraving by Franz
Hogenberg in Michael Aitsinger's "De Leone Belgico" (Cologne, 1588)
Image: Wikipedia

MYTH EIGHT

Calvinism Undermines
the Creative Arts

AT A CRITICAL POINT LATE IN the winter of 1522, Martin Luther left the fortress of Wartburg (to which he had been whisked by "kidnappers" working in service of his own supportive prince, Frederick of Saxony) and returned to his university city of Wittenberg. He could hardly afford to stay away longer, because the young reform movement he had defended at the Diet of Worms, in the prior April, now stood at a crossroads. In Luther's absence, his associate Andreas Bodenstein von Carlstadt (c. 1480-1541) in company with an acquaintance Gabriel Zwilling (1487-1548) had begun to elaborate what they sensed were the practical implications of Luther's reforming ideas. What happened next?

Films in the early twenty-first century such as *Luther* (2003), starring Joseph Fiennes, give the impression that the duo of Carlstadt and Zwilling had, in Luther's absence, created an open season on not only religious custom (such as the Latin Mass) but also artwork and statuary associated with the churches at Wittenberg.[1] Luther is portrayed, at his return to Wittenberg, standing inside a church building that has been utterly gut-

---

[1] *Luther*, directed by Eric Till, RS Entertainment, 2003.

ted. Windows are broken, sculpture and woodwork is cast down and pulverized. Yet this is a very embellished telling of the story. As such, the film has given new life to existing perceptions that the advance of the Reformation necessarily brought with it a comprehensive "climate change" for the arts. Thus, the cultural historian Will Durant, writing in 1957, stated that "art had to suffer from the Reformation, if only because Protestantism believed in the Ten Commandments."[2]

There is no disputing about what changes Carlstadt and Zwilling *proposed;* the question is about what they *accomplished.* Regarding religious customs, they contended that both the bread and the cup should be offered to the laity in the Communion Mass; the Mass itself should give way to a simpler Lord's Supper presided over by pastors wearing no distinctive clerical garb. To make the reforms he described concrete in the public mind, Carlstadt had gone so far as to celebrate the Lord's Supper in shirt sleeves while speaking the words of institution only in the German tongue. Next, students sympathetic to Carlstadt began to harass priests in Wittenberg who were unsympathetic to Carlstadt's program of reform. Regarding religious art, the students began to take to heart Carlstadt's argument, set out in a treatise, *On the Putting Away of Pictures,* that the churches should be cleared of religious images.[3]

But in point of fact, Luther, detecting the early tremors of such disturbances while at Wartburg Castle, determined that the time had come to resume life and ministry at home. He returned in March 1522 and immediately began to pour oil on the troubled waters.[4] He was there before any widespread iconoclasm could be carried out and saw to it that this would not be tolerated in Wittenberg and Saxony.[5] The practical implications of Luther's revolt against Rome would still be worked out (including the implications for the arts), but at a pace

---

[2]Will Durant, *The Story of Civilization,* vol. 6, *The Reformation* (New York: Simon & Schuster, 1957), p. 820.

[3]David C. Steinmetz, *Reformers in the Wings* (Philadelphia: Fortress, 1971), p. 181.

[4]Here, I follow the more cautious narrative provided by Hans J. Hillerbrand in *The Division of Christendom: Christianity in the Sixteenth Century* (Louisville, Ky.: Westminster John Knox, 2007), pp. 78-79. Hillerbrand indicates that popular accounts of widespread iconoclasm in Wittenberg serving as the catalyst for Luther's return are overblown.

[5]The term *iconoclasm* will be used repeatedly in this chapter. A compound of two words of Greek origin, it literally means the breaking or shattering of images.

set by Luther and not his underlings. And Carlstadt, having had his wings clipped at Luther's return, would eventually move on to become a catalyst for more radical reform in south Germany and German Switzerland.

My purpose in this chapter is to untangle myth from reality and to show that the Reformation's response to the various arts in fact varied considerably by region and by brand of Protestantism. Before I can proceed to do so, we must first glance backward from the sixteenth century to grasp the situation that the Reformers of the sixteenth century inherited vis à vis the arts. Doing so will require us to take up the question of the sponsorship of the arts.

PATRONAGE OF THE ARTS BEFORE AND AFTER THE REFORMATION

The question of the Reformation and the various arts is to a great degree tangled up with the related issue of who provided sponsorship or patronage for the arts. The sponsorship of musical composition, painting and sculpture, and dramatic production is largely an economic reality. These arts must, of course, first of all be desired; but artists, musicians and actors must eat. The emergence of the Protestant Reformation in the sixteenth century followed (but did not itself introduce) a change in the sponsorship of the arts, which was about two centuries old.

Until the fourteenth century the sponsorship of the arts in Europe had been largely the domain of the church.[6] The church in Western Europe and the Mediterranean world was the chief sponsor of art because, through the donations of the faithful and through revenues produced both through tithes of agricultural products and revenues from lands which had been bequeathed to the church, it had the financial means to do so. With these means the sponsorship of architectural and artistic works became a way of "summarizing the interaction of God with worldly reality."[7] Ecclesiastical buildings (churches, cathedrals, rectories, monasteries) were erected; both in their external fabric and in their internal décor they required the skill of architects, artisans and

---

[6]The exception to this pattern, of course, would be found in monarchy in the medieval period.
[7]Daniel W. Hardy, "Calvinism and the Visual Arts: A Theological Introduction," in *Seeing Beyond the Word*, ed. Paul Corby Finney (Grand Rapids: Eerdmans, 1999), p. 6.

artists. Regarding artists in particular, church buildings were adorned with murals and frescoes depicting scenes taken from the Bible; there were also portraits to be painted of church dignitaries. This kind of patronage had preceded and would continue beyond the dawn of the Reformation within the Roman Catholic world.

Yet in the late fourteenth century two developments challenged the church's virtual dominance in the sponsorship of art. The first was the growth of mercantile capitalism, which allowed individual families, rooted in the emerging cities and city-states of Europe, to amass very large fortunes through banking, trading textiles, and importing and selling luxury goods obtained from the Indian Ocean region.[8] Families such as the Fuggers of Augsburg, the Medicis of Florence, and the Sforzas of Milan soon had the wherewithal to commence the private sponsorship of art and of fine public buildings. Thus in the city of Padua, Donatello (c. 1386-1466), the Italian sculptor, wrought both a fine bronze crucifix for the high altar of the San Antonio church and a famous public statue showing a prominent warlord Gattamelata astride a war horse.[9] Michelangelo (1475-1564) worked first at Florence, where he produced a wide variety of Madonnas and holy families for private patrons in the city. Summoned to Rome by the pope, Michelangelo was commissioned to design and sculpt a fantastically elaborate tomb (barely begun when the pope decided to build St. Peter's Basilica instead). He sculpted the famous statue *David*, intended to grace one of the buttresses of Florence's cathedral, only to see it repositioned in front of the city's palace after deliberation by leading citizens.[10] Once more in Rome, he created the ceiling frescoes of the papal Sistine chapel.[11] When wealthy citizens sponsored art, they did so not in direct competition with the sponsorship of the church but in a way that augmented it. Sometimes the painting or sculpture commissioned by these private

---

[8]See the description of mercantile capitalism's Italian rise in Lewis W. Spitz, *The Renaissance and Reformation Movements*, vol. 1 (St. Louis: Concordia, 1987), chap. 5.

[9]This public sculpture was provided for in the will of the late Gattamelata and authorized by the council of Florence.

[10]Bard Thompson, *Humanists and Reformers: A History of the Renaissance and Reformation* (Grand Rapids: Eerdmans, 1996), pp. 258-59.

[11]Spitz, *Renaissance and Reformation*, 1:208, 220, 221; Bard Thompson, *Humanists and Reformers*, chap. 11.

patrons took up biblical themes (as with Michelangelo's *David*); sometimes citizen-sponsored art was placed in churches. But clearly, the ownership and enjoyment of art would now be no longer so concentrated in church buildings and focused so entirely on religious purposes. This bifurcation of sponsorship long preceded religious reform.

The second factor was remarked on earlier in a different context: the emergence of territorial governments (both at the national and city-state level), which made it their business to resist the claims to universal jurisdiction enunciated by successive bishops of Rome.[12] As these national and regional governing authorities enunciated their own claims to wide jurisdiction (extending over the church also) ever more forcefully, they also took it upon themselves to become the patrons and sponsors of large public buildings (whether palaces or halls of government), of paintings (portraits and murals), and of sculpture. Our question of interest, however, is whether such emergent governments gave comparable priority to the promotion of the arts such as had characterized the earlier period of ecclesiastical dominance.

THE DIFFERENCE THE REFORMATION MADE

Other things being equal, the division of Western Christendom into the various forms of Protestantism on the one hand and Roman Catholicism on the other *might* have simply ensured that the double sponsorship of art (public as well as ecclesiastical) would continue as before. But things were not equal and so the sponsorship of art did not simply continue in the former way. And the reason for this alteration of former patterns of sponsorship of art was itself twofold: monetary and theological. It is difficult to determine which of these should be given precedence over the other, on account of their interdependence.

Church finances under Protestant reform. Because Protestantism was largely introduced into various European regions with the endorsement of monarchs or the support of representative governments, it soon became the case that the management of Protestant church resources (whether gathered from collections, agricultural tithes or land rents)

---

[12]This issue of the counterclaims of emergent governments to jurisdiction has been described on pp. 179-80, dealing with the question of theocracy.

was included in the purview of the state. If under this system a church building had a leaky roof or a parsonage was in disrepair, the necessary expenditure for repair now had to be approved by an appropriate person within the sponsoring government. Revenues collected from agricultural tithes or from the leasing of church lands were not, as formerly, directly at the church's disposal. And so, just as with the care of church fabric, the patronage of the arts, which had formerly been in the purview of the church itself, was now, to a far greater extent than earlier, a matter to be considered by political authorities.

The point to be grasped then is that it was one thing for Protestant authorities to agree to maintain ecclesiastical buildings (a duty they in fact performed very indifferently), and a clear step beyond this for these authorities to serve as the patrons of religious art. We have clear reason to doubt that this right of patronage was very widely exercised. The net effect of government lethargy toward the arts in Protestant territories meant that the onus fell almost completely on persons of independent wealth to assume the support and sponsorship of the arts.

Theological issues raised under Protestant reform. But we come now to the theological issue. Without consideration of this, it is hypothetically conceivable that Protestant magistrates, superintending the affairs of the Christian churches in their regions, might have been just as robust in their endowments of the arts as various Catholic authorities had been earlier. But in actuality this was seldom the case, for theological factors worked to make it unlikely. We shall shortly make distinctions between the outlook on these questions by comparing the supporters of Lutheran and Reformed Protestantism. But before we do, it is safe to say that irrespective of Protestant confessional groupings, *all* Protestants were more wary of ostentation in buildings, furnishings and ceremony than their Roman counterparts. They were less likely to build cathedrals where none existed, and they were less likely to allow ceremony or regalia to divert attention from the divine Word read and preached.

Supremely, they were much more likely to perceive that the majesty and transcendence of God were compromised through artistic representations that violated the commandment against idolatry: "You shall not make for yourself an idol in the form of anything in heaven above or on the earth beneath or in the waters below" (Ex 20:4). Now, even when it is granted that medieval religious art seldom attempted to directly portray the unseen God, the fact that religious art furnished Europeans with paintings and sculptures that invited their adoration and devotion focused on Jesus, Mary, the twelve apostles and exemplary Christian martyrs meant that the question of potentially idolatrous use could not be evaded.

THE PRE-REFORMATION CHURCH AND THE ARTS

Yet, it was not as though, prior to Reformation times, the Roman Church had pursued a rudderless course in its sponsorship of the arts; there had been an existing general consensus that the arts should relay and amplify the teaching of the Scriptures and an orthodox understanding of the faith.[13] There had also been outspoken advocates of the position, later associated with Protestantism, that the visual representation of things divine was to be avoided and that ostentation in the things of God ought to be shunned. Bernard of Clairvaux (1090-1153) pressed this perspective on the Cistercian order and against wealthy abbeys associated with the great Cluny.[14] Yet, for as long as general literacy was beyond the reach of the bulk of the population, it was accepted that the visual arts had a role to play in conveying the characters and stories of the Scriptures through images; art, it was said, was "the Bible of the unlearned."[15] But this general approach, while not to be rejected out of hand, left a rather wide margin of error, for great discretionary powers were extended to the artisan who, however great the technical skills, may have lacked real biblical insight. Particularly in the realm of architectural stonework, tradesmen emblazoned many churches and cathedrals with faces and symbols with no transparent meaning.

---

[13]Daniel W. Hardy aptly says of the medieval Catholic tradition that it featured "a concerted effort to preserve Christian faith from degradation" in regard to images ("Calvinism and the Visual Arts: A Theological Introduction," in *Seeing Beyond the Word*, p. 6).

[14]H. Daniel-Rops, *Cathedral and Crusade* (London: J. M. Dent, 1963), pp. 108-10.

[15]This oft-repeated theme, sometimes alternately worded "of the poor," is a statement traceable to Pope Gregory the Great (540-604) in his *Letters* 9.105 and 11.13, according to the editor of Calvin's *Institutes* (Philadelphia: Westminster Press, 1964), 1.11.5 n. 11.

The best example of this anomalous art is the celebrated "green man" motif found in the exterior stonework of many ancient cathedrals and abbeys. The "green man" may actually have been pagan in origin.[16] Similar questions are raised about gargoyle figures, so prominent in the external façade of cathedrals. In stained glass windows, little distinction was drawn between characters and stories drawn from the Holy Scriptures and those drawn from the apocryphal books (some of which were nonhistorical); saints and martyrs were also depicted in glass.[17] The underlying question, really, was whether the artists and artisans who were entrusted with this work possessed sufficient discernment about their subject matter. Surely the medievalist G. G. Coulton was warranted in asserting that "medieval art was, from the point of view of religious teaching, an imperfect substitute for the spoken word."[18]

In religious painting and sculpture the role of the Virgin Mary was steadily exalted, and the likeness of the Son of God was routinely depicted.[19] The question was, did the second commandment, which forbade the making of images of the divine, in fact prohibit artistic representation of the persons of the Trinity in general and the incarnate Son in particular? To such daunting questions, the churches of the Reformation gave more than one answer.

REFORMATION RESPONSES

Conservative reaction: Lutheranism. Volatile Carlstadt, whom Lutheran Saxony sent packing, had been an avid reader of the writings of Erasmus; he had accepted that writer's principle of "interiority," that is the principle that true worship and devotion primarily required an internal right attitude of the heart and mind, which were to be arrived at quite independently of external aids (whether in ceremony, stone, on

---

[16]On the origin and symbolism of the "green man," see "Green Man," *Wikipedia* <http://en.wikipedia.org/wiki/Green_man>.

[17]On the ambiguities of much ecclesiastical art in the Middle Ages, see G. G. Coulton, *Art and the Reformation*, 2nd ed. (Cambridge: Cambridge University Press, 1953), chaps. 15-16. Coulton's verdict is stated at p. 319.

[18]Ibid., p. 319.

[19]There has long been disagreement among Christians about whether it is appropriate for art to depict (albeit imaginatively) the likeness of the incarnate Son of God. The early church routinely did this in mosaic tile.

glass or canvas).[20] Carlstadt had been encouraging the elimination of these external aids when he was interrupted by Luther's return.[21] But this iconoclasm was not to be the abiding face of the young Lutheran movement. The position Luther then articulated represented a step back from this abyss of self-appointed destruction.

Of course any openly idolatrous use of religious images was frowned upon, but short of this, Luther modeled a position that could be called one of "indifference to images." Religious images that remained in Lutheran churches would thereafter be treated with caution; as a rule religious images (whether painted or carved) were not destroyed. They were permitted to continue their former role. Luther believed that a proper emphasis on the Word of God would curb wrong use of such things.[22] In Lutheran territories, where this approach prevailed, there continued to be ecclesiastical commissions for artists. Thus we learn of fine altar pieces created by Lucas Cranach and others;[23] these did work characterized by a fuller concern for fidelity to the Scripture narrative than had characterized pre-Reformation art; art on this renewed basis became an extension of proclamation of the Word.[24] This conserving role fostered by Luther preserved an honored place for the artist within Lutheran territories.

There was added a new and expanded role for artists skillful in the making of woodcuts, for as Luther exercised his prodigious literary abilities and kept printing presses steadily employed, there was a much-

---

[20]We find this interiority already in Erasmus's 1503 treatise *Handbook of the Militant Christian (Enchiridion Militis Christiani)* in which the Christian humanist cautions his reader not to rest content in repeated attendance at the Mass or in baptism, the viewing of relics, or the performance of fixed acts of charity, while lacking inner faith and love. See the work in John P. Dolan, ed. *The Essential Erasmus* (New York: Mentor, 1964), pp. 62-69.

[21]Carlos M. N. Eire, "Iconoclasm," in *Oxford Encyclopedia of the Reformation*, ed. Hans Hillerbrand (New York: Oxford University Press, 1996), 2:303. Eire does allow that iconoclasm was characteristic of various Baltic Lutheran cities such as Danzig, Konigsberg, Riga, Stockholm, Stralsund, Stettin, Pernau, Braunschweig and Malmö.

[22]Eire, "Iconoclasm," p. 303.

[23]Carl C. Christenson indicates that these altar pieces were frequently commissioned from the 1530s onward. While princes and municipal authorities were frequently the sponsors, they were also commissioned by wealthy laypersons ("Art," in *Oxford Encyclopedia of the Reformation*, 1:76).

[24]William A. Dyrness, *Reformed Theology and Visual Culture: The Protestant Imagination from Calvin to Edwards* (Cambridge: Cambridge University Press, 2004), p. 55.

heightened demand for illustration in printed works, whether Bibles, theological treatises or handbills. The conserving role illustrated in Luther's approach to art was shown also in relation to music and drama. Unlike the developments we will shortly note in Swiss territories, music continued to enjoy an honored role in Lutheran churches. Instrumental music, choral music and congregational song (the latter in the vernacular) were maintained and enhanced, provided of course that they assisted the communication of the Word. Drama maintained its place in religious life provided that it maintained a standard of biblical fidelity and did not lead to public disorder.[25]

Disruptive reaction: Zurich. Earlier, I alluded to the influence that Erasmus's ideas of religious interiority had on Carlstadt, who made himself so unwelcome in Lutheran territories. These same ideas were soon detectable also among early advocates of the nonmagisterial Reformation in southern Germany and German-speaking Switzerland, the Anabaptists.[26] And such ideas of inwardness were simultaneously influencing Ulrich Zwingli at Zurich, who was himself a great admirer of Erasmus.[27] Zwingli's humanist orientation meant that he came to the task of church reform with a greater readiness to question the customs that had been handed down from medieval times than did his contemporary Luther. Acts of iconoclasm were reported in Zurich as early as 1520 (earlier than the onset of the crisis at Wittenberg, which brought Luther home); Zwingli was openly preaching against images

---

[25]James A. Parente, "Drama," in *Oxford Encyclopedia of the Reformation*, 2:4-6. Some, but not all, religious drama was performed in public squares and open places, and it was in such venues that disorders sometimes occurred. Bartlett L. Butler indicates that the Lutheran and Anglican expressions of the Reformation felt free to utilize (often after suitable adaptation) much of the existing musical repertoire already current in the Roman Church. But it was held to a high biblical standard ("Music," 3:109-10).

[26]Eire notes that the Anabaptist attitudes to religious images were seldom acted out in public just because this expression of the Reformation had no territorial aspect, apart from notorious episodes such as the uprising at Münster in 1534-1535 ("Iconoclasm," 2:303).

[27]Ulrich Gabler explicitly notes Erasmus's influence on Zwingli from the year 1515, singling out the treatise *Handbook of the Militant Christian* as being of special significance (*Huldrych Zwingli: His Life and Work* [Edinburgh: T & T Clark, 1987], p. 39). The Erasmus-Zwingli influence is helpfully elaborated on by Charles Garside, *Zwingli and the Arts* (New Haven, Conn.: Yale University Press, 1966), pp. 33-39. Carl C. Christenson suggests that Carlstadt, who fled Saxony for Switzerland also influenced Zwingli's thought through the intermediation of another radical, Ludwig Hätcher ("Art," 1:74).

in 1523. Already by 1524 the Zurich churches had their images (statuary) removed in an orderly procedure mandated by the city council. In pursuit of this same simplicity, Zwingli even substituted wooden Communion ware in place of the traditional silver items. The Lord's Supper was no longer served to kneeling worshipers; actual wooden tables were installed in the churches so that the semblance of a meal could be recovered.[28]

We are most concerned with Zwingli's attitude toward the creative arts. Beyond the removal of statuary and carvings, Zwingli also insisted on the removal of paintings (such as altarpieces) and that wall frescoes and murals be painted over. Even the symbol of the cross was not permitted.[29] Though Zwingli was familiar with the use of congregational singing in the Reformed city of Strasbourg, he made no provision for its implementation in Zurich. In search of simplicity, church organ music was also prohibited.[30] However, we gain a very one-dimensional perspective regarding Zwingli's attitudes unless we are aware that what was forbidden in church was encouraged in the home and community. There is evidence that Zwingli was himself highly musical and that he composed a number of religious songs; he allowed that there might be art of a religious kind (including pictures of Jesus) in the home, so long as these depictions were meant to be of a historical kind.[31] What he would not tolerate in church or home was that any art

---

[28]The transmission of this approach forward in the Reformed tradition finds some expression in the perspective of the notable Abraham Kuyper (1837-1920), who in writing on the subject "Calvinism and Art" spoke of the way the Swiss Reformation "preferred a worship of God in spirit and truth, to sacerdotal wealth," and the aim of the Reformation to "release religion and divine worship more and more from its sensual form and to encourage its vigorous spirituality" (*Lectures on Calvinism* [1931; reprint, Grand Rapids: Eerdmans, 1978], pp. 145, 149).

[29]Gabler, *Zwingli*, pp. 105-7.

[30]Ibid., p. 108. It is important to note two qualifiers of the principle that Zwingli opposed congregational singing within the city of Zurich. First, this restriction was enforced only within the city itself; elsewhere in Canton Zurich in such towns as Winterthur, Stein am Rhein and Schaffhausen congregational singing was a regular feature of church services. Second, Zurich itself reversed its opposition to congregational song in 1598. On these points see Roland Diethelm, "Bullinger and Worship: Thereby Does One Plant and Sow the True Faith," in *Architect of Reformation: An Introduction to Heinrich Bullinger, 1504-1575*, ed. Bruce Gordon and Emidio Campi (Grand Rapids: Baker Academic, 2004), pp. 142-43.

[31]Zwingli's musical adeptness and proficiency is elaborated at length in Garside, *Zwingli and the Arts*, chap. 1. Bartlett L. Butler indicates that of the three major Reformers, Zwingli easily had the most extensive musical training and experience ("Music," p. 105).

or music would be allowed to become a diversion for worshipers, whose great need was to hear God's Word.[32]

It is especially when we remember that the adoption of the Reformation in Zurich provided a portal through which it, in time, penetrated other German-speaking Swiss regions that we must expect that Zurich's influence will have been powerful. Bern in particular was indebted to the forceful participation of Zwingli in their sponsored debates of 1525, after which the city declared for the Reformation. In Bern, as in St. Gall, Basel and Schaffhausen, the destruction of images soon followed. The influences of Zurich and of Zwingli were by no means confined to German-speaking Switzerland. French-speaking regions within and beyond Switzerland, such as Neuchatel, Geneva and Strasbourg, were affected by the spread of this strong opposition to religious images. Already by 1526 Erasmus—by then resident at Basel (which had embraced the Reformation)—was writing letters of introduction for the Basel-based artist Hans Holbein the Younger. Holbein needed to go elsewhere to find work, noted Erasmus, "for here the arts have grown cold."[33]

We have noted in an earlier chapter that the influence of Zwingli and his successor, Bullinger, was very powerful indeed for friends of the Reformation in England over a half-century period in the sixteenth century. We are on firm ground in believing that some of the austere approaches to church architecture, religious art and song among many English Puritans were clearly informed by positions earlier taken in the Swiss city.

THE SHORT-TERM EFFECTS OF CALVIN'S MODERATION

It would be pleasant, indeed, to be able to recount that the Reformer of Geneva—and those who looked to his example—occupied a middle ground regarding the role of the various arts within a purified Christianity. But the evidence seems to suggest instead that while Calvin's position on these questions was more nuanced than that of Zwingli, nevertheless the long-term direction of Reformed thought in the cen-

---

[32]Christenson, "Art," p. 74.
[33]Erasmus, quoted in Charles Christensen, "Art," 1:74.

tury following was influenced more by Zwingli's austerity than by any moderation Calvin represented on the subject.

There had been incidents of iconoclasm at Geneva in advance of Calvin's initial arrival there in the summer of 1536. But Calvin, the great opponent of public lawlessness, would have nothing to do with any mobs bent on the destruction of statues, windows or paintings. Yet what Calvin did add to the discussion was a spate of biblical and theological writings that elaborated just how unthinkable were human attempts to depict the divine by artistic media. Unaided human understanding cannot approximate the likeness of God transcendent; the freedom has lain with God to disclose himself to us in acts of revelation and through his incarnate Son. Calvin was arguing to this effect as early as the first edition of his *Institutes* in 1536. That early, he was busy refuting the traditional defense of images, which posited that they are "the books of the uneducated":

> We shall answer that this [i.e., images] is not the method of teaching the people of God whom the Lord wills to be instructed with a far different doctrine than this trash. He has set forth the preaching of his Word as a common doctrine for all. What purpose did it serve for so many crosses—of wood, stone, even of silver and gold—to be erected, if this fact had been duly and faithfully taught: that Christ was offered on account of our sins that he might bear our curse and cleanse our trespasses? From this one word they could have learned more than from a thousand crosses of either wood or stone.[34]

Having struck such a note early in his career, it is hardly surprising that later Calvin needed to respond to the suggestion that he had helped create a Christian society inhospitable to gifted artists. He protested both that

> sculpture and painting are gifts from God: I see a pure and legitimate use of each, lest those things which the Lord has conferred upon us for his glory and our good be not only polluted by perverse misuse but also

---

[34]John Calvin, *Institutes of the Christian Religion*, trans. Ford Lewis Battles, 1536 ed. (Grand Rapids: Eerdmans, 1986), 1.11.7. The warnings against images, given in connection with a treatment of the second commandment, would grow exponentially by the time of the final 1559 edition; in which this theme is addressed in 1.11.1-16.

turned to our destruction. We believe it wrong that God should be represented by a visible appearance because he himself has forbidden it (Ex.
20.4) and it cannot be done without some defacing of his glory.

Furthermore,

> It remains that only those things are to be sculptured or painted which
> the eyes are capable of seeing: let not God's majesty, which is far above
> the perception of the eyes, be debased through unseemly representa-
> tions.[35]

It seemed, in consequence, that the ecclesiastical uses of art were virtually nonexistent. No more than Zwingli did Calvin agree that religious
art might be displayed in churches—though he would allow scriptural
texts to be inscribed on interior church walls; like Zwingli he allowed a
role for religious art in the homes of Christians. He accepted that biblical
themes might also provide subject matter for public art.[36] Yet the overlap
of the ideas of the two Swiss Reformers was not complete.

Calvin's position on music in the church was somewhat closer to that
of Luther than that of Zwingli. He wanted God's assembled people to
sing, and he had witnessed this capably done in his 1536 sojourn at
Basel, where his first edition of the *Institutes* was launched. He saw
more of the same during his three-year exile from Geneva at Strasbourg in the 1538-1541 period.[37] With such examples before him, he
saw to it that Genevan congregations were provided with suitable settings of the Psalms matched with stirring tunes especially composed
for the purpose. Yet organs were not to be used, and he made no provision for the continuation of church choirs. In this, in particular, Calvin's approach was largely taken up and embraced by Reformed churches
across Europe. Editions of the *Geneva Psalter* were widely used across
France too,[38] and comparable collections were produced for use in Eng-

[35]John Calvin, *Institutes of the Christian Religion*, 1559 ed. (Philadelphia: Westminster Press, 1960), 1.11.12. The Reformer's overall treatment of the danger of idolatry through use of religious images is ably analyzed by Carlos M. N. Eire, "Calvin's Attack on Idolatry," in *John Calvin and the Church*, ed. Timothy George (Louisville, Ky.: Westminster John Knox, 1990), pp. 247-76.
[36]Christenson, "Art," p. 75.
[37]Butler, "Music," p. 106.
[38]The printing of the *Genevan Psalter* in 1561-1562 is described by Monter as the largest print-

land, Scotland, the Netherlands and Hungary in rapid succession.

Calvin's own dislike of iconoclasm as an expression of lawlessness seems to have carried very little weight in the international Reformed movement. Especially in those territories of northwest Europe, such as France and the Netherlands, where Reformed Protestants would constitute a religious minority and were subject to frequent brutal harassment at the hands of political and religious authority, there were frequent waves of iconoclasm against church buildings associated with Catholic oppression and against works of art displayed in them. In France, Huguenot attacks on religious images venerated in Catholic worship intensified after 1560; it would intensify further once the Wars of Religion opened in 1562. Similar concerted iconoclasm was characteristic of Reformed Protestantism in the Low Countries, commencing in 1566; such was the intensity of it throughout the seventeen provinces of the Netherlands that it provoked King Phillip II, the Spanish ruler, to send an army to quell the disturbance. Such destructive action was characteristic also of the early Scottish Reformation up to the year 1559.[39]

NEEDED: SOME PERSPECTIVE ON THE SIXTEENTH CENTURY

The paradox that this rapid survey confronts us with is this:

- Only *one* of the three major branches of early Protestantism surveyed (the Swiss-German, led by Zwingli) aggressively promoted the removal or destruction of religious images from church buildings.

- Two of the three Reformers who lent no direct support to iconoclasm (Luther and Calvin) also tried to speak affirmingly of the various arts.

- Nevertheless, the known influence of Zwingli (who was most hostile to artistic images in churches) and Calvin (who himself would not countenance lawless acts of iconoclasm) seemed to merge with regard to besieged Reformed minorities in Western Europe. It would

---

ing enterprise of the entire sixteenth century (*Calvin's Geneva*, p. 181 n. 43). Geneva alone printed 27,400 copies of the *Psalter* by 1562, and additional editions were produced in Paris and Lyon. Copies were sold to French-speaking Protestants as far afield as Antwerp.
[39]Eire, "Iconoclasm," p. 304.

be the next century before, having gained tolerated status, these Reformed movements could move on from iconoclasm to pursue more positive concerns (among which were the positive values of the arts). There is strong evidence that they did so.

To this survey, we need to add one factor before turning our attention to the at least partial restoration of the arts once the Reformation was established. That one factor might have been guessed at, from my earlier admission, that the magisterial branches of the Reformation entailed that the pace and scope of Reformation was supervised by governing authorities (whether monarchs or elected). This very jurisdiction of magistrates over the churches of Protestantism had unwittingly opened the door to a virtual iconoclasm that targeted church lands, church buildings, furnishings and construction materials for plunder—not at the hands of zealous reformers—but at the hands of those who sought gain by stripping away the assets of a bloated late-medieval church. Visitors to Europe who have seen roofless medieval abbeys and ruined monasteries—the lamentable sights that Shakespeare called "bare ruined choirs"[40]—need to understand that these evidences of spoliation testify not to the work of religious mobs but of monarchs, nobles and revolutionary governments that obtained jurisdiction over church properties in order to use them and their materials for nonreligious purposes. The perpetrators of this spoliation range from England's King Henry VIII, commencing in 1536, to France's post-1791 revolutionary government.[41] In our judgments

---

[40]Shakespeare, Sonnet 73.

[41]England's King Henry VIII closed England's monasteries, beginning in 1536 with the weakest and least inhabited, claiming corruption and inefficiency in their operation. They, with their lands, were sold to enrich the royal treasury. See the description of this in J. J. Scarisbrick, *Henry VIII* (London: Eyre Methuen, 1968), pp. 337-38. Not all the fine buildings were destroyed, but many were gradually stripped of their valuable building materials and left to decay. In France the famous monastery of Citeaux (home of the Cistercian order) was seized by the French revolutionary government in 1791 as a part of its general repatriation of ecclesiastical property—an attempt to deal with the nation's accumulated indebtedness. The still older monastery at Cluny (founded A.D. 910) was largely destroyed in the revolution. Of this era the monastic historian David Knowles wrote "at the height of the Napoleonic domination of Europe an almost clean sweep had been made of the Benedictine abbeys, completing for the southern half of the continent the work begun by the Reformers in the north. In 1810 there were fewer monasteries in existence in western Europe than at any time since the age of St. Augustine" (*Christian Monasticism* [London: Weidenfeld & Nicholson, 1969], p. 158).

about the destruction of art and architecture, we must be able to make distinctions between those motivated by religious principle and those motivated by hope of material gain.

THE REDIRECTION OF THE ARTS AFTER THE HEAT OF REFORM

Protestant iconoclasm was still a force to be reckoned with by the dawn of the seventeenth century in regions of Europe where Protestant governments had not implemented the austerities that prevailed in much of Switzerland. This was nowhere so true as in late Elizabethan and early Stuart England.[42] Yet, in time, the advance of Protestantism gradually encouraged the fuller emergence of something that had already been operative since the fourteenth century, that is, that persons and families of means were able to take up the support of the arts. It was the slowness of persons in Protestant regions of south Germany and Switzerland to show this private initiative in the early decades of the Reformation era that contributed to a temporary underemployment of artists.

The arts and the Reformation had never utterly parted ways. This was so not only in Lutheran territories where the art of Lucas Cranach and Albrecht Dürer was supported but beyond.[43] The Swiss Holbein the Younger remained Protestant in orientation when, no doubt, a Catholic allegiance would have attracted more commissions for his artistic work. It was possible for an artist to accept the Reformation critique of late medieval religious art and yet to face poverty for lack of patronage.[44]

I have referred in passing to Erasmus, who in 1526 was busy writing

---

[42]The moderate church reforms introduced in Tudor times fell short of utterly removing ecclesiastical traces of Roman Catholicism in matters of church furnishings, elaborate clerical dress and religious art. Arch-Protestants, wishing for closer approximation to Swiss austerities, called these the "dregs of Popery."

[43]Dürer is an example of a Reformation-era artist who, while Protestant in sympathy, took artistic commissions from Catholic patrons also. See Coulton, *Art and the Reformation*, pp. 408-9; Lee Palmer Wandel, "The Reformation and the Visual Arts," in *The Cambridge History of Christianity*, ed. R. Po-Chia Hsia (New York: Cambridge University Press, 2007), 6:352. Anne Roberts has explored the stance of Cranach toward Luther in "Cranach and Luther," *Evangelicals Now*, May 2008, <www.e-n.org.uk/p-4206-Cranach-and-Luther-htm>.

[44]The allegiance of Holbein the Younger to the Reformation cause is explored by Anne Roberts, "Hans Holbein and the Reformation," *Evangelicals Now*, August 1997 <www.e-n.org.uk/p -95-Hans-Holbein-and-the-Reformation.htm>.

letters of recommendation from Basel for Holbein the Younger. Such advocacy seems to have opened doorways for Holbein, for we know that he gained many commissions for portraits in England, where he lived 1532-1543.[45] Among his subjects were King Henry VIII, archbishops of Canterbury Wareham and Cranmer, government ministers Thomas More and Thomas Cromwell, and King Henry's fourth wife, Anne of Cleves.[46] England's own sixteenth-century painter of renown was Nicholas Hilliard (c. 1547-1619). Reckoned a follower of Holbein, Hilliard was a member of a staunch Protestant family that had weathered the storms of persecution in the reign of Mary Tudor in the safe haven of Geneva. He is most famous for a portrait of Queen Elizabeth I.[47]

The provinces of the then-Spanish Netherlands were another region which, substantially embracing the Reformation, rapidly provided opportunities for painters, engravers and designers of woodcuts. Interestingly, a specialty of Dutch artists sympathetic to the cause of the Reformation were elaborate displays showing Moses standing with the Tables of the Law; these sometimes replaced earlier artwork that had been removed or destroyed simultaneous with the conversion of the churches from Catholic to Protestant use.[48]

Some prominent artists associated with Antwerp (Karel van Mander, Frans Hals and Hercules Seghers) left, not because of a paucity of work but because the Spanish obliged them to support Catholicism or else depart. The net effect of such policies was the elevation of Amsterdam as the artistic center of the region. Rembrandt van Rijn (1606-1669) is but the best-known example of artists of this era who used their artistic gifts in a Reformed context. The artistic trend implicit in such developments was one that no longer looked on painting and statuary as an aid to worship (especially for the unlettered) but considered it as both an extension of Christian teaching and proclamation, and as an aid to religious devotion in settings such as the home.[49]

---

[45]Dyrness, *Reformed Theology and Visual Culture*, pp. 104-5.
[46]The portraits are reproduced in Scarisbrick, *Henry VIII*.
[47]Dyrness, *Reformed Theology and Visual Culture*, pp. 106-9.
[48]James R. Tanis, "Netherlandish Reformed Traditions in the Graphic Arts, 1550-1630," in *Seeing Beyond the Word*, ed. Paul Corby Finney (Grand Rapids: Eerdmans, 1999), p. 385.
[49]Wandel, "Reformation and the Visual Arts," p. 353.

CONCLUSION

The centuries-old complaint that the Reformation dealt a bad hand to the arts contains several layers of confusion and misrepresentation as well as some elements of truth. Those who continue to repeat the charge that the Reformation brought unmitigated trouble for the arts *could* be taken as favoring what was still true as the sixteenth century dawned. Then, the church exercised a virtual domination of art in Western society, with independently wealthy patrons only augmenting the income of artists largely in the employ of the church. It is not clear that such an arrangement was in the interests of the arts then; it is still more clear that such an arrangement would be unworkable now—when by all accounts Christianity in all its forms has a diminished role in Western societies. It was and is important that the survival of the arts not be overly dependent on any single constituency—whether that constituency be the church or the state.

The turnstile through which the Reformation era required the arts to pass in the sixteenth century was, at its root, a requirement for biblical accountability. Artistic depiction could not offer likenesses of the God, who is unseen and who has revealed himself by prophets, wisemen and, supremely, the incarnate Son—all now offered us through Holy Scripture. Music too was required to serve the interests of biblical fidelity and gospel communication. The application of this principle of fidelity varied in its intensity between Protestant territories that reckoned the arts indifferent, provided that they were exercised chastely (notably Lutheran Germany and Tudor England, on the one hand), and others (the Reformed of Switzerland and beyond) that wanted to see the arts governed (as to ecclesiastical use) by biblical precept and precedent. Both tendencies of thought fully allowed that the arts also had wide applications to society and the home, in addition to those appropriate in the churches. It is also true that in Protestant lands, literacy proliferated exponentially in societies where the right and privilege of citizens to read the Bible for themselves was upheld and safeguarded. In such societies the old adage that "art is the Bible of the unlettered" had steadily less application.

Yet I do not propose here to utterly exonerate the heroes of the Reformation and their descendants in this matter. It is fair to say that, other than Lutheran and Anglican expressions of the Reformation, the Reformed and Anabaptists have been clearer in indicating the potential snares the arts represented for the Christian and the church than in articulating any positive role which they might fulfill.

Discussion Questions

1. If you began to read this chapter having already heard or read the suggestion that the Reformation had the effect of discouraging the arts, can you recall what the source was?

   Was it hearsay, a textbook, a popular article? What would you say now?

2. It is true that, prior to the Reformation, the church was the primary sponsor of the arts in Western society. What factors created this large role for the church? What would have been the consequences, positive and negative, if the church had continued to be the primary sponsor of the arts?

3. The Reformers were wary of the idea that people would draw their chief ideas about God and Christ from images rather than the Holy Scriptures. Was their fear an exaggerated fear? Unpack the multiple reasons for their wariness.

4. Prior to the Reformation the heavy use of images in the churches was justified on account of illiteracy. Would art today in the service of Christianity accept this role, which can slight art's intrinsic value and make it seek its validation in its usefulness?

5. In Western societies, at least, illiteracy has been virtually eradicated, and yet, if anything, moderns are more likely than a generation ago to draw their ideas from images (whether photographic or cinematic). Discuss this persistence of the image in the forming of opinion and conviction.

Further Reading

Coulton, G. G. *Art and the Reformation*. 2nd ed. Cambridge: Cambridge University Press, 1953.

Dyrness, William A. *Reformed Theology and Visual Culture: The Protestant Imagination from Calvin to Edwards.* Cambridge: Cambridge University Press, 2004.

Eire, Carlos M. N. *War Against the Idols.* New York: Cambridge University Press, 1989.

Finney, Paul Corby, ed. *Seeing Beyond the Word.* Grand Rapids: Eerdmans, 1999.

Christine de Pizan (1363-1434) Lecturing
Image: Wikipedia

MYTH NINE

Calvinism Resists Gender Equality

IT IS HARD TO IMAGINE THAT anyone would point to the movement in which John Calvin holds such a prominent place and suggest that it had helped to pioneer the advancement of women. After all, so much anecdotal evidence to the contrary is available that it would appear to be possible to maintain the complete opposite: that is, that Calvinist movements in various places have *retarded* the advancement of women in society. Did early twentieth-century Calvinists do anything to promote women's voting rights—whether in Europe or North America? Isn't it true that many churches in the Presbyterian and Reformed tradition were even slow to allow women to vote in *church* affairs? And why is there ongoing reluctance in many branches of the Reformed tradition to permit women to enter the recognized ministries of the church?

The paradox before us is that while we can acknowledge the substantial truthfulness of these pieces of anecdotal evidence, we will find that focusing on such isolated pieces of information takes us almost no distance toward discovering what has been the Reformed tradition's *intentional* stance. The fact of the matter is that Calvinism and gender is an amazingly complex topic—embracing a wide range of divergent attitudes. It is one thing to demonstrate that Calvinism has been associated with certain views on gender; it is another (and more difficult thing) to try to demonstrate that such attitudes *originated* within Calvinism or found their life support in the Reformed tradition, as in no other expression of Christianity. Association is *not* origination; association is *not* causation. In this chapter, we will discover many things contrary to our initial expectations.

IDEAS OF GENDER IN RENAISSANCE EUROPE

Those who have seen the drama *A Man for All Seasons* in a theatrical or cinematic production may be able to remember the remarkable relationship Thomas More, the central character, had with his daughters (none more so than oldest daughter, Meg).[1] More (1478-1535), being the man of the Renaissance that he was, had come to espouse the new view that women were fully capable of a mastery of the same classical curriculum young men like his son were exposed to; the Thomas More home was therefore a school. Not only Latin but Greek was a subject of common delight for father and daughters. The daughter, Margaret (Meg), eventually translated into English the theological writings of her father's close friend Erasmus of Rotterdam.[2] This revolutionary development was more widespread in the sixteenth century than is generally appreciated.

In general terms Europe in the previous medieval era had a conception of women we could call "confining." Females were reckoned to be the weaker sex in every sense; their natural sphere was reckoned to be the home and childbearing. Consistent with this view, young girls, while still in their adolescence, were customarily married by parental arrangement to men much their senior and with whom they had no prior relationship. Consequently, marriage emphasized not companionship but the procreation of children—many children—in an era of

---

[1]The Robert Bolt play was performed from 1960; a 1966 film version starring Paul Scofield as More won Scofield an Academy Award. The theme of the drama was the resoluteness of More, an Erasmian who himself sought the purification of Catholicism, in face of King Henry VIII's pursuit of a divorce of his first wife Catherine. The monarch's determination to have his divorce and remarriage in spite of resolute papal opposition found More determined to support the stance of the pope and the Roman Church.

[2]J. K. Sowards, "Erasmus and the Education of Women," *The Sixteenth Century Journal* 13, no. 4 (1982): 81-83; Jane Dempsey Douglass, *Women, Freedom and Calvin* (Philadelphia: Westminster Press, 1985), p. 71.

high infant mortality. The unmarried adult female, on the other hand, represented a perceived element of sexual danger to medieval society— a danger which had to be addressed in societies that had no real place for the single adult; convents and less formal female religious communities provided honorable roles for the unmarried. A widow represented the same anomaly in medieval society. Because it was not granted that women might live independently in society, such persons either returned to their parental home or—like the single unmarried—entered a religious house. Women who entered convents generally took with them, at entry, something equivalent to the dowry (a modest portion of the father's estate, the majority of which would be gifted to the oldest son) that she would have carried into a marriage. There was a far greater likelihood of a woman becoming literate in a medieval convent than in society at large.[3] The accessibility of education for females was something highly dependent on the social and financial situation of the family; the best known examples of educated females in medieval and late-medieval Europe come from families of means.[4]

Women who entered convents gained not only access to basic education but also opportunities to show leadership and to utilize their spiritual endowments. Within this bounded sphere of the cloister, women could lead other women as an abbess or mother superior. They could also pray and read the Scriptures aloud, and give spiritual addresses to fellow sisters. In a convent chapel they could also freely lift their voices in song—something quite unwelcome in churches in the world beyond. The enjoyment of these opportunities came at the price of "claustration."[5] Only very exceptional nuns could speak beyond the boundaries of their retreats; they could do this in voice or writing only

---

[3]Margaret L. King, "Women," in *Encyclopedia of the Renaissance*, ed. Paul F. Grendler (New York: Charles Scribner's, 1999), 6:318-20. The exception to this generalization is provided by the wealthy or noble family, which might have provided a good rudimentary education for daughters.

[4]Patricia H. Labalme, introduction to *Beyond Their Sex: Learned Women of the European Past*, ed. Patricia H. Labalme (New York: New York University Press, 1980), p. 2. The same point is made later in the same volume by Paul Oskar Kristeller in his essay "Learned Women of Early Modern Italy" (*Beyond Their Sex*, p. 96).

[5]This interesting term, *claustration* (a word related to "cloister"), is utilized in the stimulating discussion of medieval convent life by Kirsi Stjerna, *Women and the Reformation* (Oxford: Blackwell, 2009), chap. 2.

by claiming an extraordinary prompting of the Holy Spirit, which served to override the general prohibition on women addressing the church at large. Hildegard of Bingen, Julian of Norwich, Catherine of Siena and Birgitta of Sweden are outstanding examples of women who gained an audience across the gender divide while residing in the framework of the cloister.[6] The rise of Europe's universities in the thirteenth century retarded rather than advanced the education of women; the rising universities had virtually no place for females (whereas the earlier monastic schools had some place). Access to education became more difficult for girls and women to obtain.[7]

Yet with the onset of the Renaissance era (to which period Thomas More clearly belonged), different ideas began to circulate slowly in Western Europe. Already in the late fifteenth century a group of women writers (as well as some men who shared their views) pursued what came to be known as *Querelles de Femmes* (Quarrels of Women). Such writers did not dispute a woman's distinct biological role, but they did oppose the reigning notion that women were intrinsically less virtuous than their male counterparts (a theory that pinned everything on the idea of Eve's having been the first to succumb to the blandishments of the tempter). They also assailed the view that women did not need the level of education offered to men or need the liberty enjoyed by men to circulate opinions in print.[8] There were those like the male writer Henry Cornelius Agrippa who were ready to argue for the actual superiority of women to men; he wrote *Declamation of the Nobility and Excellence of the Female Sex* (1509). In a sarcastic vein he maintained that Eve had been created *in* Paradise, Adam earlier *beyond* Paradise; her name meant "life," his meant "earth"; she had been God's final and ultimate creative act in the original world.[9]

No one should exaggerate the influence of this writer or the circle he

---

[6]Ibid., p. 13.

[7]Joan M. Ferrante, "The Education of Women in the Middle Ages," in *Beyond Their Sex: Learned Women of the European Past*, p. 17.

[8]This circle of female writers and their male supporters is described in King, "Women," p. 324; and Douglass, *Women, Freedom and Calvin*, pp. 68-71.

[9]The paraphrase of Agrippa is provided by Douglass, *Women, Freedom and Calvin*, p. 68. Douglass (ibid., p. 69 n. 22) points out that Calvin read Agrippa and examined his views in his *Commentary* on 1 Peter.

was a part of, as though such Renaissance attitudes to gender rapidly stood conventional European gender prejudice on its head. But there is no denying, either, that questions about gender, which were considered closed a century or two earlier, were being pressed on European consciousness in fresh ways. It certainly became socially acceptable for Renaissance thinkers and writers to advocate that women, being also made in God's image, were educable and capable of sound judgment and expression.[10] It became common to assert that marriage was meant to serve not only the purposes of reproduction but of love and companionship. Given the widely acknowledged way that the world and ideals of the Renaissance helped to prepare the way for the early sixteenth-century Reformation movements (Catholic and Protestant), we should not be surprised to find that Renaissance attitudes toward gender left their imprint on the new religious movements.

IDEAS OF GENDER IN REFORMATION EUROPE

Jane Dempsey Douglass has aptly written that whatever else the Reformation introduced about the prospects of women, the movement brought fundamental changes because of three doctrines:

> The Protestant doctrines of Christian vocation, and the priesthood of all believers, along with a new view of marriage, did in fact tend to change the image and role of women in the direction of greater personal freedom and responsibility, both immediately and over the centuries.[11]

In keeping with the first (Christian vocation), marriage, childrearing and domestic life were reckoned to be as truly a venue for living a holy life

---

[10]J. K. Sowards points out that the "blind spot" in the advocacy of Erasmus and his contemporaries for female education is that they did not advocate also a revolution in social roles for the two genders. "Learning was simply to add erudition to those (domestic) roles, to equip a noble-woman to rear her children more capably" ("Erasmus and the Education of Women," *Sixteenth Century Journal* 13, no. 4 [1982]: 79).

[11]Jane Dempsey Douglass, "Women and the Continental Reformation," in *Religion and Sexism: Images of Women in the Jewish and Christian Traditions*, ed. Rosemary Radford Ruether (New York: Simon & Schuster, 1974), p. 314. This verdict stands in some contrast to the opinion of Richard L. Greaves, who began the introduction to his edited work *Triumph Over Silence* that "The Protestant conviction that Scripture alone is the sole authority in matters of religion reinforced traditional biases against the participation of women in most positions of leadership in the church" (*Triumph Over Silence: Women in Protestant History* [Westport, Conn.: Greenwood, 1985], p. 3).

of significance as any cloistered life in earlier times—just as the honest Christian workman in his trade was assured that working with his hands was as noble in God's sight as the life of the monk or hermit. In light of the second (the priesthood of believers), Christian men and women— without respect to gender—were urged to raise their sights and to consider that they had responsibility not only to read the Scriptures and maintain a life of prayer for their own soul's good, but also for the benefit of their Christian acquaintances who stood in need of their prayers and admonitions. This concept would prove to be a great spur to literacy, for this mutual priesthood presupposed knowledge of the Bible.

As to the third, marriage was now urged as normative and honorable for the adult woman or man, irrespective of income, wealth or social position. In the understanding of the early Protestants, marriage existed not simply for the purpose of procreation or even the containment of sexual vice, but for love and companionship. One could have found these fundamental principles present in any and every expression of early Protestantism.[12] In each expression of Protestantism, women formerly committed to conventual life entered the new sphere of influence we now call "pastor's wife."[13] The best known, though by no means a solitary example, was Katharina von Bora (1499-1552), who left a convent and eventually became the spouse of Martin Luther.[14] Was there any distinctive, in addition, which was characteristic of the Reformed theological tradition?

REFORMED PROTESTANTISM COMPARED TO OTHER PROTESTANT TRADITIONS

In certain definite respects Christian women figured more prominently

---

[12]Douglass, "Women and the Continental Reformation," p. 295; Barbara J. MacHaffe, "Women in the Reformed Tradition: 16th-18th Centuries," in *Encyclopedia of the Reformed Faith*, ed. Donald McKim (Louisville, Ky.: Westminster John Knox, 1992), p. 398; Stjerna, *Women and the Reformation*, chap. 3.

[13]From this fact I do not mean to infer that all who left convents married, that all nuns (even in Protestant territories) left their convents or that those who remained committed to cloistered life uttered no criticism of those who departed. See the incisive analysis of Stjerna, "The Monastic Option: The Struggle of the Convents," *Women and the Reformation*.

[14]The life of von Bora is sketched out in Roland Bainton, *Women of the Reformation in Germany and Italy* (Minneapolis: Augsburg, 1971), chap. 1; and Stjerna, *Women and the Reformation*, chap. 5.

in the European regions that embraced Swiss-style Reformed Protestantism than in regions that embraced other expressions of the Protestant movement. Let us enumerate four.

Education. In Protestant territories generally, steps were taken to ensure that at least rudimentary education was made available to children without respect to gender. It was so in Geneva from 1536 onward, and children were welcomed at school irrespective of their ability to pay fees. By 1541 young girls of Geneva had an institution of their own.[15] This does not mean that the curriculum in schools for girls necessarily matched that found in boys' schools, but the essential point is that Reformed territories took seriously the rightness of educating both genders. In this instance it appears that when Protestant territories instituted general education without respect to gender, they were following a trajectory set out first by humanist writers of the Renaissance.

Marriage and divorce. In Reformed territories concern for the promotion of marriage as a social norm, which was meant to encourage not only lawful reproduction but also to provide for a relationship of love and companionship, led to fresh attention to the question of what could *end* a marriage. Whereas Europe under medieval Catholic jurisdiction had found divorce well-nigh impossible to obtain and annulment possible only on the narrowest of grounds, in territories where Reformed Protestantism took hold this situation was reversed. No one will call the alternate arrangements introduced by Reformed Protestantism lax (because divorce still remained difficult to obtain, except on certain explicit grounds), but they might fairly be called "principled." Because Protestantism did not consider marriage a sacrament (which seemed to make marriage utterly indissoluble) but a divine provision, it was reckoned that marriage could end for the reasons enumerated by Christ and the apostle Paul: adultery and desertion.[16]

The motive for this Protestant alteration was one of compassion; where marriage contracts had been violated through infidelity or desertion, the injured party (female or male) was assisted to go on in life with

---

[15]Douglass, "Women and the Continental Reformation," pp. 304-5.
[16]The relevant Scriptures appealed to are Mt 19:9; 1 Cor 7:15.

the possibility of remarriage.[17] Marriage in Protestant territories was under the jurisdiction of civil authorities; these acted on the advice of church authorities when requests for divorce were made. Both the Strasbourg reformer Bucer (from whom the young Calvin had learned so much in the years of exile from Geneva) and Calvin came to favor access to divorce by women who had been wronged, just as for men in the same circumstances. By 1561 Geneva codified this provision and opened a process that broke new ground in permitting a wife as injured party to be the one to launch a divorce proceeding.[18] This quite unprecedented step tells us something about the relative improvement of the lot of women in such societies, compared to formerly.

Martyrdom. Certain writers have worked hard to draw attention to the numbers of persons who met their deaths for their principles under various Catholic and Protestant regimes in the sixteenth century; they have aimed to show that the other party demonstrated the greatest inhumanity in executing persons who held wrong beliefs.[19] While the martyrdom of Anabaptist women, for instance, was statistically very significant (with up to 35 percent of Anabaptist martyrs being female), we are here concerned with the significant representation of women among the Calvinist religious martyrs of the sixteenth century. In regions of Europe where persecution grew hot against Protestantism (France, England, the Spanish Netherlands) in the 1550s, it is remarkable to note how many were women.[20]

---

[17]Douglass, "Women and the Continental Reformation," p. 303. Douglass notes that Martin Bucer tried without success in both Strasbourg and (subsequently) England to convince authorities that the loss of heartfelt love should also constitute a ground for divorce.

[18]Douglass, *Women, Freedom and Calvin*, p. 86; and her "Women and the Continental Reformation," p. 304. Charmarie Jenkins Blaisdell, "The Matrix of Reform: Women in the Lutheran and Calvinist Movements," in Greaves, ed., *Triumph Over Silence*, p. 29 notes that by 1600, Geneva rescinded this progressive measure, leaving the initiative in divorce proceedings to the male.

[19]For example, Lacey Baldwin Smith indicates that a comparison involving the reign of the Catholic monarch Mary Tudor with France, Spain and the Spanish Netherlands in the period between 1555-1564 showed that English executions for heresy surpassed those of her Catholic neighbors in frequency (*This Realm of England: 1399-1688*, 8th ed. [Boston: Houghton Mifflin, 2001], p. 165). By contrast (ibid., p. 217) Mary's half-sister, the Protestant Elizabeth, had a forty-five year reign in which approximately two hundred persons were executed for similar reasons.

[20]Stjerna relies on the work of early seventeenth-century chronicler Thieleman Jansz van Braght, who composed *The Martyr's Mirror* between 1625-1664 (*Women and the Reformation*, pp. 16-

This frequency of occurrence points beyond itself to the question of what behaviors made these individuals vulnerable to arrest and prosecution. It would at least have involved a preparedness to join an assembly of Protestant Christians and to have been apprehended in such Protestant company; yet such records as we have indicate that those most vulnerable to such arrests were persons (male and female) who openly spoke about their gospel hopes and their trust in the Scriptures. There is the clear implication that adherence to the Reformation cause moved a considerable number of Protestant women (and men) to be very forthright about their faith. This consideration leads to yet another.

The spontaneous ministry efforts of Reformed women. It is only recently that homage has begun to be paid to a group of Protestant women who, in their civic and national settings, exercised a powerful spoken and sometimes written influence in the earliest decades of the Reformation period. Here we can focus only on two individuals who exercised this influence in territories associated with the Reformed expressions of Christianity.

Pride of place must surely go to the native of Strasbourg, Katharina Schütz Zell, who having embraced Luther's writings, took the bold step in 1523 of being the first woman to marry a Strasbourg priest (himself an advocate of reform).[21] By this marriage to Matthias Zell, Katharina came to be on friendly terms with not only the other reforming clergy of her city but their counterparts in Zurich, Basel, Geneva and beyond. A prolific letter-writer, Schütz Zell conducted serious cor-

---

17). Bainton points to just how great was the documentation of female witness-martyrs originating with John Foxe's *Acts and Monuments*, first published in 1563 (Bainton, *Women and the Reformation in France and England* [Minneapolis: Augsburg, 1973], chap. 12). Richard L. Greaves posits the following statistic: "More than fifty of the nearly three hundred martyrs under Queen Mary I (of England) in the 1550s were women, mostly poor widows" (preface to *Triumph Over Silence*, p. 6).

[21]The preeminent source of information on Katharina Zell is the two-volume work of Elsie Anne McKee, *Katharina Schütz Zell: The Life and Thought of a Sixteenth Century Reformer* (Leiden, U.K.: Brill, 1998). The first volume is biographical; the second provides a critical edition of her major writings. Katharina's marriage ceremony was conducted by the as-yet-unmarried priest Martin Bucer at 6:00 a.m. on a December day; the hour was intended to help avoid public controversy over the then-unprecedented step. Details are supplied in ibid., 1:49; and Stjerna, *Women and the Reformation*, p. 112.

respondence on theological questions with both Lutheran and Reformed leaders; she also took up her pen to compose theological treatises. When her pioneering marriage to the priest drew criticism from the city authorities, Katharina penned an able apology upholding the rectitude of her husband, of their marriage and of clerical marriage in general.[22] Katharina wrote devotional works, conducted an active ministry of pastoral visitation (especially to women) and compiled a hymnbook. After the death of her husband, and near the end of her own life, she gained notoriety by conducting funerals for persons that Strasbourg's religious establishment took a dim view of. She sometimes described herself as "church mother."[23]

In the first chapter of this book, attention was drawn to the fact that another woman, Marie Dentière (1495-1561), was honored in 2002 when her name was inscribed on Geneva's "Wall of the Reformers." Of French birth, she entered an Augustinian convent in her home city, Tournai, in 1521. By 1524 she had embraced Lutheran teaching, left her convent and gone as a refugee to Strasbourg. There she married ex-priest Simon Robert, and together they set out from Strasbourg in the company of Guillaume Farel (the man who would prevail on Calvin to help him at Geneva in 1536), who was focused on the evangelization of French-speaking Switzerland. Marie Dentière, widowed in 1535 with five children, married a second time, in this case to another Francophone pastor, Antoine Froment. In the year of their marriage, this couple took up residence in Geneva—on the eve of the city's 1536 embrace of the Reformation cause. Marie, having been a nun herself, took it upon herself to visit the city's convents and to exhort the sisters to follow her example.

Apparently the Protestant leaders of Geneva were taken somewhat aback by the exhortatory role Dentière had assumed, yet they did not match her zeal for this particular line of missionary work. Though she was aware that her attempts at public ministry were not in line with

---

[22]The defense of her husband is reproduced in chap. 2 of McKee, *Zell*, vol. 2. See also Stjerna, *Women and the Reformation*, p. 119.

[23]Stjerna, *Women and the Reformation*, chap. 6, shows how remarkably like the influence of Schütz Zell was that of Argula von Grumbach (1492-1563/8), a Bavarian noblewoman who worked as an apologist for the Lutheran faith.

what Calvin and Farel expected in a woman, she was loyal to them in any case. After this pair was banished from the city in 1538, Dentière pseudonymously wrote her own eyewitness account of what it had been like when Geneva first embraced the Reformation and made it clear that she supported the banished ministers. She interpreted Geneva's breaking free from the corruptions of medieval Catholicism in categories provided by the Hebrew liberation from Egypt in Moses' day.[24]

Three years later, Dentière published once more, this time under her own initials, M.D., and in the form of an extended letter to the noblewoman Marguerite of Navarre (a small French principality near the Spanish border), who—as one sympathetic to John Calvin—wished to know the reasons for his banishment from Geneva in 1538. This met with terrible opposition in Geneva, both on account of the writer's sympathy for the banished Calvin and her gender. Most available copies were seized and destroyed. The treatise had not disguised that Marie favored the right of women to preach and teach in support of the Reformed cause. Her husband, a minister of canton Geneva, Antoine Froment, defended his wife's literary labors, though he maintained that he had not been consulted as to the actual contents. By 1561 Calvin, who had earlier been standoffish, was prepared to request that Dentière write a preface to a sermon he had preached on female apparel.[25]

About this issue, we can simply conclude that in the opening decades of this Protestant era, there were found both in the female Protestant population at large and particularly among those women who left convents to embrace the Reformed faith, women of pronounced literary and pastoral gifts who sought to advance the Reformation in their own ways, to some good effects.

CALVIN AS A PROGRESSIVE ON GENDER FOR HIS TIME

What has been intimated thus far would not really lead us to expect that John Calvin was associated with progressive ideas about the elevation of women in his society. His relationship with Marie Dentière

---

[24]Stjerna, *Women and the Reformation*, pp. 137-38; Douglass, *Women, Freedom and Calvin*, p. 103. The treatise of 1536 was *The War for and Deliverance of the City of Geneva*.
[25]Stjerna, *Women and the Reformation*, pp. 142, 144.

of Geneva could not be described as warm, and though in his travels to Strasbourg he had known the hospitality of (and subsequently exchanged correspondence with) Schütz Zell, we know of no particular endorsement by Calvin of her varied attempts at public acts of ministry. And yet on closer examination we find that, judged within his cultural milieu, Calvin held some highly interesting opinions.[26] Let us consider three.

Man and woman in God's image. In Calvin's time there was still popular support for the idea, passed down from Aristotle, that woman was a "defective male"; Calvin would have none of this. The Reformer was a very firm defender of the principle, enunciated in Genesis 1:26-27, that man and woman were equally endowed with the divine image. Perhaps it was the Renaissance humanist background of his pre-Protestant days at work (in the section above titled "Ideas of Gender in Renaissance Europe," we have observed the Renaissance concern to elevate women), but Calvin was not enthusiastic about reasoning that made Eve a recipient of the divine image only in some lesser, derived sense. It was common for late medieval theologians to reason in that way in light of Paul's difficult saying of 1 Corinthians 11:7 that "man . . . is the image and glory of God; but the woman is the glory of man." Calvin gave the upper hand to the Genesis 1:26-27 passage in dealing with that difficult saying; he insisted that whatever Paul meant, he could not be taken as meaning that woman was less than an equal recipient of God's image. Woman was made to be companion to man and shared the dignity derived from bearing God's image.

But such considerations did not move Calvin from his conviction that in the married state and in the church, a certain order ought to prevail. He took seriously the biblical admonitions requiring the silence of women in the church (1 Cor 14:34; 1 Tim 2:12) while allowing that God, who is over all, intermittently spoke through women, such as the prophetess Anna (Lk 2:36) and the four daughters of Philip (Acts 21:9).[27]

---

[26]Of special significance is the insistence of Douglass that "Among the leaders of the mainstream Reformation deeply influenced by the changed intellectual climate, Calvin was among the most deeply touched" (*Women, Freedom and Calvin*, pp. 81-82).

[27]From Calvin's treatment of such New Testament passages as these Douglass draws the conclusion that Calvin "is ambivalent on this question" (ibid., p. 88). I do not find this ambivalence.

Women as deacons. Second, Calvin—more than any other magisterial Reformer—was ready to provide opportunity for recognized ministry for women within the Reformed churches. In the manual of church policy he wrote for Geneva in 1542, the "Draft Ecclesiastical Ordinances," he had maintained that the apostolic office of deacon ought to consist of two aspects: those who gathered alms for the needy (the procurators) and those who distributed charity—whether in institutions for the needy or those dwelling in their own homes (the Hospitallers).[28] By the next year (1543), Calvin was ready to espouse the view that this second aspect of diaconal work, the work of distribution, could be fulfilled by female members of the diaconate. He believed that such diaconal work had been performed in apostolic times by the order of widows Paul wrote of in 1 Timothy 5:9-10.[29] It was Calvin's genuine belief that this form of ministry had existed in the early church before the time when other-than-biblical cultural forces (such as Hellenistic philosophy) diminished the role of women in the church. His aim was to restore the late medieval church to its early vigor, and the restoration of this recognized ministry by women was an important element of that. It is no reflection on the sincerity of Calvin who proposed this form of recognized ministry that this practice was embraced neither in his adoptive city of Geneva nor in most other places. It seems that Calvin's readiness to include women in this way in the ministries of the church awaited rediscovery in the twentieth century.[30]

All that I believe can be safely said is that Calvin made an honest effort to deal with the implications of each passage on its own terms.

[28]See the "Draft Ecclesiastical Ordinances" (1542) in J. K. S. Reid, *Calvin: Theological Treatises* (London: SCM Press, 1954), p. 64.

[29]The 1559 *Institutes* (trans. Ford Lewis Battles) indicate by their textual apparatus at 4.3.9 that Calvin had advocated this procedure in the earlier 1543 edition of the same work. There, as in the work of the preceding year, Calvin makes the identical distinction between the two aspects of diaconal work.

[30]Elsie Ann McKee indicates that Calvin never succeeded in implementing a female diaconal ministry in his adoptive city ("Deacon," in *Encyclopedia of the Reformed Faith*, ed. Donald K. McKim [Louisville, Ky.: Westminster/John Knox, 1992], p. 96). I find it odd that among so many self-consciously conservative followers of Calvin at the present time, more note is not taken of the possibilities latent in this view of Calvin. The oddity is that whereas usually conservative followers of Calvin are ready to quote him unquestioningly, without regard for what his contemporary Reformers may have said or thought on a subject, in this instance they are inclined to dismiss Calvin's views on diaconal ministry as eccentric and out of the mainstream.

Calvin's correspondence with noblewomen who aided the reform.
There seems to be a widespread willingness to suppose that Calvin
leaned to misogyny; after all, his approach to marriage was quite utili-
tarian. The primary qualification he sought in a spouse was her ability
to keep house.[31] But this is hardly the whole story. We see Calvin in
quite a different light when we observe his readiness to meet and cor-
respond with noblewomen of influence in the expectation that they
were in positions where they could advance the cause of reform.[32] Unlike his sometime-associate John Knox—who from his temporary perch
in Geneva wrote a tract warning against the usurping tendencies of
female monarchs such as Mary Tudor of England—Calvin's own position was that female monarchs, while extraordinary, were still to be
accepted and given appropriate respect.[33] This attitude is displayed in
his relationships with a range of female monarchs and noblewomen.

Already in Calvin's early adulthood he had, as a student of law and
of classical civilization, been brought into contact with Renée of Ferrara, queen of the region that remains to this day a north Italian province of the same name. This daughter of French King Louis XII had
married Ercole II, ruler of Ferrara from 1534-1559. Known to be
sympathetic to the Reformation from the years of her early adult life
spent in Paris, Calvin, on the basis of this, sought temporary refuge
in Ferrara in February 1536 (a time when his life was endangered in
France). Yet the sanctuary at Ferrara had been short-lived because
King Ercole was clearly hostile to the reform and determined that no
heretics would be welcomed in his territory. Nevertheless, the contact

---

[31]It is interesting to see this characterization placed on Calvin's attitude toward marriage in the
recent, excellent work of Herman Selderhuis, *John Calvin: A Pilgrim's Life* (Downers Grove,
Ill.: IVP Academic, 2009), chap. 7.

[32]Charmarie Jenkins Blaisdell indicates that Calvin corresponded with eighteen noblewomen
(most of them French); regarding these, sixty letters have been preserved ("Calvin's Letters to
Women: The Courting of Ladies in High Places," *The Sixteenth Century Journal* 13, no. 3
[1982]: 67-69).

[33]Knox, in his *First Blast of the Trumpet Against the Monstrous Regiment of Women* (1558), did not
anticipate that the death of the persecutor Queen Mary in the same year would leave him
vulnerable to the inference that he was just as adamant in his opposition to Mary's half-sister,
the Protestant Elizabeth Tudor. Calvin had been aware of Knox's preparation of the treatise
and, with Bullinger of Zurich, had cautioned him not to go into print with it (see Douglass,
Women, Freedom and Calvin, p. 96). Calvin worked to disassociate himself from Knox's views
in subsequent correspondence with the government of Elizabeth.

established between Calvin and Queen Renée at this time supplied a basis for ongoing correspondence commencing in 1542 and extending to the year of Calvin's death (1564). Renée had been forced to sublimate her Reformed sympathies by King Ercole through the year of his death in 1559. Prior to that date Calvin had pleaded with her by letter to make an open declaration of loyalty to the Reformed cause; only subsequent to her husband's passing and her own return to France did she request that Geneva send her a Reformed pastor. In this, as in other such relationships, it seems that Calvin's primary motivation was the expansion of the reform movement and the strengthening of it by encouraging his well-born correspondents to make their Protestant allegiance public.[34] He sought of well-placed noblewomen exactly what he sought from their male counterparts: visible endorsement and defense of the cause.

Along similar lines, Calvin had a long relationship of correspondence with Marguerite, Queen of Navarre (a territory just north of the Pyrenees). Marguerite (1492-1549) was in fact sister to Francis I, the king of France between 1515-1547, and had in common with her brother an upbringing at Paris that stressed education and exposure to Renaissance ideas. The royal family also displayed—in the period to 1534—a definite openness to religious reform of the type associated with Erasmus of Rotterdam and Jacques Lefèvre d'Étaples.[35] From the time of her marriage in 1509 to the Duke of Alençon, she was queen of the territory abutting the Pyrenees, and it was there that she displayed most openly her sympathies with the Reformed movement, which was increasingly centered at Geneva. Widowed in 1527, she soon thereafter married again, and by this union with the younger Henri d'Albret bore the daughter (Jeanne) who would in time succeed her as monarch.

Correspondence between Calvin and Marguerite almost certainly began in the 1530s, in the aftermath of Calvin's seeking refuge there after a wave of persecution broke out against those accused of sympathy

---

[34]The visit of Calvin to Ferrara is pinpointed to February 1536 by Wulfert De Greef, *The Writings of John Calvin* (Grand Rapids: Baker, 1989), p. 26. Blaisdell casts doubt on whether Calvin was ever formally introduced to Renée at court in Ferrara, yet allows that their correspondence reflects "some prior acquaintance" ("Calvin's Letters to Women," pp. 67-84).

[35]Blaisdell, "Calvin's Letters to Women," p. 75; Stjerna, *Women and the Reformation*, p. 152.

toward Luther in 1533.[36] As in the case of Renée of Ferrara, Calvin sought to move Marguerite to a still more open espousal of the Reformed faith and church; again—like Renée—Marguerite sought to exert her support subtly, not running the risks associated with open endorsement. While there was never great doubt about Marguerite's sincerity, it was left to her daughter, Jeanne d'Albret (1528-1572) to make the open espousal of Reformed Christianity that her mother had been unwilling to make. Calvin's cordial correspondence with her led in time to the dispatching of Calvin's own associate Theodore Beza to serve as court preacher for the young queen. Jeanne d'Albret was instrumental in gaining representation for leaders of the Reformed movement in the Colloquy of Poissy, a gathering organized by Catherine de Medici in 1561, in the hope of securing common ground between Catholic and Protestant movements. When this initiative was unproductive and open hostilities broke out, Jeanne was then instrumental in securing the short-lived "Edict of Tolerance" in the next year.[37]

We should be alert to the larger picture that Calvin's correspondence with noblewomen is a part of. Plainly, sixteenth-century Europe (and especially France) had a growing number of women who, by virtue of their family ties, social position and wealth, were positioned to offer tremendous assistance to the struggling Reformed movement. In pursuit of their assistance, Reformers such as Calvin engaged in what might be called ecclesiastical diplomacy to direct them toward certain courses of action. And exercise their influence they did. We have reports that when they utilized their influence to secure and appoint preachers for struggling congregations within their vicinity (and they contributed substantially toward their upkeep) this exercise of womanly influence in the churches was noted, and sometimes resented. Be that as it may be, Calvin and others in his position sought to ensure that the considerable influence of such women would be utilized to the Protestant movement's benefit. Whether in his dealings with the French noblewomen named or in similar dealings with the young Queen Elizabeth of England, Calvin's conduct showed a real readiness to deal con-

---

[36]Stjerna, *Women and the Reformation*, p. 153
[37]Ibid., p. 165.

structively with those who, under providence, had been made "mothers" to the Protestant movement.

THE CONTRAST BETWEEN THE PIONEER PHASE OF THE REFORMATION AND LATER CONSOLIDATION

However, having related these details regarding the new state of affairs introduced when Renaissance writers who advocated the elevation of women had their ideas trickle into the Reformation movements, and noting how the early Reformation both re-ennobled marriage and afforded women largely unprecedented opportunities to exert influence on behalf of the gospel, we are left to contemplate the fact that the legacy of this period did not produce long-term change in attitudes about gender. Considerable momentum was lost. We must face up to the fact that in our time the perception exists that the writings of the Genevan Reformer provide what Willis DeBoer aptly called "an arsenal of weapons [to be used] to stem the tide of the new role for women."[38] It has indeed become a common thing, given the Reformed tradition's overly deferential attitude toward Calvin, to read and to hear him summoned as a kind of "expert witness" on why women should not aspire to certain forms of recognized ministry closed to them in past.[39] But there is something unnatural, something forced, about such appeals.

While no doubt there is a potential danger that Calvin would be appropriated and appealed to by those seeking to enlist him in causes he would never have endorsed, it is as necessary for us now to recognize that portions of the Reformed world today fall well behind Calvin's own demonstrated sixteenth-century readiness to capitalize on the then-expanding influence of women in kingdom work. It is not enough to quote Calvin on what he resisted; to be fair we must observe what he helped forward. The evidence supports the conviction that he encouraged an enlarged role for believing women in society (on behalf of the church) and in the ministries of the church itself. In subsequent centu-

---

[38]Willis P. DeBoer, "Calvin on the Role of Women," in *Exploring the Heritage of John Calvin: Essays in Honor of John Bratt*, ed. David E. Holwerda (Grand Rapids: Baker, 1976), p. 238.
[39]This tendency has been shown to be unwarranted in the first chapter of this book, "Myth 1: One Man (Calvin) and One City (Geneva) Are Determinative."

ries there has been a periodic recurrence of some of the factors which Calvin grappled with in his own century, that is, both wider cultural changes providing for an expanded role for women in society and notable Christian women seeking an expanded role for ministry and service. Several can be named as stimuli for reflection.

Eighteenth-century evangelical awakenings. In a way quite unforeseen the eighteenth-century religious awakenings we especially associate with the careers of John Wesley, Charles Wesley, George Whitefield and Jonathan Edwards brought to the fore select females who exercised authority on a scale comparable with those "mothers" of the French Reformed churches John Calvin corresponded with at such length. Two (both from the United Kingdom) call for special comment.

Selena Hastings, Countess of Huntingdon. Selina Hastings, Countess of Huntingdon (1707-1791), was converted under the preaching of the awakening and began to use her patrician influence to reach members of her social class with the gospel.[40] While her first initiatives involved inviting prominent evangelical Church of England ministers to hold preaching services in her stately homes, in time she began to acquire properties where buildings suitable for church services were renovated or erected. In time, these sixty-four chapels were served by pastors she appointed and subsidized. The flavor of this connection of churches was the evangelical Calvinism of George Whitefield (appointed as her official chaplain). At a later date, congregations were established as far afield as the colonies of Newfoundland, Nova Scotia and Upper Canada (today's Ontario), as well as Sierra Leone (West Africa). Selina Hastings was nothing if not comprehensive in her planning; she determined after taking advice that a theological college ought to be begun to supply suitable preachers for her chapels and for the wider evangelical movement. By 1768 that pastor's college was established in Trevecca,

---

[40]The Countess of Huntingdon has been the focus of intensive research since 1990. At least three major biographical works have appeared: Boyd S. Schlenther, *Queen of the Methodists: The Countess of Huntingdon and the Eighteenth-Century Crisis of Faith and Society* (Durham, U.K.: Durham Academic Press, 1997); Faith Cook, *Selina, Countess of Huntingdon* (Edinburgh: Banner of Truth, 2001); and John R. Tyson and Boyd S. Schlenther, eds., *In the Midst of Early Methodism: Lady Huntingdon and Her Correspondence* (Lanham, Md.: Scarecrow, 2006).

Wales; her educational concern would extend across the Atlantic, where she contributed financially to the founding of Dartmouth College and Princeton University. Just prior to her death she entrusted her network of chapels to three trustees, one of which, Lady Agnes Erskine, was cut from the same cloth as herself. This church "mother" thus provided for a kind of succession that ensured that another woman, selected by herself, would have a capacious role like her own.[41]

Lady Willielma Glenorchy. Lady Glenorchy (1741-1786) had a life and career, which uncannily replicated elements in the life of her contemporary, the Countess of Huntingdon. She, like the countess, was converted in adult life and had a spouse who was unsympathetic to evangelicalism. She, like the countess, entered her greatest period of Christian usefulness when, upon being widowed, she devoted her time and fortune to gospel causes. In the case of Lady Glenorchy this trajectory began with the building of an evangelical chapel in the city of Edinburgh in 1774. She undertook this endeavor while maintaining her own link with the national church of her country, the Church of Scotland, and while affirming its traditional Calvinist theology. Then, in short order, Lady Glenorchy (who traveled for considerable parts of the year in England) opened additional chapels in Exmouth, Buxton, Carlisle, Matlock, Bristol, Newton Burhill (Devonshire) and Workington.[42] Prior to her death in 1786, Lady Glenorchy (like the countess) had the foresight to entrust the management of her connection of chapels to another; and like her she chose another woman to be this superintending figure, Lady Darcy Maxwell.[43]

---

[41]Peter Lineham, "Huntingdon, Selina Countess of," in *Dictionary of Evangelical Biography: 1730-1860*, ed. Donald M. Lewis (Oxford: Blackwell, 1996), 1:585-86; J. D. Douglas, "Countess of Huntingdon's Connection," in *New International Dictionary of the Christian Church*, ed. J. D. Douglas (Grand Rapids: Zondervan, 1974), p. 266; "Selina Hastings, Countess of Huntingdon," *Wikipedia* <http://en.wikipedia.org/wiki/Selina_Hastings,_Countess_of_Huntingdon>. Edwin Welch makes plain that Agnes Erskine, while made the chief administrator of the Connection after Selina's death in 1791, labored under the grave difficulty of having virtually no money of her own to sustain the cause—on which her predecessor had lavished a good part of the £100,000 she gave to various charities in her lifetime ("Erskine, Lady Anne Agnes," in *Dictionary of Evangelical Biography*, 1:361).

[42]E. Dorothy Graham, "Glenorchy, Lady Willielma," in *Dictionary of Evangelical Biography*, 1:449-50.

[43]E. Dorothy Graham, "Maxwell, Lady Darcy," in *Dictionary of Evangelical Biography*, 2:757.

We should not seek to prove principles by relating anecdotes. This caution applies to the eighteenth century (from which these examples are furnished) and just as equally to the sixteenth. Nevertheless, what such stories illustrate is that friends of the Reformed tradition seemed able in both centuries to recognize the providential elevation of such individuals as the countess and the lady into positions where they could do considerable good for the cause of the gospel. There is no evidence that contemporary Calvinists stood in the path of such church "mothers" and instructed them to cease and desist on the ground that what they proposed to do could not possibly be the work of God.[44] We see here then, as in the sixteenth century, an example of adaptation to providential developments; it was granted that God could raise up friends and advocates of the gospel in whatever fashion he chose.

IN THE GREAT CENTURY OF MISSIONARY ADVANCE

For good reason, Kenneth Scott Latourette (1884-1968), the notable historian of world mission, titled the segment of his seven-volume *History of the Expansion of Christianity* devoted to the nineteenth century "The Great Century."[45] In a way somewhat analogous to the sixteenth century, this period of missionary advance would be characterized by an extending of the influence of believing women.

A door gradually opened to women in mission. In the earliest stages of this profusion of modern missionary effort, women were only welcome to be involved in world missions in the supporting role of spouse. Males experienced a "call" to missionary service, while their wives were expected either to accompany them in a supportive role or (sometimes) to remain in the sending country while taking full responsibility for the

---

[44]At the same time, it is only fair to say that some preachers in each century found the directive role in church affairs assumed by these church mothers to be contrary to their liking. The Countess of Huntingdon and Lady Glenorchy did not stand alone in this exercise of patronage in church planting. Late eighteenth-century evangelical ministers Roland Hill (1744-1833) and Robert Haldane (1764-1842) also built up large networks of churches in the west of England and Scotland (respectively), pouring a considerable amount of their own wealth into the enterprises.

[45]Kenneth Scott Latourette, *The History of the Expansion of Christianity* (London: Eyre & Spottiswoode, 1944). The nineteenth-century "advance" is generally reckoned to have commenced with the sending of William Carey to India in 1793 and to have ended with the outbreak of the Great War in 1914.

rearing of their children. Yet this early nineteenth-century framework soon proved to be inadequate; missionary experience demonstrated that females in the culture receiving missionaries were unreachable apart from a female messenger, thus the role of the missionary spouse needed to be expanded. The first wife of Adoniram Judson (1788-1850), Ann Hasseltine Judson (1789-1826), was the trailblazer in this respect; she accompanied her husband to Burma in 1812 with her own sense of missionary calling, rapidly acquired the local languages, did Bible translation work and was successful in evangelism with women.[46] As the sending churches in Europe and North America assimilated the wider implications of the pattern of missionary usefulness demonstrated by Ann Judson and others, the door was gradually opened for a second type of woman to find usefulness in crosscultural mission: the single woman who, by helping with the care and education of the children of missionaries, could free female missionary spouses to exercise direct ministries of their own. Then, when single women in mission had proved their usefulness as educators to missionary children, it occurred to some in 1827 that such female missionary workers might extend the gospel also by teaching indigenous women and children.[47]

Now the expansion of this missionary ministry by women in the nineteenth century was largely advanced by many recently founded women's missionary societies in the sending countries.[48] The existence of these societies, which had begun to appear around the year 1800, testified to the slowness of existing missionary agencies (founded in the aftermath of the founding of the Baptist Missionary Society in Eng-

---

[46]Marguerite Kraft, "Women in Mission," in *Evangelical Dictionary of World Mission*, ed. A. Scott Moreau (Grand Rapids: Baker, 2000), p. 1021.

[47]Ibid. And Janice Holmes, "Women Preachers and the New Orders: A: Women Preachers in the Protestant Churches," in *The Cambridge History of Christianity: World Christianities c. 1515-1914*, ed. Sheridan Gilley and Brian Stanley (Cambridge: Cambridge University Press, 2006), pp. 86-90.

[48]These were sometimes denominational women's societies and sometimes transdenominational. Their foundations, stemming from 1800 onward, are helpfully surveyed in R. Pierce Beaver, *All Loves Excelling* (Grand Rapids: Eerdmans, 1968), chap. 1. Of the purely denominational women's societies, Kraft reports that "by 1900 over forty denominational women's societies existed with over three million active women raising funds to build hospitals and schools around the world, paying the salaries of indigenous female evangelists, and sending single women as missionary doctors, teachers, and evangelists" ("Women in Mission," p. 1022).

land in 1792) to properly gauge and enfold the rising missionary zeal of women. The women's societies, originally founded to support domestic needs (such as Bible distribution and evangelism among American aboriginal peoples), soon found opportunity to support foreign missionary work by women, who still found ministry opportunity difficult to locate in their homelands. The proliferation of such women's societies was especially notable after 1870. In time the growth and influence of such societies provoked open disagreement about whether their existence tended to undermine denominational agencies, but as denominational agencies would scarcely countenance a major leadership role for women, the problem seemed intractable.[49] After 1910 pressure was exerted to combine such denominational women's societies with preexisting denominational mission agencies. But whatever economies of administration may have been realized by this amalgamation, there was considerable dynamism lost in the process.

Across those decades of great missionary expansion, a point had been hammered home: in the call for laborers during the era of expansion, women had responded in vast numbers—first as childcare workers and teachers of missionary children, then as teachers and evangelists of indigenous women and children, then as medical workers. Women had found their ways into ministry roles abroad that would not readily have been open to them in their homelands. It was only a matter of time until this discrepancy of ministry worked, leaven-like, to force difficult questions on the attention of Reformed churches at home. No issue was more urgent than the failure of the church at home to embrace women in official ministries, given the proven indispensability of the ministry of women abroad.[50] As it had proved useful on the mission field, among American Presbyterians, a consensus emerged by 1892 that it would be proper to authorize a "deaconess" movement special-

---

[49]Lois A. Boyd and Douglas Brackenridge, "American Presbyterian Women: 1870-1980," in *Triumph Over Silence*, pp. 206-7.

[50]L.O. Macdonald emphasizes that it was furloughing missionaries who were "often in the vanguard of moves to achieve equality of office and status for women in the Church (and several were prominent suffragists too)" ("Women in Presbyterian Missions," in *Dictionary of Scottish Church History and Theology*, ed. Nigel M. de S. Cameron [Downers Grove, Ill.: InterVarsity Press, 1993], p. 890).

izing in the home visitation and help of the needy.[51]

At the dawn of the twentieth century. In the same decades of the nineteenth century that had seen Christian women win expanded acceptance in foreign missions roles, great social changes were affecting the Western societies from which they had gone abroad. In major conflicts, such as the Crimean War (1853-1856), the U.S. Civil War (1861-1865) and the Great War (1914-1918), women served with distinction, and at considerable risk, as military nurses and in military-related industry. The colossal loss of life on the battlefields had, as one consequence among many, an actual depletion of the male labor force and a continuing opportunity for post-war female employment outside the home.

The growth of universal public education in this period created an insatiable demand for school teachers with postsecondary preparation. Already by 1890 more young American women than men were finishing high school.[52] But the staffing of the growing number of public schools presented a challenge because female teachers were in demand and there were few institutions in existence ready to train them. There had already been select institutions, such as Oberlin College (founded 1833) that had always accepted male and female students on equal terms, yet for most of the nineteenth century aspiring women were obliged to seek admission to exclusively female institutions. Major universities in North America and Europe, formerly male-only enclaves, began to admit women only after 1870; some waited until after 1920.[53] By the close of World War I, widespread agitation for women's voting rights (which had preexisted the war) resumed again, and most Western democracies granted this right by 1930. Between the missionary

---

[51]This was in the context of the Northern Presbyterian Church; Boyd and Brackenridge, "American Presbyterian Women," pp. 208-9.

[52]Barbara Miller Solomon, *In the Company of Educated Women* (New Haven, Conn.: Yale University Press, 1985), p. 46.

[53]Ibid., p. 51. Boston University, a Methodist-supported university, led the way with this policy in 1870. By contrast, British universities moved far more deliberately. Cambridge University would grant no woman a degree until 1921, while Oxford had granted the privilege one year earlier. But both universities had for some decades permitted students, enrolled in adjacent unaffiliated women's colleges, to write their standard exams ("Fact Sheet: Women at Cambridge: A Chronology," *University of Cambridge* <http://www.admin.cam.ac.uk/news/press/factsheets/women2.html>; "Women at Oxford," *University of Oxford* <www.ox.ac.uk/about_the_university/introducing_oxford/women_at_oxford/index.html>.

advances demonstrated in the nineteenth century and the changing social attitudes toward women in the new century, how would the
churches respond? They did so cautiously.

In the early decades of the twentieth century, churches in the Reformed family began, gingerly, to take up the question of the appropriate uses of the gifts entrusted to believing women. One Scottish denomination, the United Free Church took a first step in 1914 by
regularizing the new office of "Church Sister."[54] Here was recognition
at home of a principle clarified in foreign missions: much ministry
among women was effectively carried out only by a woman. By 1919 the
same denomination (which was clearly progressive by the standards of
the time) made provision for the office of deacon to be open to "men
and women appointed for three years."[55] Prior to that denomination's
reunion with the Church of Scotland in 1929, it had already debated
(inconclusively) a proposal to open all offices of the church to women.
By 1935 the now-united body went so far as to open only the diaconate
to both genders. That body eventually admitted women as elders in
1966 and as ministers in 1968. Other denominations in the Presbyterian family had taken up the same questions too. The Presbyterian
Church in England had begun to ordain women ministers in 1917.

In the same post–World War I era, such discussion began in earnest
within North America. The United Church of Canada, a 1925 union
of Methodist, Presbyterian and Congregational churches ordained its
first woman to the ministry in 1936. The Presbyterian Church in the
U.S.A. began discussion in 1919 about opening the offices of deacon,
elder and minister to females. The offices were dealt with separately
and over an extended period of time; by 1920 consensus was reached on
opening the office of deacon to women; by 1930 the office of elder; by
1956 the office of pastor.[56]

---

[54]The United Free Church was a 1900 union of the majority of the Free Church of Scotland and
the United Presbyterian Church.

[55]Macdonald, "Women in Presbyterian Churches," p. 886. This provision was offered as an alternative to the preexisting policy of male deacons appointed in perpetuity. The new provision
was optional. Macdonald also makes plain that, as early as the 1860s, Scottish Presbyterian
churches were using "Bible women" in their outreaches to the poor. This seems to have been
the recovery of an office or title of ministry found in the early church.

[56]Lois A. Boyd, "Women in the Reformed Tradition: 19th & 20th Centuries," in *Encyclopedia*

It must at once be acknowledged that the adjustments in the twentieth century just described did leave many unsatisfied. The changes described here had come in response to multiple contributing factors: one, of lessons learned in world missions; another, of insights derived from the observation of a changing society in which women were steadily better educated, had gained the power of the ballot, and had shown the invaluable character of their work in times of World War. But there was also, and concurrently, a change of attitudes toward the Bible—such that what were formerly taken to be biblical prohibitions on women in official ministries were now being reinterpreted or set aside.[57]

Of those denominations that have responded to these changes by maintaining the old prohibitions of women in ministry, the question can fairly be asked: Are there still no lessons learned in world missions that ought to ameliorate our ideas about the practice of ministry at home today? Does the usefulness of women in early Reformed history and the observable changes in gender roles across the twentieth century not require *any* rethinking on the part of today's churches? Of those denominations that have made the changes in ministry described in this chapter, the questions can fairly be asked: Was it indeed the input of mission principles that moved your church to adopt this change, or was it the other factor—observed societal change—that was the prime mover? If prohibitory statements of the New Testament were set aside in the process of widening ministry opportunity for women, how does biblical authority fare in your churches today?

CONCLUSION

The Reformation-era recovery of the priesthood of all believers (which in principle set men and women on an equal spiritual footing), combined with the newfound zeal to proclaim the Word of God to a population unfamiliar with it, introduced into European Christian life a new momentum. Women as well as men were moved to undertake

---

of the Reformed Tradition, pp. 400-401; Boyd and Brackenridge, "American Presbyterian Women," pp. 210-11.

[57]Among these New Testament Scriptures are the following: 1 Cor 14:34; 1 Tim 2:12; 3:1-13. I, the author, am affiliated with the Presbyterian Church in America, which upholds these prohibitions. I do not accept that the New Testament conceives of the diaconate as male-only.

forms of proclamation. But intervening centuries have not necessarily
nurtured these original impulses well. Subsequent periods of spiritual
zeal (such as the eighteenth-century awakenings and the rise of the
missionary movement in the nineteenth century) have shown the need
for cross-gender collaboration to be maintained in the worldwide cause
of the gospel. Whatever our denominational situation, it is still necessary for these recovered insights to be pursued.

There is considerable common ground available to be shared between the Reformed churches that have and those that have not opened
their official ministries to both genders. All can observe that the New
Testament shows ways of including women in some forms of recognized ministry under the rubrics of "fellow worker" (Euodia and Syn-
tyche in Phil 4:3), and of "deacon" or "servant" (Phoebe in Rom 16:1).
All can verify that the early church soon instituted an order of ministry
called "Bible woman" and "church sister."[58] In the Reformation era and
since, it is a matter of record that Reformed churches have also chosen
to *add* to the number of recognized offices in the church in light of
pressing emergent circumstances.[59] Today, as before, we can readily
point to persons we might honor as "church mothers." What scruples
still remain that hinder the recognition of the principle that the work of
the gospel warrants colabor of a recognized kind?

DISCUSSION QUESTIONS

1. Historian Kirsi Stjerna has written that "teaching courses on the
   Reformation is no longer feasible without the inclusion of women as
   subjects in the story of the Reformation and its evaluation."[60] Is this
   statement welcome? Problematic? Objectionable? Discuss.

2. In reading this chapter, what struck you as the single most important
   contribution, of which you had been previously unaware, of women
   to the Reformed tradition?

---

[58]T. M. Lindsay, *The Church and Its Ministry in Early Centuries* (London: Hodder, 1902), pp.
181-82.

[59]Examples of such additions would include the office of "doctor," introduced by Calvin at Geneva in his "Draft Ecclesiastical Order" of 1542, and the Scottish Reformed Church's introduction of the offices of "superintendent" and "reader" in 1560.

[60]Stjerna, *Women and the Reformation*, p. 1.

3. Of the several factors that have helped the Reformed tradition enlarge its understanding of the role of women in Christian service, which do you think is the most significant?

4. The idea of "church mothers" is not one that has had much recognition in the Reformed tradition. It certainly summed up well the influence of some sixteenth-century Christian women. Who might be added to this category in more recent times, and why?

FURTHER READING

Bainton, Roland. *Women of the Reformation*, 3 vols. Minneapolis: Augsburg, 1971.

Beaver, R. Pierce. *All Loves Excelling.* Grand Rapids: Eerdmans, 1968.

Douglass, Jane Dempsey. *Women, Freedom and Calvin.* Philadelphia: Westminster Press, 1985.

Greaves, Richard L. *Triumph Over Silence: Women in Protestant History.* Westport, Conn.: Greenwood, 1985.

Stjerna, Kirsi. *Women and the Reformation.* Oxford: Blackwell, 2009.

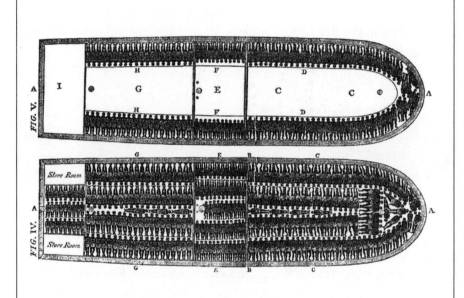

Plan of the British Slave Ship, "Brookes," 1789

*Image: wad1, as shown on www.slaveryimages.org, sponsored by the Virginia
Foundation for the Humanities and the University of Virginia Library,
http://hitchcock.itc.virginia.edu/Slavery/details.php?categorynum=5&category
Name=Slave Ships and the Atlantic Crossing (Middle Passage)&the
Record=11&recordCount=78*

MYTH TEN

Calvinism Has Fostered
Racial Inequality

As in chapter nine, we begin by admitting that there is an abundance of anecdotal evidence that would seem to tie the Calvinist or Reformed movement to oppressive policies on race. Those who want to disparage the Calvinist movement can readily enough do this on the basis of things easily known about racial inequities perpetuated in regions of the United States, regions once associated with slavery and subsequently known for the withholding of civil rights. And then there is the Republic of South Africa, in which racism and the segregation of the races dominated national politics until 1994. Calvinism was a force in both regions, and racism and segregation were facts of life in both. Is that not proof enough? But association is not causation. The European Christian practice of enslavement long pre-dated the birth of Protestantism, and the branches of Protestantism (the Reformed among them), once they arose, eventually differed over the legitimacy of these practices. These issues would eventually divide Baptists and Anglicans, Methodists and Presbyterians.

EUROPEAN ENSLAVEMENT PRIOR TO THE RENAISSANCE AND REFORMATION ERA

The sober fact is that slavery was practiced and perpetuated by European Christians for many centuries before the era of the Protestant-Catholic divide. No one should pretend that this pedigree—extending back into the Roman era and the subsequent period in which the empire's boundaries were penetrated by barbarians—lends any legitimacy to slavery as an institution.[1] As these warring tribes moved across Europe, they took prisoners from among their defeated enemies, and these became slaves—even when the warring sides both claimed adherence to forms of Christianity. The church itself held slaves in this post-Roman era, and utilized them to cultivate lands from which they drew important revenues. Only gradually, as medieval Europe was threatened again (by Viking invaders), did this very widespread enslavement of former enemies give way to the practice of serfdom. The latter practice displaced the former because, in uncertain feudal times, serfs (who, compared to slaves, profited by their own agricultural labor) could be better counted on to fight off invaders, and serfs required far less supervision in their work than the enslaved did. Thus Phillips has written, "Master and serf were bound together in a web of mutual rights, obligations and economic relations."[2]

Early Italian enslavement of Central Europeans. By the tenth century, slavery began to be revived in Western Europe by traders who introduced to the West large quantities of Slavs (inhabitants of a region extending from the Baltic through Poland and south to the Balkans)—from which all modern European languages have derived the term *slave*.[3] These Slavs, in addition to being sold as far to the west as Spain (still substantially under Muslim control), were taken south to Mediterranean ports; some of these ports came temporarily into Muslim hands. And such ports as Marseille and later Venice became great export centers of European slaves to the Muslim world. Meanwhile in Eastern Europe, a similar trade in slaves was carried on by Scandina-

---

[1]Slavery in the earliest Christian centuries is surveyed in R. H. Barrow, *Slavery in the Roman Empire* (New York: Barnes & Noble, 1968).

[2]William D. Phillips Jr., *Slavery from Roman Times to the Early Transatlantic Trade* (Minneapolis: University of Minnesota Press, 1985), pp. 55-57. The same point is made by Erwin Fahlbusch and Esther Szabo, "Slavery," in *The Encyclopedia of Christianity*, ed. Erwin Fahlbusch et al. (Grand Rapids: Eerdmans, 2008), 5:30.

[3]Phillips, *Slavery from Roman Times*, p. 57, lists the following cognates: slave, *esclave, esclavo, escravo, schiavo* and *sklave*.

vian traders down the Dnieper River, across the Black Sea to Constantinople and to Itil on the Caspian Sea.

The Slavs were not alone in being sold into the Muslim world; Saxon peoples from northwest Europe sometimes endured a similar fate. In these centuries Western Europe (as the less economically developed region) had little of value to trade with the eastern Mediterranean and the Muslim world, and thus experienced what we would call a balance of payments deficit. The availability and export of European slaves redressed this economic imbalance. Payments for slaves, taken in gold, enabled the European purchase of luxury items, such as silks, ivory, spices and sugar from Muslim traders.[4]

Muslim slave-trading as an abiding norm. At first, in the wake of the conquest of non-Muslim territories and subsequently through trade, the taking and trading of slaves in the Muslim world was a constant through what Europeans have called the Middle Ages. Christians and Jews who surrendered their communities to Muslim invaders were allowed to live in peace (albeit under significant taxation), but those who offered armed resistance to Muslim conquest and were captured in battle were likely to be sold as slaves. Once Muslim territories had reached their geographical zenith in the east and west (so that there was little further territorial conquest), the taking and sale of slaves had more to do with trade. We read of sub-Saharan Africans transported to the Persian Gulf region, where they worked as slaves on large sugar plantations; others from the same region labored in Egyptian gold mines;[5] and north European Slavs comprised whole armed units in the troops of eastern caliphs.[6] Considering only the recruitment of slaves from the African continent, Ralph A. Austin estimated that in the me-

---

[4]Ibid., pp. 61-62.

[5]It is absolutely essential that from this point onward we understand that the export of sub-Saharan Africans for the purposes of slavery—whether to the Muslim world, Europe or the Western hemisphere—was a matter of trade in which one party to the exchange was always an African chief or tribe that had captured Africans of another tribe with a view to profiting by their sale. Phillips has also documented how Portuguese slave traders obtained Niger Delta, Congo and Angolan slaves on this basis and resold them to tribal chiefs in the region we now call the Gold Coast, where they did forced labor for the African traders who brought goods for trade (spices and gold) from the interior (ibid., p. 143).

[6]Ibid., pp. 79-86.

dieval era, Muslim slave traders removed 7,450,000 sub-Saharan Africans for various slave purposes. This number did not include those who perished in transit.[7] The vast scale of this market in slaves and the tie between enslavement of Africans and large-scale agriculture and extraction of raw materials was thus well-established and known well before the era of European transoceanic exploration.

Italian city-states and slavery. At the time of the launch of the Crusades in 1095, an existing involvement in trading slaves from Slavic and Balkan regions within Italy mushroomed as city-states such as Venice, Florence and Genoa began to gather and market slaves for use in Palestinian territories, where victorious Crusaders seized and expanded the existing production of sugar. Crusaders who remained in the Holy Land after the initial European victories had seized these enterprises from Muslim owners. Not only were the crusading landholders supplied with slaves in such locales as Tyre, Sidon and Acre by these Italian middlemen, but so also did Muslim authorities in the East Mediterranean in such locales as Alexandria turn to the same Italian middlemen for a supply of slaves, gathered in the Black Sea region.[8] And as this Italian foreign trade in slaves expanded, so also did the sale of foreign slaves within these Italian city-states. Genoa had its own slave market for the domestic market commencing in 1190; in this domestic market Muslim black slaves were soon for sale.[9]

The growth of intra-European slavery was dramatically accelerated by the decimation of the population of Western Europe in light of the spread of the Black Death after 1346. The labor shortage that followed on the heels of the loss of up to one third of the population resulted in a dearth of persons willing to serve as domestic servants (those surviving the plague who had formerly filled these roles now moved on to more lucrative employment). The city-state of Florence,

---

[7]Ralph A. Austen, "The Trans-Saharan Slave Trade: A Tentative Census," in *The Uncommon Market: Essays in the Economic History of the Atlantic Slave Trade*, ed. Henry A. Gemery and Jans S. Hogendorn (New York: Academic Press, 1979), quoted in Phillips, *Slavery from Roman Times*, p. 87. Albert Wirz reports an aggregate of seventeen million slaves traded by Muslims to North Africa and the Middle East over the period from the seventh to the twentieth centuries ("Slavery," *Encyclopedia of Christianity*, 5:31).
[8]Phillips, *Slavery from Roman Times*, pp. 93-95.
[9]Ibid., p. 103.

in consequence, allowed the unrestricted importation of slaves from outside Italy beginning in 1363.[10]

Spanish and Portuguese enslavement of West Africans precedes transatlantic discovery. Spain and Portugal had participated in the intra-European slave trade that had revived in the tenth century. These nations also took Muslim slaves in the course of their ongoing military conflicts with the Islamic kingdoms that controlled southern portions of the Iberian peninsula until the year 1492 (when the reconquista was completed). Beyond this, both countries transported African slaves—obtained either by trade with African merchants or by direct capture—to their various Atlantic island colonies (such as the Cape Verde Islands, Madeira and the Canaries). Such was the influx of African slaves into Portugal itself that by 1480 a slave market was established in the capital, Lisbon. In consequence African slaves came to comprise 2.5-3 percent of the Portuguese population, while in Lisbon itself the proportion sometimes reached 10 percent.[11] In the Spanish city of Seville a 1565 census showed that 7.4 percent of the population was African and enslaved. In the Iberian Peninsula itself, most slaves were put to domestic rather than agricultural uses, yet in the Atlantic islands, both Spain and Portugal began to use slaves in the large-scale plantation settings that slavery would soon be connected with in the Western Hemisphere.

Having allowed that Spain joined Portugal in this late-fifteenth-century expansion of the use of sub-Saharan African slaves, it must still be acknowledged that Portugal was the trailblazer in this development. Beginning with its capture of the Moroccan coastal city of Ceuta in 1415, Portugal began its incremental advance southward on Africa's Atlantic coast in search of grain, gold and slaves. In each respect it was determined to eliminate past reliance on trans-Saharan Muslim traders who had brought these items to the Mediterranean coast of North Africa by camel train. As the Portuguese influence extended southward from Ceuta, the off-shore Cape Verde Islands

---

[10]Ibid., p. 105.
[11]William Phillips, "Slavery," in *Encyclopedia of the Renaissance*, ed. Paul F. Grendler (New York: Scribner's, 1999), 6:40.

became a main staging area for the use of sub-Saharan slaves in agriculture (the products of which were then used in African and European trade) and the re-export of slaves to other destinations.[12] By
1525 Portugal was gathering slaves for export from Morocco in the
north to as far south as Angola.

The massive expansion of transatlantic slavery in the age of Colum-
bus. It is quite well known that the importation of African slaves to the
Western Hemisphere was an improvisation designed to address two
problems the European explorers did not properly anticipate. First, the
European explorers attempted to force the labor of the aboriginal peoples of the Caribbean and Central America in growing sugar cane and
mining precious metals, only to find that this population was unaccus-
tomed to the intense labor required by these enterprises. The people
were industrious, but their manner of existence had not required this
kind of day-in-and-day-out labor. Monarchs in Spain and Portugal,
once alerted to the abuse of the aboriginals, pressed to prevent their
enslavement so long as they undertook no military resistance. Yet, the
royal wish was as often honored in the breach as in the observance.[13]
Second, even as the Europeans, so interested in the extraction of resources, were finding the local labor force unequal to the challenges
this posed, terrible infectious diseases (inadvertently introduced by the
Europeans themselves) proceeded to decimate the native population.
Smallpox was the most devastating of these diseases.

Modern studies of the decline of population in colonial Mexico have
indicated that the period from 1519 to 1605 saw a decrease from 25.3

---

[12]Ceuta continued to be under Portuguese control until 1580, when it became a Spanish possession (Phillips, *Slavery from Roman Times*, pp. 136-41).

[13]Phillips, *Slavery from Roman Times*, pp. 179, 181. A significant role was played in alerting
the Spanish monarchy to the peril faced by the aboriginal peoples by the renowned Bartolomé de las Casas (1474-1566). The latter, having profited by the "encomienda" system
(which required the colonist to provide basic education and religious instruction to natives,
while receiving their labor in return) agitated for an end to such arrangements. His advocacy
on behalf of natives helped move the papacy to declare (in 1537) that native peoples were
rational beings entitled to the same basic rights as Europeans. See A. Scott Moreau, "De las
Casas, Bartholomew," in *Evangelical Dictionary of World Missions*, ed. A. Scott Moreau
(Grand Rapids: Baker, 2000), pp. 553-54. However, as Phillips points out, part of the plea
of de las Casas in seeking the amelioration of conditions for the native population was that
African slaves be imported in order to lift this inhuman labor from their shoulders (*Slavery
from Roman Times*, p. 180).

million to 1 million persons, whereas in colonial Peru the decrease was from 3.3 million persons in 1520 to 601,000 in 1630.[14] These two factors, when taken in combination, might have required both Spain and Portugal to fundamentally recalculate—and even abandon—their objectives in the hemisphere. But in fact, both countries moved to resolve these problems related to the supply of labor by looking to Africa. Spaniards advocated as early as 1516 that African slaves be imported to their colonies; the Portuguese call for slaves for Brazil arose in 1549.[15] In the period to 1650, some 350,000 African slaves reached the ports of Spanish America, and 250,000 reached Brazil. Before long, Catholic France would send nearly equal numbers to its Caribbean colonies.[16]

Transition: Slavery and Protestantism. In opening this chapter a caution was given that we not construe the eventual association of Reformed Protestantism with slavery as if it were the causation of slavery. It is only now, after reflecting on the more than half-millennium of Christian European involvement in intra-European and sub-Saharan slavery, that we can even begin to consider the question of Reformed Protestant association—inasmuch as all the groundwork for the rapid post-1500 expansion of slavery into the New World had been so clearly laid out by Catholic nations Spain and Portugal, and imitated by various north Italian city-states. Generally, but not completely, abiding by the dictum that European Christians ought not to enslave other Christians, the Spaniards, Portuguese and Italians had readily enslaved and sold Eastern Europeans (which they conveniently reckoned as non-Christians), Muslims and sub-Saharan Africans.

These nations had also grasped the principle that the cultivation and production of sugar could not be supported, large scale, by free labor—a very scarce commodity in the aftermath of the Great Plague. The

---

[14]Phillips, *Slavery from Roman Times*, p. 178.

[15]Ibid., pp. 180, 182.

[16]Ibid., p. 192. Albert Wirz supplies a number of eleven million Africans forcibly shipped to America in the period up to the end of the nineteenth century ("Slavery," 5:31). Hugh Thomas agrees with the eleven million number, and shows that Portugal led all other European nations in this trade by a margin of more than 2 to 1 (*The Slave Trade: The Story of the Atlantic Slave Trade 1440-1870* [New York: Simon & Schuster, 1997], pp. 804-5). Leading European slaving nations were Portugal: 4,650,000; Britain: 2,600,000; Spain: 1,600,000; France: 1,250,000; Holland: 500,000; and British North America: 300,000.

pre-Reformation Western Church had offered minimal resistance to the expansion of this trade in humans and had very frequently held its own slaves to work its expanding landholdings. Christian voices were scarcely ever raised to insist that slavery was degrading, inhumane and inconsistent with the possession of the divine image by all humans. With this understanding in place, we may take up the question of how nations associated with Reformed Protestantism eventually came to be associated with this degrading practice of such long standing. The two nations associated with Reformed Protestantism that led the engagement with the slave trade were the British and the Dutch.

BRITISH AND DUTCH INVOLVEMENT IN AN EXISTING TRANSATLANTIC SLAVE TRADE

Already in the period 1562-1568, English privateers John Hawkins and John Lovell seized both cargoes of slaves en route from Africa to the New World and of refined sugar in transit on the return journey.[17] The slaves in question were not put to any British use but sold in slave markets in Spanish America; it would be some decades until there were British plantations in need of slave labor. British colonies in the New World (North American and Caribbean) did not move to utilize African slaves until well into the seventeenth century, and for two reasons. The British did not yet have unrestricted access to the west coast of Africa, from which Spain and Portugal (which were jointly ruled by a single monarch from 1580 to 1640) enjoyed a monopoly of trade. The British did not yet have the capital necessary for the importation of slaves and attempted to launch their colonies relying on indentured labor. This changed after 1650.[18]

But meanwhile, Dutch navigators—whose homeland was ruled by Spain (then united with Portugal)—began to aim to undermine the commerce of the joint Iberian nations by seizing coastal African sites associated with Portuguese trade in gold and slaves, Caribbean sites associated with Portuguese trade, and other Portuguese trading sites, such as the African Cape of Good Hope, Ceylon and the Spice Islands.

---

[17]Phillips, *Slavery from Roman Times*, p. 200.
[18]Ibid., p. 183.

In the period up until Portugal terminated joint rule with Spain (1640), the Dutch consequently had free access to many of the sources of African slaves drawn on by the other country and to many sugar-growing regions on the Brazilian coast. They also made slaves in Southeast Asia and transported them to the region we now call South Africa.

Yet by 1648 the Portuguese excluded the Dutch from Angola, and by 1654 also from Brazil.[19] Thereafter, the Dutch presence in the Caribbean was focused on the islands of St. Martin, Curacao, Aruba, and Bonaire and the coastal region of Suriname; to these sites African slaves were imported and an extensive plantation culture built up, which was not really displaced until slavery ended in these colonies in 1863.[20]

The plantation culture in the British colonies in America. Writing his 1719 epic *Robinson Crusoe*, Daniel Defoe depicted his shipwrecked, long-surviving hero as having departed from a successful sugar plantation on the coast of Brazil in search of additional African slaves to work in his enterprise. In the course of this journey he survived a wreck and lived twenty-eight years on an island, imaginatively positioned by Defoe off Venezuela's coast.[21] Evidently, at least by the time of Defoe's writing, there had come to be fixed in the British mind the notion that a plantation cultivated by slaves represented the road to riches. In short order British port cities such as Bristol, Liverpool and Glasgow became the depots where the produce of the transatlantic plantations was offloaded (sugar, cotton, tobacco, coffee) and trade goods (particularly textiles) taken aboard to be shipped south to African ports, where Africans, captured by members of rival tribes, awaited exchange.

In due course, these same ships—now laden with slaves—completed the "triangle" and crossed the Atlantic from Africa's west coast to slave markets extending from the Caribbean in the south to the thirteen American colonies to the north. Novelist Defoe, a theologically informed writer whose training might as easily have prepared him for the Presbyterian ministry as for his life as a merchant and journalist, raised

---

[19]Ibid., p. 191.
[20]"Dutch Empire," *Wikipedia* <http://en.wikipedia.org/wiki/Dutch_Empire>.
[21]Daniel Defoe, *Robinson Crusoe*, ed. Michael Shinagel (New York: Norton, 1975), p. 168.

no ethical questions about his hero's rapid road to riches.[22] Rather, by the eighteenth century, the fruits of this Atlantic triangle had assumed such a large role in British trade, industry and the creation of wealth that it had become nearly immune to criticism. And in the American colonies, African slaves were sold freely; in northern climes they were often domestic servants and apprentice artisans, while in the southeast, the large-scale cultivation of cotton and tobacco claimed their labor. But a reaction against slavery was coming in the second half of the eighteenth century.

The Eighteenth Century: A Parting of the Ways Regarding Slavery

One of the primary reasons that the practice of slavery did not alarm more Europeans is that so few had the opportunity to directly observe it in practice in the regions where plantation agriculture and mining (two of the most brutal versions of slavery) were in process. It is worth acknowledging that the Europeans who conducted plantation agriculture on the islands of the Caribbean generally did not live there but resided in Europe in the genteel company they preferred. This class only observed plantation slavery directly on their periodic visits from Europe; the actual management of their plantations was delegated to managers the owners appointed. (By contrast, plantation agriculture in the American South was much more extensively conducted by persons and families who lived on-site.)[23] Very often, those who did observe plantation slavery were revulsed by what they saw. It was utterly unlike the domestic slavery Europeans had learned to tolerate. It would be heartening to be able to report that the Protestant opposition to slavery was led by individuals associated with the Presbyterian and Reformed churches; yet this honor in fact goes to others.

John Wesley and Charles Wesley, the recent Oxford graduates, witnessed it briefly, firsthand, in South Carolina in 1736-1737. They even-

---

[22]Paula R. Backscheider, *Daniel Defoe* (Baltimore: Johns Hopkins University Press, 1989), p. 15.

[23]Eugene D. Genovese, *The World the Slaveholders Made* (Hanover, N.H.: Wesleyan University Press, 1988), p. 31.

tually recorded their adverse reaction in published journals—with Charles, the hymn writer, soon penning lyrics against slavery in 1758.[24] George Whitefield, their contemporary, paradoxically obtained slaves to till the gardens of the Orphan House he set up in Savannah, Georgia, even while penning a fierce "Letter to the Inhabitants of Maryland, Virginia and the Carolinas" that took them to task for their harsh treatment of their slaves.[25] A considerable impetus for further Christian efforts, however, seems to have been provided by a famous court case (the "Somerset case") in England in 1772, in which the presiding justice, Lord Mansfield, declared that as England had no laws providing for or governing slavery, no person "in English territory" could be held in such servitude. The ambiguities inherent in this ruling regarding what constituted English territory unfortunately permitted slaves to still be sold in England until 1792. During that lapse of time the ruling did little or nothing to curtail slavery elsewhere in lands held by Britain.[26]

In the period surrounding the Somerset case, members of the Society of Friends (the Quakers) began to raise their voices against the slave trade from within both Britain and America. At the forefront of the Quaker literary campaign in favor of the termination of slavery stood Anthony Benezet (1713-1784), himself a refugee of French Huguenot origin, living in the vicinity of Philadelphia. Beginning with the publication of *Observations on the Enslaving, Importing and Purchasing of Negroes* (1759) and in other publications extending forward through 1771, Benezet became one of the foremost authors advocating the abolition of slavery in Britain and America. His writings certainly strengthened John Wesley's resolve.[27] But it is not as though writers from within the Reformed theological tradition were silent in this period.

In colonial New England, the Congregationalist pastor-theologian

---

[24]Warren Thomas Smith, *John Wesley and Slavery* (Nashville: Abingdon, 1986), pp. 41-46.
[25]Ibid., p. 51. It needs to be stressed that the modern historian of the Great Awakening, Thomas S. Kidd, credits Whitefield, the evangelist, with being the first person in the colonies to energetically seek the evangelization and Christianization of America's slave population (*Great Awakening*, chap. 14).
[26]Smith, *Wesley and Slavery*, p. 77.
[27]Ibid., p. 81.

Samuel Hopkins had written at the time of the Revolutionary War to support the freeing of slaves and of their resettlement to West Africa. Though persons of great influence on Hopkins, such as Jonathan Edwards, had themselves held domestic slaves, sometime between 1770 and 1773 Hopkins had had a change of heart and began to speak and write about the necessity of ending this evil. By 1776 he published *A Dialogue Concerning the Slavery of the Africans*.[28] Within England, the former slave trader and now Church of England minister John Newton (1725-1807), himself clearly oriented toward Reformed theology, wrote *Thoughts Upon the African Slave Trade* (1787).[29] Newton, like the aged John Wesley, was the strong encourager of William Wilberforce, who after his conversion to Christianity, devoted his parliamentary career to the abolitionist movement.[30] In these same decades, within the young United States early protests began to be heard against the institution of slavery. A study committee brought to the General Assembly of the Presbyterian Church in 1787 the following recommendation "in warmest terms, to every member of this body, and to all the Churches and families under their care, to do everything in their power consistent with the rights of civil society, to promote the abolition of slavery, and the instruction of negroes, whether bond or free."[31]

NINETEENTH-CENTURY DEVELOPMENTS

In both countries, however, the destabilizing effects of the French Revolution made progress against the great evil of slavery highly difficult. The public disorder in France that characterized the decade of the

---

[28]David Torbett, *Theology and Slavery: Charles Hodge and Horace Bushnell* (Macon, Ga.: Mercer University Press, 2006), p. 46; Joseph Conforti, *Samuel Hopkins and the New Divinity Movement* (Grand Rapids: Eerdmans, 1981), p. 128; and Mark A. Noll, *The Civil War as a Theological Crisis* (Chapel Hill: University of North Carolina Press, 2006), p. 57.

[29]The preference of Newton for an irenic Reformed theology is emphasized in Bruce Hindmarsh, *John Newton and the Evangelical Tradition* (Grand Rapids: Eerdmans, 2001).

[30]Newton's *Thoughts on the Slave Trade* was released in conjunction with the early efforts of William Wilberforce to repeal slavery through legislation in Britain's House of Parliament.

[31]*Records of the Presbyterian Church in the United States of America Embracing the Minutes of the General Presbytery and General Synod 1706-1788 Together with an Index and the Minutes of the General Convention for Religious Liberty 1766-1775* (Philadelphia: n.p., 1904), pp. 456, 458-59, as quoted in Irving Stoddard Kull, "Presbyterian Attitudes Towards Slavery," *Church History* 7, no. 2 (1938): 102.

1790s raised the specter of potentially freed slaves becoming involved in insurrection. There were in fact slave uprisings in colonies such as Sainte Domingo (present-day Haiti). Yet by 1807 it was finally possible for legislation to be passed making any further British trade in slaves between West Africa and the Caribbean unlawful; it was henceforth also unlawful for British ships to transport slaves to any destination whatsoever. In the following year the United States also forbade further importation of slaves.[32] There were discernible signs of movement, for by 1818, the General Assembly of the Presbyterian Church went so far as to state the following conviction:

> We consider the voluntary enslaving of one portion of the human race by another, as a gross violation of the most precious and sacred rights of human nature; as utterly inconsistent with the law of God, which requires us to love our neighbors as ourselves, and as totally irreconcilable with the principles and spirit of the gospel of Christ which enjoin that all things whatsoever ye would that men should do to you, do ye even so to them.[33]

While slavery was fully abolished throughout the British Empire in 1837, it is well known that this was not the case in the United States. In fact, the period from the 1830s onward saw the United States polarized as never before over the question of the future of slavery. While some individual states, such as Pennsylvania, had acted unilaterally to decree an end to slavery inside its regional boundaries (in this case in 1780), eleven states resisted all discussion of slavery's eventual abolition. And it was in this polarized situation that there became manifest the most stark disagreements pitting Northern and Southern Christians of almost all denominations at odds with one another. Naturally, our concern here is chiefly with the fortunes of the Presbyterian and Reformed

---

[32]Garth Lean, *God's Politician: William Wilberforce's Struggle to Abolish the Slave Trade* (Colorado Springs: Helmers & Howard, 1987), p. 67.

[33]*Records of the Presbyterian Church in the United States of America Embracing the Minutes of the General Presbytery and General Synod 1706-1788* (Philadelphia: n.p., 1904), p. 539, in Irving Stoddard Kull, "Presbyterian Attitudes Towards Slavery," *Church History* 7, no. 2 (1938): 103. The 1818 declaration is printed in fuller form in H. Shelton Smith, Robert T. Handy and Lefferts A. Loetscher, eds., *American Christianity: An Historical Interpretation with Representative Documents* (New York: Charles Scribner's, 1963), 2:179-82.

family of churches; but what transpired in that branch of the Protestant family can only be properly appreciated when it is seen in relation to developments beyond that communion. The Methodist Episcopal churches were divided, North and South, in 1844; within a year Baptists polarized into Northern and Southern Baptist Conventions. Presbyterian division was complete by 1861 (the year in which war began), while Lutheran churches did not divide until midway through the war, 1863.[34]

In the public mind of today there is a definite perception that Presbyterians were not on the side of the angels in this prolonged conflict. This perception needs to be qualified at several levels. On the one hand, while it is true that able theological defenders of the practice of slavery within those Southern states took up arms to defend its continuation in 1861, these same regions also had their antislavery theological writers. With the Presbyterian theological defense of Southern slavery, we easily associate the names of James Henley Thornwell (1812-1862) and Robert Dabney (1820-1898),[35] yet we take less note of their opponents, such as the Kentuckian Robert Breckinridge (1800-1871).[36]

It should be more widely known that there were Northern Presbyterian voices as forthright in the defense of slavery as could be found in the Southern region.[37] Further, it is mistaken to assume that Northern

---

[34]Erwin Fahlbusch and Esther Szabo, "Slavery," *Encyclopedia of Christianity*, 5:33. It is interesting to note that Northern Methodism, separate after 1844, did not satisfy all its adherents that it was sufficiently in earnest about seeking an end to slavery. "Free" Methodism, explicitly devoted to abolition, stood apart from Northern Methodism after 1860. The splintering effects of the slave question on Methodism are documented in Donald G. Mathews, *Slavery and Methodism* (Princeton, N.J.: Princeton University Press, 1965).

[35]Ernest Trice Thompson indicates that in 1860 Thornwell modified his position and was prepared to support gradual emancipation of slaves (*Presbyterians in the South* [Richmond, Va.: John Knox Press, 1963], 1:553). In the event, however, his change of mind was overtaken by developments in his state of South Carolina, the first to declare its secession. Thornwell drafted the extensive rationale justifying the existence of the new Southern Presbyterian body, excerpts of which can be seen in Smith, Handy and Loetscher, *American Christianity*, 2:206-10.

[36]Mark Noll, *The Civil War as a Theological Crisis* (Chapel Hill: University of North Carolina Press, 2006), p. 55. Robert Breckinridge was the maternal grandfather of Benjamin Breckinridge Warfield (1851-1921), long professor of theology at Princeton. Warfield followed his grandfather in being a supporter of emancipation.

[37]Noll points to Brooklyn Presbyterian Henry Van Dyke as an example of this Northern viewpoint. Tremendous wealth was created through the New England textile industry, which was itself utterly dependent on Southern cotton, cultivated by slave labor (*Civil War*, pp. 19, 32).

opponents of slavery, allied with the Presbyterian and Reformed tradition in Northern states, were necessarily abolitionist (i.e., committed to the immediate liberation of the enslaved). While abolitionism had its advocates among New England Congregationalists and New School Presbyterians (a movement separated from the main Presbyterian body in 1837), it was just as common for persons in Reformed and Presbyterian churches in the North to be associated with the position termed *emancipationist* (i.e., committed to the gradual liberation of the enslaved).[38] These abolitionists and emancipationists differed among themselves over the wisdom of colonization schemes under which freed slaves would be encouraged and assisted to emigrate to West Africa.

One particular Northern Presbyterian supporter of emancipation, the Rev. Gardiner Spring of the Brick Presbyterian Church, New York, helped to bring nearer the division of American Presbyterians in the Civil War era by proposing a motion in his denomination's General Assembly of May 1861. The motion called on Presbyterians everywhere in the nation to support their federal government and the Constitution of the United States. Armed hostilities had already begun, with the Confederate attack on Fort Sumter, South Carolina, in the preceding month, but Presbyterians had not yet (like the denominations mentioned previously) divided into Northern and Southern factions. The passage of this motion, however, was perceived as obliging Presbyterians in seceding states to maintain obligations of loyalty to the federal government at a time when their state legislatures had repudiated that government's authority. It is hard to believe that Spring could have been surprised by the subsequent division of the denomination, since the very General Assembly he pressed his case in had heard strong counterarguments and—in the event of the support of his motion by a majority—received a strongly worded dissent.[39] On the whole, American Presbyterianism has to be judged severely lacking in nerve in this pe-

---

[38]This abolitionist point of view came to be especially associated with one theological school, Lane Seminary of Cincinnati, Ohio. See Lawrence Thomas Lesick, *The Lane Rebels: Evangelicalism and Antislavery in Antebellum America* (Metuchen, N.J.: Scarecrow, 1980), chap. 3; and Bertram Wyatt-Brown, *Lewis Tappan and the Evangelical War Against Slavery* (New York: Atheneum, 1969).

[39]Thompson, *Presbyterians in the South*, 1:571.

riod; having gone on record, twice in previous generations, in calling for slavery's end, this body seems to have exercised a limitless charity on the question of the actual practice of slavery by its members. Slaveowners were deferred to; the enslaved were kept waiting until the declaration of war and the eventual Emancipation Proclamation took the matter out of the hands of church assemblies.

The aftermath of war. The two executive orders of the Emancipation Proclamation (1862 and 1863), which declared the freedom of slaves held in Confederate states, followed by the ratification of the Thirteenth Amendment to the Constitution in December 1865, which freed all slaves outside the former Confederacy, were dramatic steps in restoring basic rights to the four million African Americans then resident in the United States. However, the restoration of these basic rights carried with it little or nothing in the way of amelioration of the social and spiritual disadvantages under which these millions had long labored. Post-Civil War society, in both the North and South was extensively unprepared for any integration of the African American population (whether just-liberated or freedmen of long-standing). The integration of churches proceeded then and still proceeds at a snail's pace. But there were also bright spots. Princeton theologian Benjamin Breckinridge Warfield (1851-1921), himself a Kentuckian of emancipationist roots, was exemplary in his involvement in the "Presbyterian Board of Missions to Freedmen," his written advocacy of the need for the racial integration of the churches, and in his pressing for the rights of African American students to enter Princeton Seminary in 1915.[40]

Summary. Calvinism no more caused slavery than the preexisting Roman Christianity caused it. But both—in company with virtually every other branch of the Christian movement—had grave difficulty in shaking off this terrible violation of human dignity.[41] The economic

---

[40]Bradley J. Gundlach, " 'Wicked Caste': B. B. Warfield, Biblical Authority, and Jim Crow," *Journal of Presbyterian History* 85, no. 1 (2007): 28-47.

[41]Pope Gregory XVI had in December 1839 issued an Apostolic Letter that "aligned the Roman Catholic Church on the side of abolitionism"; and yet in 1840-1841, the Catholic bishop of Charleston, S.C., John England, wrote in defense of the institution of slavery, which he claimed his church had always sanctioned. See the document in Smith, Handy and Loetscher, *American Christianity*, 2:201-5.

advantages to be reaped by this exploitation of other humans deadened the conscience of Western societies (and their Christian churches) far longer than can be justified. But the failure was one of condoning for too long, and the failure to uproot for too long, something contrary to Christian and biblical principle.[42] Yet, while many Calvinists were to be found in company with the Christians of other persuasions condoning slavery, we can celebrate the sizeable number who (in company with Christians of other denominations) went against the stream and called for dramatic change.

CALVINISM AND SOUTH AFRICA

In a strange juxtaposition with the events in the nineteenth century we have been considering, the region we today call South Africa was proceeding steadily down a road that would lead to more than a century and a half of racial disharmony. It did this even as Western Europe and the United States were attempting to dismantle slavery in legislatures and on battlefields. The South African intransigence in this matter has itself been attributed to the Calvinism which that country's earliest European immigrants brought with them from the Netherlands in 1652.[43] *Surely*, the tenacious hold of racist ideology in this southern region of Africa until 1994[44] cannot be explained without reference to the Calvinist framework that the Dutch (and later, French Huguenot) immigrants brought with them?[45]

---

[42]Key Scriptures on this question include Genesis 1:26-27; Acts 17:26; and Galatians 3:28.

[43]My thinking about this subject is indebted to the senior research paper of my former student Chris Barker, "The Dutch Reformed Israelites: Deuteronomy, Sphere Sovereignty, and the Hermeneutics of Apartheid in the Dutch Reformed Church" (Covenant College, 2008).

[44]1994 marks the year when the Nationalist Party, which had upheld the range of oppressive laws collectively termed *apartheid*, was swept from power by the African National Congress.

[45]A most-thorough review of the claim, circulated since the mid-nineteenth century, that the Dutch South African racist attitudes were an outworking of their Calvinism, is carried out by André du Toit, "No Chosen People: The Myth of the Calvinist Origins of Afrikaner Nationalism and Racial Ideology," *American Historical Review* 88, no. 4 (1983): 920-52. Du Toit shows that until mid-nineteenth century, the standard explanations for these racist attitudes (especially in the new territories beyond British control, Transvaal and the Orange Free State) stressed the rusticity and backwardness of the settlers who had gone there decades earlier. Du Toit demonstrates that it was the missionary statesman David Livingstone (1813-1873), himself a Calvinist, who helped to popularize a new explanation for the South African attitude to race (i.e., stern Calvinist principles)—and that by the early twentieth century this explanation was taken up and adapted in a self-serving way by South Africans of Dutch descent ("No

The question is indeed a complex one, and it is necessary to return (yet again) to a distinction already employed: association compared to causation. There is no question whatsoever that the Calvinist heritage was associated with racist attitudes and policies in this region from the earliest period of European immigration. But to admit this association is to stop far short of an admission that these very attitudes and policies could never have been generated if the European immigrants had been Roman Catholic or Anglican or Baptist.

The early immigrants, sent to live in what was then the Cape (of Good Hope) Colony, were convinced, like other seventeenth-century Europeans, of the superiority of their European culture, religion and way of life when compared to that of an indigenous population. They were determined to press on with the development and improvement of the territories surrounding the Cape of Good Hope. In pursuit of this development, slaves of West African and Southeast Asian extraction were introduced into the colony after 1707.[46] The colonists enjoyed considerable success in a period leading up to 1806, when control of the colony passed from Holland to Great Britain. In the preceding period there was some intermarriage of aboriginal people with the European immigrant community; there was no objection to this intermarriage provided that the aboriginals had embraced Christianity. Yet by 1857 such earlier policies of comprehensiveness, across racial lines, by the Netherlands Reformed Church, were in clear retreat. In that year it was agreed that there were to be separate congregations for different races. There followed separate Reformed churches for "colored people" (mixed descent), blacks and East Indians. On the one hand, this new policy was a reflection of the success with which the Christian message was being welcomed by non-European peoples, but at the same time it was an indication that "racial prejudice and the interests of labor and land

---

Chosen People," pp. 939-43). Livingstone's intended depiction of the reason for Dutch South African intransigence was put to new positive purposes by those who wished to wrap their racist attitudes in theological garb.

[46]Susan Rennie Ritner, "The Dutch Reformed Church and Apartheid," *Journal of Contemporary History* 2, no. 4 (1967): 18; John W. de Gruchy, *The Church Struggle in South Africa* (Grand Rapids: Eerdmans, 1979), pp. 7- 8.

clashed with theology."[47] The Dutch Reformed community was not at ease with churches that embraced racial diversity in an era when the economic advancement of their community presupposed their own preferential position in society.

The change to British control in 1806 had set in motion ripples that would extend across a century or more. For one, settlers and missionaries came into the Cape Colony in large numbers after that year.[48] On the one hand Protestant churches *other* than the Netherlands Reformed Church began to proliferate, such that its former near-monopoly was ended; these churches, while by no means fully racially integrated, certainly had a place for nonwhites (as did their British mother churches at this stage). On the other hand, the aboriginal people were being evangelized at a much more rapid rate under British missionaries than had been the case in the preceding Dutch era. The missionaries, whether Methodist, Baptist or sent by the denominationally inclusive London Missionary Society, regularly defended the interests of the aboriginal people they were trying to reach. This advocacy tended to exacerbate the strained relationships not only between the native people and the colonists of Dutch extraction, but between the native people and British settlers.[49]

Further, the series of steps taken by Britain to inhibit the sale of slaves within the United Kingdom, to ban the transport of slaves on British ships, and ultimately to decree the freeing of slaves everywhere in its empire cut across attitudes ingrained in the original South African Dutch community. A portion of this community, extensively unwilling to accept a society where there was equality in the sight of the law for all free persons and resentful of the cultural imperialism exerted by their British masters, determined to try to move to the north, beyond the frontiers of British influence; so the "Great Trek" resulted.

---

[47]De Gruchy, *Church Struggle in South Africa*, pp. 7, 9.

[48]The most illustrious of the missionaries who entered South Africa after 1806 was Robert Moffat (1795-1883) of the London Missionary Society, regarding whom see the entry in the *Evangelical Dictionary of World Mission*, ed. Scott Moreau (Grand Rapids: Baker, 2000). A Dutch appointee of the same mission society, Johannes Van der Kemp (1747-1811), had entered South Africa in 1799.

[49]De Gruchy, *Church Struggle in South Africa*, p. 13.

Those undertaking the trek did so against the counsel of their Nether-lands Reformed churches.[50] In the new independent republics of Trans-vaal and the Orange Free State, which were set up by the trekkers, at-titudes to race took their own course—rather than the one required by Britain.

In the Cape Colony the churches in the Reformed tradition serv-ing British immigrants (Presbyterian, Congregational, Baptist) as well as the Anglican, Methodist and Catholic churches were increas-ingly ready to support the legal and property rights of South Africa's black, mixed-race and Southeast Asian peoples in the middle de-cades of the nineteenth century—even as the historic Dutch immi-grant community entrenched itself in support of ideas of separate (and unequal) development for the races. The eventual political union of Cape Colony and Natal with the northern republics of Transvaal and the Orange Free State (which resulted in the 1909 Union of South Africa) did not serve to secure the political, territorial and economic rights of nonwhites because a continuation of the existing inequitable racial policies of the two republics were insisted on as the price of their participation in the political union.[51] From this point onward the proportionate number of South Africans of British de-scent relative to the entire population declined, and with it any nu-meric advantage these immigrants had enjoyed in pressing for a change in race policy.

In this postunion era the National Party was founded, which when it came to form the government in 1948, enacted racist poli-cies with which a strong proportion of the historic Dutch popula-tion had long been associated. The Netherlands Reformed Church, with two other majority-Dutch denominations in the Reformed tra-dition, had never been univocal in support of these race policies (with mission programs among nonwhites often led by persons who sought to modify them), yet in the aftermath of 1948 the policies known as apartheid were enacted and racial discrimination was institutionalized.

---

[50]Ibid., p. 19.
[51]Ibid., p. 27; Ritner, "Dutch Reformed Church and Apartheid," p. 21.

White and nonwhite voices of Dutch descent and other descent, from within the Reformed tradition and from within other South African churches, continually called for the overthrow of this system.[52] In time, the Dutch sister church of one South African, Reformed denomination (the *Gereformeerde*) issued a rebuke to the South African sister church for its ongoing involvement in apartheid. There were also criticisms uttered by the international Reformed Ecumenical Synod (to which the Dutch Reformed Church belonged) for the same reasons.[53] By 1984 the World Alliance of Reformed Churches, having heard a convincing indictment of the Reformed churches of South Africa and their endorsement of apartheid from the black South African, Reformed theologian Alan Boesak, condemned apartheid as heresy and suspended these denominations from membership.[54]

The sad juggernaut of apartheid careened onward until the early 1990s. The stubborn maintenance of it until that time had cost South Africa its reputation in the Christian world and much of its economic momentum and prosperity (as it became subject to severe economic sanctions instituted by the United Nations). Finally, in 1994 the National Party (which had been in power since 1948), agreed to grant the vote to nonwhites and was swept from power by the African National

---

[52]Thus, for example, the Presbyterian Church of South Africa in 1948 protested the elimination of African representation in the parliament of the nation. The Anglican bishops of the country also protested this development. By 1960, progressive voices within the Dutch Reformed Church broke ranks and indicated their dissent from the racial policies being pursued by their denomination, and by extension, the national government (see Ritner, "Dutch Reformed Church and South Africa," p. 34). South African, Reformed theologians B. B. Keet and Beyers Naudé were outspoken in their opposition to these policies pursued by their churches and their government. By 1974 the promising young, African, Reformed theologian Alan Boesak was contributing to the protest within South Africa (see De Gruchy, *Church Struggle in South Africa*, pp. 54-55, 74, 82, 103); and Alan Boesak, "Black and Reformed: The South African Challenge," in *Black and Reformed: Apartheid, Liberation, and the Calvinist Tradition* [Maryknoll, N.Y.: Orbis, 1984], pp. 83-99).

[53]De Gruchy, *Church Struggle in South Africa*, pp. 81-83. Susan Rennie Ritner, "Dutch Reformed Church and Apartheid," p. 30, points out that this censure by foreign churches did serve the positive purpose of stirring up dissent within the Dutch Reformed Church as to these race policies. David J. Bosch, "The Afrikaner and South Africa," *Theology Today*, 43 (July 1986), p. 213 credits the Reformed evangelical wing of the Dutch Reformed Church—the wing working most closely in missionary outreach to South Africa's nonwhites—with leading agitation against apartheid from within the denomination in the 1960s and beyond.

[54]Allister Sparks, *The Mind of South Africa* (London: Arrow, 1997), p. 287.

Congress, which it had long tried to throttle.

Did Calvinism stand like an *éminence grise* (gray eminence) behind the introduction and maintenance of these hostile racial policies by South Africans of Dutch descent? The available evidence only warrants us to accept that a certain *strand* of Calvinism was strongly associated with these policies—a strand that faced opposition even within the Reformed denominations, within other Christian churches of South Africa (churches in the Reformed tradition among them), by international bodies of Reformed Churches (the Reformed Ecumenical Synod and World Alliance of Reformed Churches) and the World Council of Churches.[55] With this explained, no one can credibly argue for a cause-and-effect relation between the Calvinist heritage per se and the views of the South African citizens of Dutch descent and their churches. This was *their* theological idiosyncrasy.

Now that the very regrettable association of some strands of the Calvinist heritage with racism and slavery has been exposed as the persistent misrepresentation that it was, there are encouraging signs that Christians of African as well as Asian descent are finding in the Reformed theological tradition resources that are of deep usefulness in the challenges that they face in the current age. In North America, Reformed theology is currently of increased interest among African American Christians.[56] At the same time, there are persistent reports of the attractiveness of this same theology to the Chinese churches, for whom this theology with its long European association, might have been held suspect.[57]

---

[55]It was as a theologian of the Dutch Reformed Mission Church (a missionary arm of the Dutch Reformed Church so closely associated with the National Party) that Alan Boesak warned in 1981, "Apartheid is the grave of the dignity and the credibility of the Reformed tradition," and "the Reformed tradition calls for resistance to so blatantly an unjust government as is the South African" ("Black and Reformed," pp. 86, 92).

[56]Anthony J. Carter, *On Being Black and Reformed: A New Perspective on the African-American Christian Experience* (Phillipsburg, N.J.: Presbyterian & Reformed, 2003); and *The Glory Road: The Journeys of Ten African American Christians into Reformed Christianity* (Wheaton, Ill.: Crossway, 2009).

[57]"Chinese Calvinism Flourishes," *AndrewBrown's Blog*, n.d. <www.guardian.co.uk/comment isfree/andrewbrown/2009/may/27/china-calvin-christianity>. The same trend was observed at an earlier stage by David Aikman, *Jesus in Beijing* (Washington, D.C.: Henry Regnery, 2003), pp. 191, 277.

DISCUSSION QUESTIONS

1. If the Calvinist or Reformed theological tradition came to be associated in the popular mind with the wrong approach to the question of race and enslavement, how do you suppose that this association came to be formed (since, as we have seen other streams of Christianity also fell down here)?

2. How did Christians in the Reformed tradition (along with others) enjoy a measure of prosperity and ease related to human enslavement, *even* when they held no slaves themselves? Consider how the same indirect benefit from the misfortune of others still permeates much of modern life: what are some things we ought to do differently?

3. Evidently, the Reformed theological tradition can take little or no credit for pioneering the opposition to slavery in the world since 1750. Did it contribute anything distinctive to the cause once the struggle had begun?

FURTHER READING

Barrow, R. H. *Slavery in the Roman Empire*. New York: Barnes & Noble, 1968.

Genovese, Eugene D. *The World the Slaveholders Made*. Hanover, N.H.: Wesleyan University Press, 1988.

Lean, Garth. *God's Politician: William Wilberforce's Struggle to Abolish the Slave Trade*. Colorado Springs: Helmers & Howard, 1987.

Noll, Mark. *The Civil War as a Theological Crisis*. Chapel Hill: University of North Carolina Press, 2006.

Phillips, William D., Jr. *Slavery from Roman Times to the Early Transatlantic Trade*. Minneapolis: University of Minnesota Press, 1985.

Thomas, Hugh. *The Slave Trade: The Story of the Atlantic Slave Trade 1440-1870*. New York: Simon & Schuster, 1997.

Recovering Our Bearings

Calvinism in the Twenty-First Century

IN LAYING OUT THE JUSTIFICATION for this book in the introduction, I indicated my concern about Calvinism's difficulty in restraining its own extremists and its penchant for treating Calvin and the Geneva of his day as the primeval standard against which all subsequent development ought to be measured.[1] I also drew attention to this movement's reluctance to admit that diversity of emphasis has been a real factor from the start (rather than just a sure sign of declension, later), and its slowness to acknowledge that its system of belief contains a complex of convictions, some of which prove highly difficult. And then there were the usual grievances that the unconvinced regularly lay at the door of Calvinists (some contain fair morsels of truth). If you have read this far in *Ten Myths*, you will have seen that my concerns were not without foundation. The question then becomes, What should we do differently, in consequence? I strongly suggest that we need to recover our bearings. This will entail both our gaining an awareness of the flow of Calvinism's tides and our growing to accept Calvinist diversity.

---

[1]Thanks to Dordt College, Sioux Center, Iowa, for the opportunity to present much of this material in the conference titled "Calvinism for the Twenty-First Century" (April 2010).

I could not have known it when I first came into the Reformed movement as it existed in the 1970s, but I now know that our Calvinist story contains as many troughs as waves, as many ebbs as flood tides. Calvinist history is the opposite of static. The setbacks in Calvinist history are just as instructive as the periods of rapid advance. The Calvinist movement would be wise to study these ups and downs, for they disclose blunders that should not be repeated and good ideas that are worth a second look.

As well as studying the ebb and flow in Calvinist fortunes, recovering our bearings entails seeing that there are Calvinisms, that is, multiple, distinguishable expressions of this Reformed faith present in the modern world. In order to note both the fluctuations and the variety of movements, I propose that we take a rapid overview of six waves of Calvinist resurgence across the past two centuries.[2] In doing so, we will begin our survey with what is currently called "new Calvinism" and proceed backward until we come to the era of the French Revolution. As we go, be open to the following suggestions:

- Some resurgences of Calvinism from long ago *still* have considerable momentum and are thus ongoing.

- Each earlier Calvinist resurgence has left a legacy of ideas and books to assist later Calvinist movements.

- No single resurgence of Calvinism in the modern world has been complete in itself (enfolding the whole of the tradition within itself), such that it will never be surpassed.

TODAY'S CALVINIST RESURGENCE: FROM WHERE?

Unless a Christian has been dozing, he or she could hardly have failed to note that since 2006 we have been seeing a resurgence of Calvinism—especially among the under-thirties generation. In September of that year *Christianity Today*'s cover displayed a T-shirt emblazoned with Jonathan Edwards. According to the magazine, Calvinism in America was "making a comeback and shaking up the church." This

---

[2]I stop in the era of the French Revolution simply for convenience. The sequence could be extended back still further, all the way to the age of the Reformation itself.

was only the beginning of a media surge. Such was the outpouring of interest in this article that its author soon completed a paperback bearing the same title as the original article: *Young, Restless and Reformed*.[3] There, he described at greater length his personal interviews with and impressions of the pastors and theologians who are leading the resurgence. Now, we could *all* say that we had been introduced to John Piper, Mark Driscoll and C. J. Mahaney. We learned too that in cities as diverse as Seattle, Memphis, Atlanta and Minneapolis crowds of younger adults ranging between five thousand and forty thousand persons were coming together to hear fervent gospel proclamation within a Calvinistic framework. We learned that in these cities massive congregations (sometimes meeting at multiple sites) of young-adult students and career people gather around Calvinistic preachers.

With these two items in print by 2008, the wider American press began to take note. By January 11, 2009, the *New York Times Magazine* began to zero in on Driscoll of Seattle. In the March 12, 2009, edition of *Time* magazine, writer David Van Biema rated this "New Calvinism" as one of the "10 Ideas Changing the World Right Now" (along with such trends as Chinese industrial investment in Africa).[4]

Yet, embedded in this journalistic buzz, an identifiable theme was beginning to emerge. It was the supposition—encouraged by the major personalities interviewed—that this upsurge of Calvinism had appeared Melchizedek-like, "without genealogy" (Heb 7:3). Of course the movement's spokesmen linked themselves to John Calvin and the sixteenth-century European Reformation. As well, both the original press coverage in *Christianity Today* and the following *Time* story harked back to Jonathan Edwards (1703-1758) as a forebear of today's movement.[5] And yet,

---

[3]Collin Hansen, *Young, Restless and Reformed: A Journalist's Journey with the New Calvinists* (Wheaton, Ill.: Crossway, 2008).

[4]See Molly Worthen, "Who Would Jesus Smack Down?" *New York Times Magazine*, January 6, 2009 <www.nytimes.com/2009/01/11/magazine/11punk-t.html>; Neal Karlinsky, "Pastor Dude's Mega-Church Draws Crowds," *Nightline*, January 23, 2008 <http://abcnews.go.com/Nightline/FaithMatters/pastor-dudes-mega-church-draws-crowds/story?id=6711206>; David Van Biema, "The New Calvinism," *Time*, March 23, 2009 <www.time.com/time/specials/packages/article/0,28804,1884779_1884782_1884760,00.html>.

[5]Seattle's Mark Driscoll is an admirer of the Victorian preacher C. H. Spurgeon. This is documented in the ABC *Nightline* interview.

a timeline of Calvinism, constructed by *Time,* was utterly *blank* between Edwards's day and 1997![6] Thus, this "new day" of Reformation Christianity seems to have "touched down" solely on the "new Calvinists" after a hiatus of centuries.[7] Amber lights should be flashing!

As represented by Piper and Driscoll, the surging movement of today shows little consciousness of how the set of Christian convictions they identify as Calvinism have traveled across time. There is even less of an idea as to why their current convictions earlier fell out of favor and needed to be recovered in our time. There are on the contemporary scene persons better rooted in the Reformed tradition, known to and respected by Piper and Driscoll, who could have depicted matters in a much clearer light.[8]

The confusion the new Calvinism has helped to create is shown in two quotations:

> Reports from various parts of the world convince us, [that] we are witnessing in our days a rejuvenescence and a rising tendency of . . . [Calvinistic] teaching. . . . The renewal of Calvinism appears to be but part of a larger phenomenon, i.e. of a general return to the teaching of the Reformation.[9]

> In our day, a time when many denominations are declining and religion is apparently losing its hold, there appears to be a renewed interest in Calvinistic theology and a resurgence of those committed to the doctrines of grace summarized in the Reformed standards. . . . Ways are being found to highlight the Reformed faith nationally.[10]

---

[6]Van Biema, "The New Calvinism," p. 51. The significance of the year 1997 lies in the fact that, in that year, the first "Passion" conference (involving John Piper) was held.

[7]In spite of the assigned significance of the year 1997 (see n. 6) it seems to me that an informal launch of the current "new Calvinist" movement might be reckoned to have occurred with the publication of Wayne Grudem's *Systematic Theology: An Introduction to Bible Doctrine* (Grand Rapids: Zondervan, 1994). This soteriologically Calvinist, mildly charismatic theology has become the handbook of many in the new Calvinist movement.

[8]I am here thinking of Ligon Duncan, Bryan Chapell, Mark Dever, Al Mohler, Kevin DeYoung and Tim Keller; these pastors and theological educators, associated with the current upsurge in Calvinism, are all well-situated to interpret and explain the Calvinist tradition as it has been transmitted across past centuries. My assertion can be supported by consulting the March 27, 2010, Josh Burek interview of Mark Dever, Capitol Hill Baptist Church, Washington, D.C., in the *Christian Science Monitor* <www.csmonitor.com/USA/Society/2010/0327/Christian-faith-Calvinism-is-back>.

[9]John Victor, "The Revival of Calvinism," *The Evangelical Quarterly* 7 (1936): 37-39.

[10]James M. Boice, "Is the Reformed Faith Being Rediscovered?" *Christianity Today,* March 28, 1975, p. 12.

Are these just further examples of the coverage that we are now accustomed to seeing in print regarding the new Calvinism? They are not; they are opinions from 1936 and 1975; the two individuals quoted (John Victor, a Hungarian, and James Boice, an American) *each* claimed to be living in a time characterized by a tremendous upsurge in Reformation teaching. Thus, whatever features the representatives of the "new Calvinism" (and those who interviewed them) may have got right, they have definitely missed others. We need to recognize that today's new Calvinism stands in succession to and dependence on five earlier movements in the past two centuries. This is part of "getting our bearings."

FIVE EARLIER CALVINIST RESURGENCES FROM THE FRENCH REVOLUTION TO 1990

1939-1990: From Lloyd-Jones to the Philadelphia Conferences on Reformed Theology. The most immediate predecessor of the current new Calvinism movement was another whose rise was inextricably related to the career and influence of Martyn Lloyd-Jones (1899-1981), minister of London's Westminster Chapel from 1939-1968. He was the figurehead over a major Calvinist upsurge throughout the English-speaking world, an upsurge that both gave birth to and was then propelled by the Banner of Truth movement and (from 1972) the Philadelphia Conferences on Reformed Theology. Lloyd-Jones, in addition to being a rising preacher in his native Wales (he had left a London medical practice in 1926 to pastor a working-class mission hall), was regularly in North America during summers from the early 1930s. His biographer indicates that it was on such a summer sojourn to Toronto in 1932 that he encountered the recently published *Works* of the late B. B. Warfield (d. 1921) in the library of that city's Knox College; theologically, he was never the same again.[11] By the time he joined G. Camp-

---

[11]Notably, however, Lloyd-Jones rejected Warfield's cessationist view on the gifts and ministry of the Holy Spirit. Is it only coincidental that this continuationist stance is now common among new Calvinist leaders of today? In a fascinating as-yet-unpublished paper of 2009, "Calvin and British Evangelicalism," professor David W. Bebbington credits Free Church of Scotland historian Donald MacLean (1869-1943) with being a seminal theological influence on Lloyd-Jones in the late 1930s.

bell Morgan on the pastoral team of Westminster Chapel, London, in 1939, he was well-versed in Reformed theology.

Beginning in 1947-1948 he came to North American prominence by his involvement with the early efforts of the International Federation of Evangelical Students (the global network of InterVarsity movements) and with the release of his *Truth Unchanged and Unchanging*, which were sermons he had preached at Wheaton College.[12] So many threads lead to and from Lloyd-Jones. Involved in the foundation of the London Bible College (now London School of Theology), the Tyndale Fellowship for Biblical Research (connected with Tyndale House, Cambridge), he was also a cofounder of the Banner of Truth movement, known throughout the English-speaking world for its monthly magazine and reprints of older theological works. It was only with the launching of this publication effort in 1955 that the United Kingdom ceased to rely, as it had had to do for half a century, on the production of Reformed theological literature from the United States.[13]

Here is an interesting demonstration of how this wave of Calvinist resurgence advanced in reliance on another that had gone before. Lloyd-Jones and his movement were the debtors of an older Reformed tradition that, by the 1920s, was having difficulty in sustaining itself, yet it lived on through its literature.[14] In the United Kingdom and the United States, Lloyd-Jones's example would point the way to the resurgence of

---

[12]The highly significant role of Lloyd-Jones in the postwar global expansion of the InterVarsity movement through the International Fellowship of Evangelical Students is helpfully elaborated in A. Donald MacLeod, *C. Stacey Woods and the Evangelical Recovery of the University* (Downers Grove, Ill.: InterVarsity Press, 2008), pp. 102-4; and the two-volume work of Lloyd-Jones's biographer Iain H. Murray, *D. Martyn Lloyd-Jones*, vol. 2 (Edinburgh: Banner of Truth, 1990), chap. 8. Not only was a somewhat earlier Calvinism from America known in Britain through its literature (largely produced in Grand Rapids), but it was also known through the visits of Americans—such as the Philadelphian Donald Grey Barnhouse (1895-1960), who spoke in Keswick—and Universities and Colleges Christian Fellowship, formerly known as the Inter-Varsity Fellowship, gatherings in Britain.

[13]This is an interesting point made in the recent treatment of this era by John J. Murray, *Catch the Vision: Roots of the Reformed Recovery* (Darlington, U.K.: Evangelical Press, 2007), p. 44. The *Banner of Truth* magazine was commenced in 1955; the wider publishing concern, the Banner of Truth Trust, in 1957.

[14]Lloyd-Jones was conscious of this older Reformed tradition. He attended the European meetings of the International Association for Reformed Faith and Action in Amsterdam (1948) and Montpellier (1953); see Murray, *D. Martyn Lloyd-Jones*, 2:155, 281. The roots of this organization in the post-WWI era are explained in the section on 1910-1950.

Calvinism *beyond* the confessionally Reformed churches. When Philadelphia's James Boice (1938-2000) spoke in 1975 of the expansion of Reformed theology, he was describing *this* very expansion of Calvinism into broad evangelicalism from the confines of the Presbyterian and Reformed denominations that had upheld these views in preceding decades. Closely associated with each of these individuals (on their respective sides of the Atlantic) was the British-Canadian, Anglican Reformed theologian J. I. Packer, who lent scholarly credibility to the "Puritan Conferences" organized by Lloyd-Jones in London each year, commencing in 1950, and the Philadelphia conferences spearheaded by Boice, beginning in the year 1972.

In this context it is important to note the contribution made along highly similar lines by Francis Schaeffer (1912-1984). Both by his Reformed theological training and especially by his long residence and ministry in Europe, he relayed to a broadly evangelical constituency across the English-speaking world the theological resources of the Reformed tradition and some of the intellectual currents associated with Dutch neo-Calvinism.[15] Clearly, this expansion of Calvinism beyond the Presbyterian and Reformed churches is continuing under new Calvinist auspices in a way continuous with what began a good sixty years ago.

1910-1950: From the Sovereign Grace Union to the International Association for Reformed Faith and Action. A still-older movement, while a carryover of late Victorian Calvinism (such as had been seen in the career of C. H. Spurgeon [1834-1892]), survived only with difficulty through the optimistic pre-Great War period. In Columbus, Ohio, the Congregational pastor Washington Gladden (1836-1918), because he construed societal progress as if it were the same as the advance of the kingdom of God, was still using each New Year's Day service to enumerate all the ways the world was steadily improving; he continued this through January 1914 (the year in which World War I broke out).[16]

---

[15]Schaeffer especially began to mingle with Dutch neo-Calvinists in the Kuyperian tradition on his arrival in Switzerland as an American missionary in 1948. I refer to the widening influence of Kuyperian ideas in the following sections. See the recent biography Barry Hankins, *Francis Schaeffer and the Making of American Evangelicalism* (Grand Rapids: Eerdmans, 2008).

[16]Garry Dorrien, *The Making of American Liberal Theology: Imagining Progressive Religion,*

This age of endless social optimism was also the age of contention for confessional revision, and stalwarts like B. B. Warfield went to their graves sensing that theological rot was setting in. Within a single decade Warfield and contemporary stalwarts James Orr (1844-1913), Abraham Kuyper (1837-1920) and Herman Bavinck (1854-1921) would all pass from the scene.

But the era also had witnessed some developments that, over time, would yield significant results. Confessional Presbyterianism was not quite a thing of the past: a portion of the Free Church of Scotland had opted out of a union scheme in 1900 that would have further distanced their churches from firm adherence to the Reformed standards. In England there were rumblings from a small high-Calvinist organization called the Sovereign Grace Union, which, founded in 1914, began in post-World War I years to urge that European Calvinists should confer at regular intervals.[17] By 1938 "International Calvinist Congresses" had been held in four European cities; these drew scholarly papers and attendees from both sides of the Atlantic as well as Eastern Europe.[18] This movement was especially notable in its uniting of Calvinists *across* the divide of conservative-mainstream denominations. Though the momentum of these conferences was halted by World War II, the movement would regroup in 1948 at Amsterdam. By 1953 this revived movement took the name "International Association for Reformed Faith and Action." In its early post–World War II years, French

---

1805-1900 (Louisville, Ky.: Westminster/John Knox, 2001), p. 329.

[17]This information is available from the website of the still-existing Sovereign Grace Union <www.sgu.org.uk/details/history.htm>. Calvinistic Conferences were held in London (1932), Amsterdam (1934), Geneva (1936) and Edinburgh (1938). Bebbington notes that it was a visit of SGU leaders to the Netherlands in 1929 and the making of contacts there that proved a catalyst for the launching of the Calvinist Congresses ("Calvinism and British Evangelicalism").

[18]*Proceedings of the Fourth International Calvinistic Congress* (Edinburgh: n.p., 1938). A survey of this conference volume, complete with a foldout, panoramic photograph of and complete listing of all delegates, provides an interesting window into the reviving fortunes of Calvinism on the eve of World War II. Present were members of the theological faculties of Edinburgh and Aberdeen universities, of several European divinity faculties and many distinguished ministers. In attendance also were future theologians George Hendry (later at Princeton) and T. F. Torrance (later of Edinburgh). An analysis of the 1938 Edinburgh Congress was offered by S. L. Hunt, "The Fourth International Calvinistic Congress," *Evangelical Quarterly* 10, no. 4 (1938): 390-96.

Reformed theologian Pierre-Charles Marcel figured prominently in its activities.[19]

One of the great motivators in the fresh appropriation of Reformed theology in the interwar period was the sense of disillusionment with the overly optimistic cultural theology that had dominated Protestant theological thinking in the pre-World War I era. The theological trajectory traveled by the Swiss theologian Karl Barth (1886-1968) is inexplicable apart from this sense of disillusionment.[20] But Barth was not a solitary figure; the Hungarian theologian John Victor, whose sentiments from 1936 I have quoted earlier,[21] saw in that decade a very bright horizon as the Reformed faith was showing new signs of vigor across Europe. Recent scholarship has demonstrated that the Calvinist revival of that decade was widely seen as bringing welcome relief from the long-reigning dominant liberal emphasis in theology.[22]

In the Netherlands in these same decades the Gereformeerde Kerken, through both its Free University of Amsterdam and seminary at Kampen, maintained a Reformed orthodoxy that was well abreast of current critical trends.[23] During this interwar period there is evidence that this theology had been taken notice of in France, for

---

[19]Marcel is still remembered for his classic defense of infant baptism, *Baptism: Sacrament of the Covenant of Grace* (London: James Clark, 1959). Note 15 of this chapter draws attention to Martyn Lloyd-Jones's involvement with these postwar conferences.

[20]On the trajectory traveled by Karl Barth after World War I, see Colin Brown, *Karl Barth and the Christian Message* (London: Tyndale Press, 1967), pp. 17-22.

[21]See p. 273. Victor's remarks had been delivered in September 1935 in his native Hungary at a European meeting of the World Presbyterian Alliance. A similar optimistic forecast for Reformed theology, linking the rising fortunes of Calvinism with the rise of Karl Barth's influence, was provided in an essay by W. Harvie-Jellie of Montreal: "Back to the Reformed Theology," *Evangelical Quarterly* 7, no. 2 (1935): 140-45.

[22]This is illustrated particularly in the essay of John L. McPake, "John McConnachie as the Original Advocate of the Theology of Karl Barth in Scotland: The Primacy of Revelation," *Scottish Bulletin of Evangelical Theology* 14, no. 2 (1996): 101-14. Bebbington has shown how the Cambridge Congregationalist theologian J. S. Whale (1896-1997) was a widely influential catalyst in refocusing attention on Reformation theology through such publications as *The Christian Faith* (1938) and *The Protestant Tradition* (1955) ("Calvin and British Evangelicalism"). From the same era might be considered W. W. Bryden (1883-1952), principal and professor at Knox College, Toronto. See John Vissers, *The Neo-Orthodox Theology of W. W. Bryden* (Eugene, Ore.: Wipf & Stock, 2006).

[23]The Gereformeerde Kerken (or G.K.N.) was the union after 1892 of two groups which had had an earlier existence. Combined, they stood distinct from the Hervormde Kerk or national Reformed Church. More details appear at n. 31.

the rising French Reformed theologian Auguste Lecerf (1872-1943) showed himself a kind of continuator of Abraham Kuyper.[24] Especially as material by Gereformeerde Kerken scholars began to be translated into English during the 1920s and 1930s, the entire Calvinist world was enriched.[25] And in the post–World War II period, translation into English would make scholars from the Gereformeerde Kerken, such as G. C. Berkouwer and Herman Ridderbos, extremely well known and influential.

The immediate post-Great War period also featured a fresh beginning for American Presbyterians who valued the Calvinist confessional heritage. In 1929, after a simmering dispute between conservative members of the theological faculty at Princeton and the broadening sponsoring denomination, the (Northern) Presbyterian Church in the U.S.A., a faculty minority—led by Dr. J. Gresham Machen—departed to begin Westminster Theological Seminary at Philadelphia.[26] It is noteworthy that from its inception this seminary drew on the theological resources of the Christian Reformed Church to fill some significant faculty posts.[27] From these small beginnings in 1929 grew one of the significant centers of Reformed theological education and scholarly writing in North America and in the English-speaking world.

It was in this era of upheavals and reverses that Arthur W. Pink (1886-1952), largely self-taught, began a prolific writing ministry. Perhaps his most influential volume was his first, *The Sovereignty of God*

---

[24]See the brief sketch of Lecerf at Wiki-protestants.org <www.wiki-protestants.org/wiki/Auguste_Lecerf>. The indebtedness to Kuyper becomes apparent in Lecerf's *Introduction to Reformed Dogmatics* (1931; reprint, London: Lutterworth, 1949).

[25]A helpful example of this scholarship's influence is the publication in English of the Free University professor G. C. Aalders's Old Testament essays in the United Kingdom-based *Evangelical Quarterly* through the 1930s. Eventually, these would be offered in the post-WWII period as *Short Introduction to the Pentateuch* (London: Tyndale, 1952).

[26]This story is ably recounted in two major biographies of Machen: Ned B. Stonehouse, *J. Gresham Machen: A Biographical Memoir* (Grand Rapids: Eerdmans, 1954), and D. G. Hart, *Defending the Faith: J. Gresham Machen and the Crisis of Conservative Protestantism in Modern America* (Baltimore: Johns Hopkins University Press, 1994). The complexity of the period, in which not all Presbyterian conservatives saw matters just as Machen did, is helpfully sketched by Bradley Longfield, *The Presbyterian Controversy: Fundamentalists, Modernists, and Moderates* (New York: Oxford University Press, 1991).

[27]The Christian Reformed Church, a Grand Rapids, Michigan–based denomination, was founded in the United States by nineteenth-century Dutch immigrants and is the sponsor of Calvin College and Seminary.

(1918). A strident protest against early twentieth-century conceptions of a nontranscendent God, Pink's volume encouraged readers to prize God's majesty, power and freedom.[28] A 1929 graduate of Princeton Seminary, Loraine Boettner (1901-1990), in this same era authored what has proved to be one of the handbooks of twentieth-century American Calvinists: *The Reformed Doctrine of Predestination* (1932). The work has never gone out of print since its original publication.[29]

But having said this, it is also necessary to say that the most influential textbook of Reformed theology published in English in the twentieth century was the *Systematic Theology* of Louis Berkhof (1873-1957) in 1932. Not only was the text used in his own institution, Calvin Seminary of Grand Rapids, but it was eventually used for a time in seminaries as diverse as Princeton and Westminster. This text, reflective of the stance of orthodox Reformed theology between the World Wars, has never gone out of print in the United States. It was eventually taken up and published in Britain by the Banner of Truth Trust in 1958, after which it circulated widely within Britain and its former colonies, just then coming to independence. Berkhof's *Systematic Theology* is for sale across English-speaking Africa today as well. One would be hard-pressed to find a more concrete example of how the resources of one wave of Calvinist resurgence (admittedly one that faced great obstacles) put a subsequent wave in its debt.[30]

Whether we think about the growing influence of Calvinism in Britain in the post–World War II years (in connection with the leadership of Martyn Lloyd-Jones) or the extension of it in the expansion of Reformed influence in America, which James Boice commented on in 1975, it is hard to imagine *either* movement accomplishing so much if it were not built on the broad foundation already laid in these difficult earlier decades of the century.

---

[28]The standard Pink biography is that of Iain H. Murray, *The Life of Arthur W. Pink* (Edinburgh: Banner of Truth, 1981).

[29]I have drawn attention in the earlier chapters on TULIP and predestination that Boettner is responsible for some questionable developments in the framing of popular Calvinism. His 1932 volume was a reworking of his 1929 Princeton Th.M. dissertation.

[30]Louis Berkhof's significance has been helpfully outlined by Henry Zwaanstra in "Louis Berkhof," in *Reformed Theology in America*, ed. David F. Wells (Grand Rapids: Eerdmans, 1985), pp. 153-71. Zwaanstra highlights the way Berkhof drew on the theology of Herman Bavinck.

1850-1900: Resurgence in the period in the face of a rising liberalism. Our references to the theological vitality of the Dutch Gereformeerde Kerken in the period between the two World Wars, first within the Netherlands and then (through translation) beyond it, have served notice of a considerable upsurge of Calvinism in late nineteenth-century Holland. We will have reason to speak of still earlier nineteenth-century development in the Netherlands, but here I draw attention to the surge of interest in Calvin and the age of Reformation in the lifetime of Abraham Kuyper (1837-1920) and the movement he led.[31] This surge advanced through the last third of the nineteenth century and beyond.[32]

While still a young minister of the national Reformed Church, Kuyper had come—by a variety of influences—to depart from the theologically liberal trajectory he had been trained in at Leiden, and to embrace both a more pietistic and confessionally Reformed position of a type already in existence within the national church. Kuyper did not interject Calvinistic teaching into an environment that was ignorant of it; rather he fanned the flames of the latent Calvinistic teaching that had long been present at the grassroots level. He also redirected it by introducing, successively, his key ideas of "antithesis" and "common grace." The first he emphasized to highlight the distinctiveness of the Christian faith and of Calvinistic teaching (in the face of late-nineteenth-century secularizing trends) while the second he emphasized to counter a residual pietistic tendency to withdraw from "worldly" culture.

By 1886 many thousands of believers and scores of congregations followed Kuyper out of the national church and eventually (in 1892) into union with the majority of an older movement, in existence since 1834, to form the Gereformeerde Kerken.[33] Immigrant communities

---

[31]Kuyper himself had written a Leiden doctoral dissertation on a contemporary of Calvin, the Polish reformer John à Lasco, who for a time was associated with the Frisian city of Emden. The term *Gereformeerde* is the equivalent of the English term *Reformed*.

[32]James Bratt speaks of a "spectacular revival of Calvinism" in these decades (*Dutch Calvinism in Modern America: A History of a Conservative Subculture* [Grand Rapids: Eerdmans, 1984], p. 14).

[33]I have followed the helpful account of Karel Blei, *The Netherlands Reformed Church, 1571-2005* (Grand Rapids: Eerdmans, 2006), chap. 6. The story of the portion of preexisting Secession

in the American upper Midwest and in South Africa would demonstrate the reach of this movement within those final decades of the nineteenth century. And in the twentieth century, Dutch immigration to Canada, the United States, Australia and New Zealand would demonstrate that this neo-Calvinist movement unleashed by Kuyper had considerable staying power. Concrete evidence of this is provided by the continued republication in English of Kuyper's *Lectures on Calvinism*, originally delivered at Princeton Seminary in 1898.[34] We cannot explain the fascination with Calvinism and politics, as well as Calvinism and art, present in the International Calvinist Congresses of the 1930s without making reference to the diffusion of Kuyperian ideas throughout the international Calvinist family. Even today, many preachers, professors and classroom teachers—well beyond the reach of Dutch Calvinism—have repeated Kuyper's words: "There is not one square inch of this earth over which Jesus Christ does not proclaim, 'That is mine!' "

Though it founded a university and a political party, it is important to reflect on the fact that this neo-Calvinist movement's strength lay in the laboring classes. Does it occur to us today to think that Calvinism will take root in such a constituency? And yet, not only in Holland but also in Britain at this time, there were large congregations made up of the working classes and united under the ministry of a powerful Calvinistic preacher. Of this phenomenon the ministry of Charles Haddon Spurgeon is simply the best-known example, but as recent research has shown, Spurgeon's Metropolitan Tabernacle, seating five thousand, was *not* an isolated example of urban Calvinist ministry to the rank and file in Victorian Britain.[35] Urban ministry in Liverpool became the great cause of the last twenty years of the life of the beloved Anglican-Calvinist bishop and writer J. C. Ryle (1816-1900). In the United States

church (which had taken the name "Christian Reformed," which did not enter into the union of 1892) is told by Hendrik Bouma in *Secession, Doleantie, and Union: 1834-1892* (Pella, Ia.: Inheritance, 1995), chaps. 1-2.

[34]The first English edition was that of Eerdmans in 1931. Bebbington shows convincingly that Scottish Church historian Donald Maclean was the preeminent mediator of neo-Calvinist or Kuyperian views into Scotland in the prewar period ("Calvin and British Evangelicalism").

[35]This is the thrust of the excellent study by Ian J. Shaw, *High Calvinists in Action: Calvinism and the City: Manchester and London, 1810-1860* (Oxford: Oxford University Press, 2002).

in this era, the Seattle Presbyterian minister Mark Matthews (1867-1940)—dubbed "America's Spurgeon"—gathered a congregation said to include nine thousand persons, launched a radio station and agitated for universal health care.[36] Yet, all Calvinist resurgence in this period needed to move against a powerful cultural stream that was increasingly informed by antisupernaturalism.[37] Late in the nineteenth century, Princeton Seminary (established 1812) acquired the reputation of being an international citadel of Calvinist orthodoxy, even as this theology had less and less traction in other places.[38]

Calvinism after the 1815 Council of Vienna. If these examples stand somewhat alone in indicating an upsurge of Calvinism in the late nineteenth century, the canvas at the opposite end of the century is very crowded indeed. If we take the 1815 Council of Vienna (which redrew the map of post-Napoleonic Europe) as our point of reckoning, we would find strong evidence of the upsurge of Calvinism in Britain, the Swiss cantons, France and Belgium-Holland.

As the year 1836 drew near, and the national Reformed church at Geneva determined to mark the official embrace of the Reformation by their canton three centuries earlier, they sent out invitations to other Reformed churches across Western Europe. They asked, Would these churches care to send delegates to the tercentenary celebration? The Church of Scotland experienced instant opposition within its annual General Assembly to the invitation. Adherence to Calvinism was so on the upswing in 1830s Scotland that contemporary Geneva (identified with the rationalism of Voltaire) was judged "deplorably corrupt in doctrine."[39] Supporters of Calvin's teaching within various English and

---

[36]C. Allyn Russell, "Matthews, Mark Allison," in *Dictionary of the Presbyterian and Reformed Tradition in America*, ed. D. G. Hart (Downers Grove, Ill.: InterVarsity Press, 1999).

[37]The challenges of the period are described in Mark Noll, *Between Faith and Criticism: Evangelicals, Scholarship and the Bible in America*, 2nd ed. (Grand Rapids: Baker, 1991), chaps. 2-3; and Mark Hopkins, *Nonconformity's Romantic Generation: Evangelical and Liberal Theologies in Victorian Britain* (Carlisle, U.K.: Paternoster, 2004). In fact, it had been the growth of this antisupernaturalism that contributed to the substantial erosion of the Calvinism of the mid-nineteenth century. This rapid eclipse of Calvinism is helpfully documented in Bebbington's "Calvin and British Evangelicalism."

[38]The posture of Princeton in the late nineteenth century is described by David B. Calhoun, *Princeton Seminary: The Majestic Testimony, 1869-1929* (Edinburgh: Banner of Truth, 1996).

[39]The account is provided in Kenneth J. Stewart, *Restoring the Reformation: British Evangelical-*

Scottish churches had banded together in 1843 to found the Calvin Translation Society, which in a short space of time issued a fresh translation of the *Institutes*, three volumes of *Tracts and Treatises*, and all of Calvin's biblical commentaries.[40] Though this edition of the *Institutes* was displaced by something more contemporary (a 1960 translation we know as the Battles edition), and the New Testament commentaries were also retranslated in the 1960s, all these Victorian editions are all still in print.[41] All English-speaking Calvinists in our times are in the debt of these early Victorian Calvin enthusiasts.

But the wave of Calvinism manifesting itself in Britain after the Napoleonic Wars had its counterparts on the Continent. When the Scottish evangelist Robert Haldane (1764-1842) made his celebrated sojourn to Switzerland and the south of France in 1816-1817, he not only won numerous students for the evangelical and Reformed faith (as he understood it) but found a number of tenacious Calvinists who were valiantly attempting to hold to the historic Reformed faith as summarized in the Reformed confessions.[42] At Geneva he met the high-Calvinist evangelist César Malan (1787-1864), who was rapidly "digging himself into a hole" (as we would say) by his preaching on Calvinistic doctrines within the national church. By 1820 Malan was

---

ism and the Francophone Réveil 1816-1849 (Carlisle, U.K.: Paternoster, 2006), p. 196.

[40]There is no monograph in existence detailing the work of this Victorian society, which roughly shadows the existence of the Anglican "Parker Society" begun in the same period. The latter existed (1840-1855) to republish the writings of the "fathers of the English Reformed Church." The Calvin Society was plainly an Anglican-Presbyterian collaborative effort. Bebbington seems to paint with too broad a brush in attributing the genesis of the Calvin Translation Society chiefly to the nascent Free Church of Scotland, born in 1843 ("Calvin and British Evangelicalism").

[41]This is the Library of Christian Classics edition (2 vols.) simultaneously published in 1960 by Westminster Press (Philadelphia) and SCM Press (London). The New Testament commentaries were retranslated and published by Eerdmans (Grand Rapids) and the St. Andrew Press (Edinburgh) commencing in 1972.

[42]Haldane, in addition to being part of the late Georgian continuation of the "British Evangelical Revival" also had loyalties that bound him to the emerging "restorationist" brand of evangelical Christianity that would manifest itself in the Plymouth Brethren and Churches of Christ. This side of Haldane's character and ministry is explored in both Timothy Stunt's *From Awakening to Secession: Radical Evangelicals in Switzerland and Britain 1815-1835* (Edinburgh: T & T Clark, 2000), and Stewart, *Restoring the Reformation*. Treatments of Haldane's European ministry, tending to the hagiographic, include a chapter in A. L. Drummond's *The Kirk and the Continent* (Edinburgh: St. Andrew Press, 1956), chap. 8, and Alexander Haldane's *Lives of Robert and J. A. Haldane* (Edinburgh: n.p., 1856).

defrocked by the canton's church and had begun ministering in an independent chapel, built with the help of foreign donors. Malan, an itinerant evangelist as well as a Genevan pastor, developed a reputation for his fervent preaching over the next four decades in neighboring Swiss cantons, France, Belgium, Holland, the Rhine Valley and Great Britain. Within the ministry of the Genevan national church was another holdover of the Calvinism of a previous age: the young F. S. R. L. (Louis) Gaussen (1790-1863). Gaussen made himself unpopular with the authorities by republishing the Second Helvetic Confession of 1566 in 1820 and by his insistence on using the old Geneva Catechism in preference to an Arian-leaning catechism just produced at Geneva. To the ranks of Malan (expelled from the national church) and Gaussen (who remained within it until 1831) were added many fervent young theological students at Geneva who had been touched by the combined ministry of Moravian evangelists and of such foreign visitors as Haldane and English Member of Parliament Henry Drummond (1786-1860). Drummond personally financed a reprinting of Calvin's *Institutes* in Geneva in 1819.

Some of these students entered the service of the cantonal church, some were called north to serve Huguenot diaspora congregations in places as far afield as Berlin, Brussels, Hamburg and Copenhagen, while others returned to their native France to accept pastoral positions in both the Reformed Church and independent congregations. Also, after 1810, Napoleon had permitted the French Reformed Church to operate its own seminary at Montauban; from there too came a supply of young men who were far more oriented to the Calvinist heritage than had been the case for many decades.[43]

Yet what was unfolding at Geneva and in France had as its counterpart similar developments elsewhere in Western Europe. Frisian pastor

---

[43]Once Napoleonic France had invaded the Swiss cantons, Napoleon decreed in 1802 that the Academy of Geneva would be the seminary of the French Reformed Church. Prior to this decree, no formal theological education of Protestant ministers had been permitted within France since the Revocation of the Edict of Nantes in 1685; such education as could be had needed to be gained clandestinely. A good number of French Reformed pastors had earlier slipped across the French-Swiss border to take an abbreviated course at Lausanne (see Stewart, *Restoring the Reformation*, pp. 42-43).

Henry de Cock underwent a drastic theological reorientation in 1829 when he discovered Calvin's *Institutes* in the library of a pastoral friend; trained in the more latitudinarian theology of the University of Groningen, de Cock was in short order marching in step with Calvinist writers from a century or more before his time. Expelled from the ministry of the national Reformed Church in 1834, he led a secession eventually numbering 120 congregations.[44] Meanwhile, in close affinity with movements at Geneva, Paris and Montauban, a movement of academics and students centered in Leiden were studying Reformed theology, holding cell groups for Bible study and thinking intently about how the intellectual and social legacy of the French Revolution could be counteracted. This was the Dutch manifestation of the Francophone "Réveil" (revival), and it would survive to coalesce with the movement Abraham Kuyper would lead in the 1880s. Not without good reason, these multiple expressions of early nineteenth-century Calvinism have been termed "the evangelical revival of Restoration Europe."[45]

Late Georgian Calvinism: The seedbed of multiple later developments. It has long been customary to suppose that the era of eighteenth-century spiritual awakening variously known as the Great Awakening or Evangelical Revival had spent itself long before the dawn of the nineteenth century. Jonathan Edwards had passed to his reward in 1758, George Whitefield in 1770, and John Wesley in 1792. But recent scholarly opinion has advanced the view that the movement's momentum actually continued into the opening decades of the new century.[46]

---

[44]The story of de Cock's theological reorientation is effectively told by Gerrit J. ten Zythoff, *Sources of Secession: The Netherlands Hervormde Kerk on the Eve of the Dutch Immigration to the Midwest* (Grand Rapids: Eerdmans, 1987), chaps. 4-5. Bratt stresses the affinity of de Cock and the early "Afscheiding" (secession movement) with the "second Reformation," Dutch pietism of the seventeenth century (*Dutch Calvinism in Modern America*). Fresh attention has also been given to the secession movement in the P. Y. De Jong and Nelson D. Kloosterman, eds. *The Reformation of 1834: Essays in Commemoration of the Act of Secession and Return* (Orange City, Ia.: Pluim, 1984).

[45]Bratt, *Dutch Calvinism*, p. 10. Henry Zwaanstra speaks of "an extensive spiritual and evangelical revival sweeping Western Europe" as the context for the movements of 1834 (*Catholicity and Secession: A Study of Ecumenicity in the Christian Reformed Church* [Grand Rapids: Eerdmans, 1991], p. 1).

[46]So, for example, Thomas F. Kidd, *The Great Awakening* (New Haven, Conn.: Yale University Press, 2007), p. xix; G. M. Ditchfield, *The Evangelical Revival* (London: University College London Press, 1998), p. 113.

In Britain the closing decades of the eighteenth century and the opening of the nineteenth was a great period of itineration, of church planting and of evangelical Calvinism. With this era we associate names like John Newton (1725-1807), Rowland Hill (1744-1833), George Burder (1752-1833) and John Angell James (1785-1859). It is from this period also that we date the onset of the modern missionary movement, marked by the departure of William Carey for India in 1793. Not to be outdone by the efforts of the fledgling Baptist Missionary Society (which sent Carey), evangelical Calvinists at London united in 1795 to form the London Missionary Society. The latter shortly had workers in China, South Africa, the South Pacific and France. The same period saw the launch of the Religious Tract Society (1799) and the British and Foreign Bible Society (1804); evangelical Calvinists were at the forefront of each of these endeavors.[47]

As in Britain, so also in America, there were signs that Christianity in the Reformed tradition was rising to the challenge of a new century. There was new evidence of spiritual vitality at Yale College under the presidency of Timothy Dwight (1752-1817). The "haystack prayer meeting" at Williams College, Massachusetts, in 1806 was the springboard that launched American foreign missionary effort in coming years. The heir of Jonathan Edwards, evangelist Asahel Nettleton (1783-1844), was still seeing substantial evangelistic harvests in the opening decades of that new century.[48] At Princeton, New Jersey, the Presbyterian Church established Princeton Seminary as an entity distinct from the college it had previously been a part of, and called Archibald Alexander (1772-1851) from a Philadelphia pastorate as pioneer professor of theology. All of these efforts were in motion throughout

---

[47]The momentous developments of this period are treated in Roger H. Martin, *Evangelicals United: Ecumenical Stirrings in Pre-Victorian Britain, 1795-1830* (Metuchen, N.J.: Scarecrow, 1983); and D. H. Lovegrove, *Established Church: Sectarian People* (Cambridge: Cambridge University Press, 1988). Insight into the principles undergirding the founding of the London Missionary Society is provided by John Morison, *The Fathers and Founders of the L.M.S.* (London: n.p., 1844); and Johannes van den Berg, *Constrained by Jesus Love: An Inquiry into the Motives of the Missionary Awakening in Great Britain in the Period Between 1698 and 1815* (Kampen, Netherlands: J. H. Kok, 1956).

[48]The latter years of Nettleton's ministry were, sadly, characterized by contention between the older style of evangelism he represented and the "new measures" brought in by Charles G. Finney.

the period of the French Revolution and Napoleonic era; the international chaos of the period, rather than justifying a wait-and-see attitude among the Reformed, was perceived as opening the way for wider gospel opportunity to come.

Drawing the Threads Together

1. Admitting interdependence. We could have traveled back further in time to locate Calvinists earlier than the French Revolution. But we have seen enough to help us get our bearings a little more clearly. This story includes setbacks as well as advances. Unquestionably, those earlier movements enrich and inform our later movements. There is no movement of our time that can pretend that Calvinist resurgence is bound up with their cause and no other. And Calvinist resurgences can extend themselves for a very long time—often overlapping with the next wave.

When we stop to think about it, what we may call *our* Calvinism is actually a kind of alloy combining ideas and emphases from three, four or more eras. Personally, while I came into the Reformed movement in the Martyn Lloyd-Jones and James Boice era, I also feel a special tie to the movements and writers I have called "late-Georgian" and "post-1815," as well (of course) as the Swiss reformers. And though I am not a "new Calvinist," I am watching this contemporary movement keenly because it holds out a promise of fresh engagement with modern culture. The question arises, What kind of an alloyed Calvinist are you?

2. Loyal to past and present. What is true of us individually is also true of the particular movements we are part of now. We need to see that every resurgence of the Reformed faith is, in fact, new-old; that is, it is a fusion of elements from long ago with contemporary elements. That blend is important because the quality and staying power of any particular wave of Calvinism will lie, in large measure, in how these two factors are held in creative tension. If a Calvinist movement stresses *only* the reiteration of ideas and doctrines from long ago, its tendency will be antiquarian and fogyish; its devotees might actually wish to be living in a different time and place! On the other hand, if a Calvinist movement glories *chiefly* in its affinities with the contemporary scene (whether these affinities are musical, in the arts, the trappings of pop culture, etc.), the necessary link with historical markers of the movement may be very hard to locate.

3. Hold the triumphalism! We have just passed the milestone of Calvin's five hundredth birthday. The broad movement we call *Reformed* is plainly still a force to be reckoned with, and a global force too. Yet our rapid survey of the last two centuries of Calvinism—whatever it may signal about the movement's ability to bounce back after seeming to be a spent force—tells us equally that Calvinism is neither a panacea (curing all ills) or a silver bullet (vanquishing all opposition). After all, *only* God is omnipotent. It is sobering to consider that the resurgences of Calvinism that I have named in the Western world have come and gone and come again even as Western Europe and North America have grown steadily more secularized and less hospitable to all expressions of Christianity.[49] It is no time for triumphalism on the part of Calvinists of *any* stripe.

But neither is it a time to lower the flag and to opt for a kind of bland, lowest-common denominator expression of Christianity that has no heritage to speak of, is lacking in a solid theological framework and is insipid. The abiding value the Reformed tradition has to offer is surely a rigorously biblical and God-centered approach to faith and life in Jesus Christ; Calvinists should see that we hold this in trust for the many sincere believers in Christ who would find it a tonic (as some of us surely did) if they could sample it, and for the many as yet unbelievers who have yet to "taste and see that the LORD is good" (Ps 34:8).

4. Unity, forbearance. It is time for more Calvinist unity and forbearance. We should be more ready to recognize that this movement is broader than our little corner of it and bigger than the circle we feel most comfortable in. We need fewer angular, sharp-elbowed Calvinists who glory in what distinguishes their stance from that of others and a lot more supporters of the Reformed faith who rejoice in what they hold in common with others. When versions of Calvinism contend with one another over which is most authentic, we have sunk to a much lower

---

[49]This is the especially sobering verdict of Bebbington, "Calvin and British Evangelicalism."

290 Ten Myths About Calvinism

level than that of the sixteenth century when the Swiss reformers and their international allies aimed at the broadest possible collaboration and widest possible mutual recognition. Calvin, after all, insisted he would if necessary "cross ten seas" if he could promote agreement in the central doctrines of the faith with fellow believers.[50]

Calvin, "Letter to Cranmer," April 1552, in *Letters of Calvin*, ed. Jules Bonnard (Philadelphia: Presbyterian Board of Publications, 1858), 2:345.

Appendix: The Earliest Known Reference to the TULIP Acronym

T^{he} Outlook

JUNE 21, 1913

LYMAN ABBOTT
Editor-in-Chief
HAMILTON W. MABIE
Associate Editor

THEODORE ROOSEVELT
Contributing Editor
R. D. TOWNSEND
Managing Editor

THE READER'S VIEW

THE FIVE POINTS OF CALVINISM HISTORICALLY CONSIDERED

The meeting of the two Presbyterian General Assemblies in Atlanta, Georgia, last month, and the retiring from the presidency of Princeton Theological Seminary of Francis L. Patton, D.D., LL.D., who has for so many years occupied with most marked ability the highest and most honorable positions within the gift of the Presbyterian Church, render this a most appropriate time to take a brief historical glance at the so-called Five Points of Calvinism.

It may not be very generally known that these articles of belief had no existence in the time of Calvin, and therefore did not originate with him. John Calvin died in the year 1564, aged fifty-five years, while these five points, called by his name, were formulated in 1619 by the Synod of Dort to controvert the Five Points of Arminius, which formed the basis of the discussions through the six months of the sessions of that Synod. These Five Points, as formulated by the Synod of Dort, according to two authorities, are as follows:

1. Personal, Gratuitous Election to Everlasting Life.	1. Divine Predestination.
2. Particular Redemption.	2. The Redemption of Men through the Death of Christ.
3. Depravity, Native and Total.	3. Total Depravity.
4. Effectual Calling, or Regeneration, by the Holy Spirit.	4. Redemption through Grace.
5. Certain Perseverance of Saints unto Eternal Life.	5. Perseverance of Saints.

Some eight years ago I had the privilege of hearing a popular lecture, by Dr. McAfee, of Brooklyn, upon the Five Points of Calvinism, given before the Presbyterian Union of Newark, New Jersey, which was most interesting as well as instructive. To aid the mind in remembering the Five Points, Dr. McAfee made use of the word Tulip, which, possessing five letters, lends itself nicely to the subject in hand, especially as it ends with the letter P, as will be seen later.

Taking the five letters, Dr. McAfee used them as follows:

- 1st, T stands for Total Depravity.
- 2d, U " " Universal Sovereignty.
- 3d, L " " Limited Atonement.
- 4th, I " " Irresistible Grace.
- 5th, P " " Perseverance of the Saints.

Of course the adoption of this word restricts the order of the five points, and perhaps throws them out of their proper order and logical sequence. However this may be, I was led to consult several theological authorities to see how they agreed with Dr. McAfee, both as to the substance of doctrine as well as to the order of their relation to each other, and I give below some of the results of such consultations.

First, going to Abbott's "Dictionary of Religious Knowledge," I found the Five Points of Calvinism listed as in the list marked A below.

Jonathan Dickinson, first President of Princeton College, states these Five Points, with their proof texts, as:

1. Eternal Election. Ephesians i. 4, 5.
2. Original Sin. Romans v. 12.
3. Grace in Conversion. Ephesians ii. 4, 5.
4. Justification by Faith. Romans iii. 25.
5. Saints' Perseverance. Romans viii. 30.

And now, to come to the living authorities, I called upon Dr. Francis L. Patton, in Princeton, in the year 1905, and, requesting him to write the Five Points of Calvinism for me offhand, he sat down at his table and began. As he hesitated a little upon the second point, I said to him that if he desired a little time to think them over he might mail the list to me the next day, when he immediately replied: "Dr. Vail, if I cannot give you the Five Points of Calvinism offhand, without taking time to consider them, I had better get out of here" (meaning the presidency of Princeton Theological Seminary).

As he wrote the last point, "Perseverance of the Saints," I remarked, "That's right, Doctor, don't leave that point out." And he quickly replied, "No, Doctor, that would never do, for even the Cumberland Brethren believe in that."

Then I asked Dr. Patton if he had noticed that from the time of the disruption of the Presbyterian Church into the Old School and

	A	B	C	D	E
1.	Original Sin	Sovereign Election	Predestination	Universal Sovereignty and Partial Election	Absolute Sovereignty of God
2.	Free Will	Total Depravity	Irresistible Grace	Total Depravity	Total Depravity of Man
3.	Grace	Limited Atonement	Original Sin	Limited Atonement	Invincibility of Divine Grace
4.	Predestination	Efficacious or Irresistible Grace	Particular Redemption	Efficacious Grace	Eternal Decrees of God
5.	Perseverance	Perseverance of the Saints	Perseverance of the Saints	Perseverance of the Saints	Perseverance of the Saints

THE READER'S VIEW

New School branches, in the year 1837, until the date of the reunion of the two schools in the year 1870, was just thirty-three years, which we were accustomed to call one generation, and that between the dates of the reunion, in 1870, and the year of the revision of the Confession of Faith, in 1903, was again just thirty-three years, another generation. He replied that he had never noticed those facts, but, said he, "Dr. Vail, it will not be thirty-three years before the Cumberland Brethren are admitted into the great Presbyterian family." And it was not. It was only three years, as they were admitted in 1906, the very next year.

The Five Points of Calvinism, as given by Dr. Patton, are in list B.

Soon after obtaining Dr. Patton's list, having occasion to write Dr. Henry van Dyke upon another matter, I requested him to give me, off-hand, the Five Points, stating that I had received them from Dr. Patton, but that I would like to have them in the order that he preferred.

He replied as follows: "The so-called Five Points of Calvinism are matters of historic theology, and you can rely upon Dr. Patton's statement of them as being correct. There is room for dispute as to what these points have been in the history of the Church, but I feel that there ought to be considerable room for difference of opinion as to whether they are true or not."

In reply to my request for a similar statement of the Five Points from Dr. Hugh Black, of Union Theological Seminary, he, after giving the list marked C, said: "I don't think Calvin himself would have summed up his system in these points. The system is one built up by rigorous logic from the one central idea of the sovereignty of God."

The Rev. George B. Stewart, D.D., President of Auburn Theological Seminary, gives the Five Points according to list D.

The Rev. Isaac N. Rendall, D.D., late President of Lincoln University, Pennsylvania, gives the Five Points as they are in list E.

It is interesting, in closing this short survey of these Five Points of Calvinism, to notice that the authorities consulted, however they may vary in the order of the points, all place "Perseverance of the Saints" as the fifth point, and while the order or wording of the other four points differs in almost every instance, no one omits this fifth point. This is significant, as it brings thus into prominence the fact that the main point of difference between the Calvinists and the Arminians at the Synod of Dort was just this fifth point, the Arminians believing that saints could fall from grace, and the Calvinists holding to the perseverance of the saints.

Whatever may be our individual position as to the merits of the Five Points of Calvinism, we must admit that they have stood the test of generations of controversy better than other statements of belief, and that Dr. Patton was about right when he said, in substance, not long since, that should Calvinism as a system of belief pass away, and man come to hold that he had found something better and more satisfactory, and in the coming ages should the antiquarian in his researches through the cemeteries dig up a skeleton of Calvinism, he would find it a vertebrate.   WILLIAM H. VAIL.
Newark, New Jersey.

Name Index

Scripture Index